# Accidentally on Purpose:

## Tripping Through Life with Regina

REGINA MEREDITH

REGINA MEREDITH

Copyright © 2018-2019 Regina Meredith

All rights reserved.

ISBN: 9781791957773

# Dedication

This book is dedicated to all of you who have chosen the path of coloring outside the lines of life. This journey is about trusting in our instincts and deepest desires.

REGINA MEREDITH

# Table Of Contents

| | |
|---|---:|
| Introduction | 1 |
| Chapter One: Life Happens | 4 |
| Chapter Two: My Family Gene Pool | 5 |
| Chapter Three: Accidental Estrangement | 13 |
| Chapter Four: The Freak | 17 |
| Chapter Five: My Life As A Pretend Nun | 22 |
| Chapter Six: A Primate Christmas | 28 |
| Chapter Seven: First Loves | 31 |
| Chapter Eight: The Boot Camp Marriage | 41 |
| Chapter Nine: A Journalist Is Born | 49 |
| Chapter Ten: Salvation Through Ballet | 57 |
| Chapter Eleven: My Son's Father Arrives | 63 |
| Chapter Twelve: "You Can Have Children!" | 65 |
| Chapter Thirteen: The Son Rises | 68 |
| Chapter Fourteen: New Mommy To News Anchor | 75 |
| Chapter Fifteen: An Eager Seeker | 85 |
| Chapter Sixteen: Past Lives Stranger Than Fiction | 90 |
| Chapter Seventeen: Paranormal Or Normal? | 94 |
| Chapter Eighteen: The Tiny Mystic | 107 |
| Chapter Nineteen: The Baptist Who Loves Kwan | 113 |
| Chapter Twenty: The Messy Origins Of Humankind | 120 |
| Chapter Twenty-One: Changing Perspectives | 128 |
| Chapter Twenty-Two: Loss Of The Elder Woman | 142 |
| Chapter Twenty-Three: The Funding Arrives | 154 |
| Chapter Twenty-Four: The Missed Metro And Retribution | 164 |

| | |
|---|---|
| Chapter Twenty-Five: Vegetables Take Center Stage | 168 |
| Chapter Twenty-Six: A Boy Grows Up | 175 |
| Chapter Twenty-Seven: An Old Man Dies | 179 |
| Chapter Twenty-Eight: Red Rock Seduction | 189 |
| Chapter Twenty-Nine: Settling into Camelot | 197 |
| Chapter Thirty: Argentina Tango | 205 |
| Chapter Thirty-One: UFO Hunting | 209 |
| Chapter Thirty-Two: Adventures Between Dimensions | 223 |
| Chapter Thirty-Three: The Connection | 233 |
| Chapter Thirty-Four: Love and Free Will | 237 |
| Chapter Thirty-Five: Time to Heal | 239 |
| Chapter Thirty-Six: Love Comes Again | 244 |
| Chapter Thirty-Seven: CMN Travels | 253 |
| Chapter Thirty-Eight: Ma'at Joins the Team | 275 |
| Chapter Thirty-Nine: India, The Sedona Afterlife | 280 |
| Chapter Forty: Reality Sinks In | 296 |
| Chapter Forty-One: Conspiracy | 302 |
| Chapter Forty-Two: Letting Go | 305 |
| Chapter Forty-Three: Entanglement | 309 |
| Chapter Forty-Four: More Letting Go | 316 |
| Chapter Forty-Five: Beginning Again and Again | 320 |
| Chapter Forty-Six: Many Hats | 325 |

# Acknowledgments

My heartfelt thanks to my family for the collective memories of our lives together and apart, particularly my sister, Denise Pappenberger. Her photo archives and memory have contributed greatly. My husband, Zeus Yiamouyiannis, has been a powerful support in helping me find my voice. Alex Storm offered his contributions with the artwork. Sandie Sedgbeer has been a wonderful and patient editor. Nancy Beckman has been an angel in helping format this book.

# Introduction

During the process of writing this book, what struck me as interesting was that some of my closest friends knew little to nothing of the experiences I share within these pages. In truth, I didn't share some of these events because I had become fatigued with the nervous 'giggle factor.' I later realized that I also had not given my life experiences much weight as I tend to live in the present. "What's behind me don't matter!" is one of my favorite lines in film from an 80's comedy in which the Italian driver in a Great Race ripped off his rearview mirror and uttered those words.

As for the perpetual giggle factor, I, along with millions of others, have had to hide my interest in the 'inexplicable' in spite of repeatedly being faced with evidence for its existence. As I developed a career in traditional media as a news anchor, reporter, columnist, documentary producer, writer, and on-air host, it was important that these interests and experiences be kept private under the threat of losing my professional credibility. This in itself creates internal stress, from which I have chosen to break free.

As a result of an inadvertent trauma at a young age, I was set free from the moorings of social or peer pressure. The downside was an early mistrust in those closest to me, which necessitated a dependence on myself. In becoming my own point of reference, I became a free thinker.

Subscribing to the theory, or reality, that each of us is in control of the creation of our life's experience, I share my story warts, glory and all. It is not meant as a congratulatory or flattering self-portrait but as a direct and honest look back at the influences that shaped my life's experience and drove me deeper and deeper into the exploration of the unknown. When paired with my lifelong instincts as a journalist, one could say that it was inevitable that I would find my way to the establishment of the video streaming site www.reginameredith.com.

This is the hallmark of most of the people I have met who have had paranormal experiences throughout their lives. There is a willingness to be separated out from their peers and family to access parts of life's mysteries that are ultimately so often killed by judgment and lack of acceptance from those around us. To speak up has meant subjecting oneself to the judgment of others and even open ridicule. This ridicule has extended to men and women - scientists, doctors, philosophers, spiritual leaders, psychologists - who I consider to be among the most brilliant people of our times, many of whom I have interviewed. They have had to maintain an absolute faith in their own knowledge and commitment to truth to stay on their path. But above all, they have had to maintain an Open Mind.

It is these inexplicable experiences that are at the foundation of my choices, interests, relationships and even professional life. I choose to live side by side with the infinite aspect of myself, my Soul, and other sources of intelligence which give me guidance and share profound wisdom with me for my own growth and clarity.

Looking back, my life may have appeared to be a comedy of accidents, bad decisions, and misfortune at times along the way, but I now understand that every single event carried me closer to my purpose. In truth, the soul is far more creative than we can imagine. If we fall away from our path or miss a cue, alternate routes will be opened to us to guide us back home.

I believe our soul never fails us and that, if we choose to know this infinite part of ourselves, it offers each of us tools beyond our wildest imaginations. More than forty years into the journey, I can't imagine living any other way! So, I invite you to enjoy the ride as both a spectator and a participant as it is my wish that you will see your own genius in my story.

## Chapter One:
## Life Happens

My little two-year-old body was frozen in what I remember as a glass room, unable to breathe as I watched the two figures, my mother and father, walking away from me with my baby sister in their arms. I was left behind, mouth stretched wide in a soundless scream. When the crying stopped, and I caught my first breath I was a different person.

## Chapter Two:
# My Family Gene Pool

My father called me Wagon Wheel by the time I could walk as I seemed to possess an air of having 'seen it all' - like a dusty, well-worn spoked wheel that had covered many miles of barren landscapes, across streams and meadows, creaking along from one outpost to another. He did not take this to be confused with the notion of old souls who actually do bring varying degrees of wisdom into this life with them. He was simply observing a confidence and stubbornness unusual for such a tiny person, a child that preferred not to be told what to do nor how to think. But then, free thinkers were a part of my family's heritage.

*'Wagon Wheel', my father's nickname for me*

## Billy Stuart Hirschfelt

Dad was raised by Alda May, a kind-hearted woman who was ultimately abandoned by her wandering, union-organizing husband, Chester. Chester made his money in the upholstery business. Chester was a bigot, sexist and a generally hateful man who believed that heaven was reserved for a select group of souls, those who occupied white men's bodies. Women were either overt or latent jezebels in Chester's eyes, waiting to snatch a man's cleanliness of heart and mind out from under him through the temptations of the flesh. For this reason, he would not allow Alda May to wear red, the color of the harlot.

*Alda May Hirschfelt, my paternal grandmother*

Upon her abandonment, now endowed with five children and no significant means of support, Alda May quietly executed perhaps her only act of rebellion in her brief life. She bought a red dress and wore it in front of God and family.

As a single mother, she taught my father, his three brothers, and sister that neither she nor God would tolerate speaking poorly of others. When one of her boys would find himself escorted home by an angry neighbor or local law enforcement authority, Alda May would merely look at them sadly with her soft brown eyes. They each vowed they would never make their mother hurt like that again, at least until the next time life offered too much temptation to resist.

Billy became, in the figurative and real sense of the word, a Texas horse trader. Known for their cleverness and creativity, another appropriate phrase might be 'a man possessing good salesmanship.' He entered the workforce toward the beginning of World War II at the age of thirteen. His older brothers had been shipped off to the war, while Billy sold tickets at the Ballinger, Texas movie theater. His salary consisted of free movie passes, which he in turn sold, pocketing just enough film passes for himself to develop a crush on Judy Garland.

At seventeen, Billy, and his best buddy Dave hit the road for the oil fields where a young man had a chance of making some real money. Billy regularly consulted with his boss, the field manager, sharing his observations about how the operation could be run more efficiently. For this, he was paid top dollar. This put him in an enviable, position with his peers, who were cussing, goofing off and causing trouble in the field.

*Billy Stuart Hirschfelt, my father as a young football player*

The more gregarious Dave was the spiritual leader of the young roughnecks, and, after mouthing off to the boss one last time, was fired from his job cleaning out the oil drums. "Come on Bill, let's get out of here. Let's go home and make a new plan." Dad couldn't resist the plea of his lifelong friend, and so quit his job in solidarity.

The pair pulled into Ballinger, Texas with a new air of

personal power, they had some cash in their pockets. There was no argument, in post-Depression and post WWII America, money was power.

Upon walking into Alda May's home, Billy was handed a letter. It was from his father and had arrived that very day. Chester had not felt it necessary to communicate with his children since his departure twelve years earlier. With his father nothing more than a distant memory, the sight of the remarkably beautiful, cursive handwriting, unmistakably formed by Chester's hand, delivered a shock to Billy.

Chester had apparently been thinking about his past, perhaps with a heavy conscience. He had written to make his son an offer. There was work to be had in San Francisco where Chester was living with his newest wife, Hazel. He ordered Billy to come at once, to seize the opportunity, no time to fiddle-faddle over his future.

A free, eighteen-year-old man with enough cash to change his destiny, Dad said goodbye to his mother, Alda May, and hitched a ride to the Greyhound depot.

**Nancy Marie Lanahan**

Henrietta Willamena Mary Krumhauer was a stoic girl. Pregnant with my mother by the age of seventeen, she labored under the judgment and abuse of her 19-year-old husband, Arthur Lanahan. Art was Irish, handsome, and exceedingly bright. As an adult, he chose the profession of law enforcement, serving as a police officer in St. Paul, Minnesota. He had been decorated for bravery in the line of duty and had been using some of his more lucid evening hours to invent things in his head.

Big, quiet, slow, 'Etta' was no match for Art and he resented it. With the frustrations of marriage and fatherhood (now supporting four children) weighing heavily on his spontaneous spirit, Arthur drank. One afternoon he made an indiscreet move in lifting his gun overhead and shooting up a local bar while in uniform. This spontaneous and exhilarating act created an instant change in his employment status.

*Henrietta Lanahan, my maternal grandmother with my mother Nancy and Uncle John*

Since change was upon him, perhaps he should make a clean sweep of it. He was already involved with a woman of means - a working woman. Perhaps this might be an opportune moment to make a bold move, to start afresh in a place where his employment references might not hold so much sway. He could also use this opportunity to lighten up his family burdens.

It was a blessing when Art left Henrietta, who was then 28, with four children and no means of support. At least the drunken beatings had stopped.

The state of Minnesota did not hold a sentimental position on the nuclear family under hardship. No man, no money. The kids were taken away from Etta and parceled out to a variety of foster families who could earn upwards of $30 a month housing the unfortunate young charges. My mother, Nancy, the eldest of the children, was taken in by Mrs. Madison, a stern woman who needed help to maintain her large home and yard. Her son Warren didn't care for house or yard work, so the duties fell to their new eleven-year old, state-sanctioned, in-house ward.

Mom painted the house, hand mowed the one-acre lawn, worked on local farms and did daily chores to earn her room and keep. She was not allowed to touch the piano she so desperately longed to play while listening to Warren's weekly lessons and practice sessions. Nor was she allowed to wear the new nylon underwear of the day, nor the new shoes, nor the new clothes.

When she was not in school, or working for Mrs. Madison, she spent her time in her small, spare room decorated with nothing other than a small portrait of Jesus. She developed a deep and abiding love for the attractive blonde, bearded man, her Savior, on the wall. She saw him as the only beautiful thing in her life.

*Nancy Marie Lanahan, my mother upon High School graduation*

There is a photograph that captures my mother's early teens. She stood in the back row of a group of teens who had just been confirmed into the Lutheran faith. The girls were seated in the front row wearing lovely, white chiffon and taffeta dresses with low heeled, matching pumps and nylons. My mother stood behind with the boys, ashamed to have anyone discover her thick, brown, work shoes, hairy legs and beige dress that appeared to have been made decades before. She didn't wear a beaming smile like the other girls. She forced a wan, tight-lipped little smile, desperate to become invisible.

At seventeen, after high school graduation, she received an invitation out of the blue from her father and his new wife Mary, to join them in their new life in San Francisco. For the past six years, the only contact from her father had been an annual birthday card.

My mom was dropped off at the Greyhound bus depot, closing a long, difficult chapter of life that genuinely can be termed as both neglectful and abusive.

Upon my father's and my mother's respective arrivals at the San Francisco Greyhound Bus Station, Chester gave Dad a job lead and put him up for a few days while Mom was shocked at the wanton advice of her father's new wife Mary, who suggested that as a single woman in the city she should become outfitted with a birth control device. Appalled at the suggestion she would have sex before marriage, Mom moved out of Arthur and Mary's apartment into a boarding house on Octavia Street, the same one to which my father had relocated after his stay at Chester and Hazel's apartment.

*Mom, Dad and Grandfather Chester on New Years Eve wedding day*

Bill ('Billy' was too juvenile for his new life in San Francisco) and Nancy married on New Year's Eve 1949. It wasn't so much a poetic gesture to start life anew at the stroke of midnight as it was good timing for my father to claim another tax deduction. I was born ten and one-half months later, conceived during the Valentine's Day revelry of the nineteen-year-old lovers.

I entered the world in what is termed the frank-breech position. In other words, butt first. I was clearly ambivalent about the prospects for this life.

## Chapter Three:
## Accidental Estrangement

My first life lesson came at the age of two. Mom was about to give birth to my sister, who was also conceived during Valentine Day festivities, and she was in a bind. She had no reliable connections or family in San Francisco to care for me for the few days she was to be in the hospital. This was at a time when my father could not afford to miss a day of work because the family budgetary margins were very thin. His meager salary as an insurance clerk didn't stretch very far and his wife would be taking maternity leave for the time being. Life in the big city carried a price tag, and $200 a month was barely enough to cover their rent on the apartment above Dixon's Dress Shop on Geary Boulevard plus heat and food.

When the time for my sister's arrival came, Mom went to the hospital, Dad to work and I to the Children's Receiving Home, which is the place where unwanted and orphaned children are taken until further arrangements can be made. My mother had come up with this solution out of desperation, having casually known a woman who worked at the facility. She felt this was her best option as her new acquaintance agreed to keep an eye on me. It was a make-do arrangement that was only to have lasted 2-3 days at most.

My sister was apparently in no hurry to begin this incarnation either, as she stubbornly held out ten days past her due date. My mom would go into labor, then it would cease. She was on tenterhooks to get this baby into the world. Not the least of her motivations was that she was concerned I would begin to feel abandoned as did my other tiny roommates. She was right to be concerned.

My new baby sister, Denise, dilly-dallied her way into the world with her birthday falling two years and one day after mine. My mother and father bundled Denise up and took a taxi to the Receiving Home to take me home. Unfortunately, I was not destined to join our newly expanded family as the entire nursery had developed a highly contagious ear infection. The facility was under quarantine, and none of the 'orphans' were allowed to join their new, or in my case old, families.

After being made aware of the situation, my now 22-year-old parents, unquestioning of authority, left with their newborn in their arms. But not before peeking in on me. The protocol for visiting an adoptee was structured toward non-invasiveness for the sake of the child. I remember it more like being in a cage at the zoo. The boy or girl was placed in a room with a glass door or windows where the potential parents could observe the child under consideration for adoption. Since the

*My sister Denise and I*

prospective parents were strangers, this was little more than a minor distraction to the child. However, when your parents, whom you love and have bonded with for two years, come to visit with your replacement bundled up in their arms, it's an entirely different thing.

I screamed and clawed at the door trying to break out of the room to be with my parents. It's a classic understatement to say that this was a harrowing scene for everybody, one I remember clearly to this day. Unable to do anything about my plight, my parents turned to go home with their new infant. Whatever sense of safety and trust I may have possessed until that time vanished as their figures receded down the hallway.

The nurse took me to the nursery and my little bed where I cried until I couldn't breathe, holding my hair with one hand and gripping my shirt with the other. I was left to "cry it out." After all, hysterical two-year-olds were nothing out of the ordinary in this place of refuge for the unfortunate.

It was another ten days before I was allowed to go home. I later learned that my parents had come to see me again, only the next time it was done through a two-way mirror to avoid the potential horror of the last encounter. It wasn't until my mid-forties when I was put under hypnosis that I remembered the 'coming home' part. This event seemed to be exerting a great deal of influence on my life, so I felt it was time to see what was going on in that bottomless and unknowable pit known as the subconscious mind.

As I found my way through the stillness and darkness that precipitates the regression experience, I remembered myself in a long corridor with green walls. I was holding the hand of a nurse wearing the official stiff white uniform. Far in front of me at the other end of the hall were my parents and the baby. At first, my heart leaped for joy - especially at seeing my father's face. In my next tiny step, I froze. I had suddenly remembered that these were the people who had turned their back on me, left me on my own among strangers and had replaced me with another baby - they had abandoned me. I clung to the nurse's skirt and leg screaming "No! No! No!" over and over. I did not want to go with those people at the end of the hall.

When I told my father after the regression what I had seen, he confirmed that it was all true and that it was one of the worst days of his life. Such pain at seeing your little child so angry and confused, your daughter who had loved you so much now distant and mistrustful.

I sat in the back of the car that drove us home quiet and withdrawn and stayed that way for the next decade. Each year the report cards came back, will not play with others. Does not participate in class, and the like. In truth, I was just watching. I watched how people acted with each other and anything else I could observe considering the fact that my vision was 20/400, which meant I watched everything that was no more than a foot in front of my face. Nobody knew that I was legally blind. That type of information is generally discovered as a result of interactions between a child and his/her family or teachers, and I didn't interact.

For all of the reasons mentioned, I spent a great deal of time in a dream world. I alternately played queen and servant living in a stone castle in a faraway place. While I didn't understand it at the time, keeping to myself kept me out from under the emotional influence and control of anyone but me. I was my own girl, invulnerable to the harshness of the world - and the goodness too.

## Chapter Four:
## The Freak

By the age of six, my body began developing at a very rapid rate. I was headed toward very early puberty. Alarmed, my parents took me to the doctor, who in turn sent me to a specialist at Stanford University. I was to become a research case for the Department of Birth Defects.

A small bag was packed with my pajamas and a couple of toys. My mother walked me into the hospital ward next to the newborns. It was precisely five years after my 'accidental estrangement' in the Children's Receiving Home.

She left me in my hospital bed, explaining that she would be back, but I didn't understand when that would be. In fact, I wasn't sure why I was even there.

I was afraid, but not so fearful that I wouldn't check out my new environment. As the days and weeks unfolded, I observed the most confusing sights and events of my life.

The memory is interesting in that it remembers in the context in which our life events transpire. If you are six when you have an experience, it recalls in the framework of a six-year-old. So, what I am about to share with you is from the mind, and through the eyes of a 6-7-year-old. I will never know the answers to the questions raised through my observations of the children surrounding me in the Birth Defects unit at Stanford University Hospital in San Francisco.

The little red headed-boy in the bed next to me, Timmy, had two additional small purple thumbs. They grew low on the fleshy part of his normal thumbs. He was quiet and kind.

The African-American girl across from me was wrapped in what looked like cellophane from neck to toe. They said she was three years old, but she was at least as tall as me, and I was tall for my age. I thought they were trying to shrink her.

Every morning I heard screaming from the glass examination room at the end of our ward. A pretty little girl with curly brown hair would be lying on her back on the examination table. The doctor appeared to be sticking what looked like a silver tube up into her nose and into her sinuses. Inside the tube would pass what looked like a long needle. Then she would scream.

There was the girl who was paralyzed from the waist down. Everyone carried her around, which I thought was cool. As for the rest of the little patients, I don't recall.

As for me, I was taken into the examination room twice a day where my blood was drawn. For each draw, I was given a purple paper heart. By the time I left, I had a string of them that was dragging on the floor when I pinned them to my shirt.

As tough as this place may sound, it was not without its happy times. Just as cookies and Kool-Aid incentivized me to attend church, I was always up for graham crackers and grape juice in the afternoons. In addition, I loved wheeling around the ward in any available wheelchair. The nurses obliged me whenever possible as there was little else to do. We weren't allowed to go outside and I don't recall any physical activity being made available to us.

*Christmas with my bridal doll, a girl's primary aspiration in the 1950s*

My favorite ritual was to wheel down to the newborn ward in the mornings and see who had arrived during the night. The black and Chinese babies made me smile. I loved their little puffy lips and cheeks and the shock of thick black hair in many cases. The white babies, on the other hand, were boring and had no engaging features for the most part, so I ignored them. But with the black and Chinese babies, I wanted to play with them and be their pretend mom as I had done a good job at that with my dolls. I had seen to it that my plastic children were strolled, fed on time and diapers changed as needed.

On weekends, my mother and father came to see me. It was apparently my birthday on one such occasion. Just as I had turned two years of age in the Children's Receiving Home, I turned seven in the hospital research ward.

Mom brought me a little girl's 'make-up' kit from a neighbor, which I thought was wonderful. It contained sweet, pink candy lipstick and may well have been the inspiration for my lifelong love of lipstick!

I didn't think much of the fact that I only had these sparse visits from my family. Since they only had one car, which my father used for work, and lived in Marin County, it was practical to wait until weekends to visit. In the 1950s children weren't considered to be complex individuals with emotional needs. Besides, I was already a free agent. I didn't expect much from other people. And, while I was a loner, I didn't feel particularly different from others - until I arrived home from the hospital.

One evening shortly after my return from Stanford University Hospital, Mom and Dad were playing pinochle with some friends. My mother lowered her voice, thinking I was asleep in the room next to the kitchen. She told their friends "They say she could end up over six-feet tall and 'homely.' She will likely never marry and will not be able to have children." She also mentioned that I might be fat and sickly. The medical name of the condition is adrenalcorticohyperplasia, a congenital hormonal defect that does not allow for the natural production of cortisol, which has had its consequences.

At seven years of age I had no way to come to terms with this unfortunate information other than developing a vague, but profound, sense of shame at being different - a freak. So, I chose to further isolate myself from others.

Each morning mom would pack a lunch box that contained a small portion of the cortisone pills I would have to take the rest of my life. It was twisted up inside waxed paper. Mortified that someone would see the little pill packet, and ask what it was and why I was taking it, I moved away from the other kids and sat by myself. If they learned that I was a freak, I wouldn't be able to bear seeing any of them again. Better to keep to myself.

Through laziness and forgetfulness, I did not take my four times daily dose of cortisone for long. By the time I reached puberty, I was down to twice a day. In spite of this, I did not end up like the image of the six-foot-tall, homely, sickly, barren woman forever etched into my very young subconscious mind.

At eighteen, an appointment was made for a follow-up visit with the diagnosing physician, Dr. Luiggi Luzatti. He was the doctor who had delivered the bad news regarding the likely unfortunate future developments my parents should expect during the maturation of my body. He had not seen me in over a decade.

I still delight in the look on his face when he walked into the examination room. First, he was confused, thinking he was in the wrong exam room. "Look at you! What happened?"

I was wearing a soft peach and white floral print knit top and mini skirt. With long flowing hair, and at 5'5" with a figure measuring 34-24-34, I was definitely not the large, ungainly girl he was expecting to see. Dr. Luzatti, my mother and I chalked it up to good drugs and some kind of miracle as this condition had never been known to self-correct. To this day, very little is known about this kind of adrenal insufficiency.

## Chapter Five:
## My Life As A Pretend Nun

Beyond the Children's Receiving Home incident and the hospital, we lived a life most easily characterized by the 1950's television series Leave it to Beaver. My father was handsome, kind, and patient, making my sister and I the envy of all of our girlfriends. Each of our little pigtailed girlfriends vowed to marry our father once they were grown up. I allowed them their dream as I was proud to have such a sought-after father, though I secretly knew I had the inside track. My sister and I also thought Dad would be the perfect man to marry when we grew up. I had decided that because I was five and Denise was only three, I would be the logical girl to marry dad. There was no question that we would have the advantage over the others since we were his daughters and he loved us.

It would be a few years before we became aware of the societal implications of marrying your father. Meanwhile, he was the nicest man we knew, and he sang 'Negro spirituals' and church hymns to us as we sat on his knee. I have no idea why he sang mournful slavery era songs of the Deep South as he did not grow up around black people. When I recently queried him about this penchant, he said he simply liked singing Swing Low Sweet Chariot, That Lucky Ole' Sun and had a particular love of Shortnin' Bread. It was a lucky day when Dad co-opted the kitchen from Mom and actually made us Shortnin' Bread (white bread fried in shortening), which we would garnish with mounds of butter.

Mom spent her time keeping the train moving forward and none too cheerfully. Her life consisted of cooking, laundry, getting the kids to school, getting the kids to church and an occasional pinochle game with friends. Her dreams had been dashed with the arrival of two little children by the age of 22. How would she ever become the professional singer she had longed to be? So, she became a nurse, a very good one.

Abandoning her dreams depressed her and put her into a survival mode that lasted about thirty years at which time she discovered a group of women who harmonized together a couple of times a week; the Sweet Adelines. She finally had a reason to wear mascara, false eyelashes even, and sing her heart out on stage.  Life was finally sweet for our mother, but she had lost a few decades of joy in the wait.

By kindergarten, I had begun to question some of the more challenging concepts about life. "You mean if a little Chinese baby dies before he hears about Jesus, he's going to hell?" I asked. "Yes. Nobody said it was fair" said my mother.

I believe it was then, at five years of age, that the two frown lines etched between my eyebrows began to form. The incongruity of this information simply could not find a peaceful landing place in my young mind, and I believe was the start of my critical thinking. Nonetheless, Denise and I went to Sunday school every week. My sister ignored the sermons, and I cherry-picked the information that I thought was interesting or exciting, burying the inconsistencies and cruelties in an increasingly doubtful part of my mind. Within in a short time, I was just in it for the cookies and Kool-Aid they served at the finish of church services. But a time came, a few years later, when feelings of devotion began surfacing.

*The pretend nun*

My spiritual turning point occurred in the darkness of a movie theater at the age of nine when I saw the film The Nun's Story starring Audrey Hepburn. She was so beautiful and kind to the Africans in the Congo. That was all the motivation I needed to commit myself to God and the Catholic faith. Never mind that I was a Missouri Synod Lutheran, which is much like Catholicism but without the incense, wine, and confession. For us, there was no luxury of the halfway state of purgatory. You were good or bad, heaven or hell, and it appeared to be weighted toward hell. You could get there by dancing to the American Bandstand show, listening to dirty jokes, stealing things (I had stolen a blue gumball a few years earlier from the Ben Franklin Five and Dime), and not sharing. Entrance to heaven was based on saying nice things to people, sharing with your siblings, gladly helping out with chores whenever possible and the like, not my favorite things to do.

It didn't take much contemplation to realize I was going to hell and I just might be able to change my fate by becoming a girl of the cloth, a nun. I would only be married to Jesus, whom, like my mother, I had a crush on due to his good looks.

The first order of business was securing the vessel for the holy water. My fellow aspirant and friend, Brooke, and I searched our kitchens. Brooke had fuzzy red hair, brown eyes, a fierce gaze, and a stutter. She was already a Catholic so it was only appropriate that she should take the lead in our spiritual rites. My "vessel" was a mason jar.

Next was the process of collecting the holy water. It turned out the bathroom tap worked just fine as long as you thought Holy thoughts while the faucet poured the chlorinated and fluoridated city water into the Vessel.

Finally, I set up a little altar on my dresser with a picture of Jesus. The ritual was to sprinkle our foreheads with the sacred waters a few times a day while looking at the face of Jesus and making promises to him and his father, God.

The demands of my new faith started wearing thin after a few days as I noticed I was sloppily hurrying through the rites, forgetting to praise God at all. Within a week, we were down to one sacred ritual a day. I was starting to feel the burdens of Catholicism as it was much more work than was demanded as a Lutheran. I was even beginning to appreciate my former faith because you didn't have to do anything to go to heaven except be baptized and say you accepted Jesus Christ as your Savior. Why had I thought a little dancing and listening to Brooke's brother's dirty jokes would prohibit my entrance to the kingdom in the first place?

By the end of the week, both Brooke and I realized that we did not have the kind of dedication that had motivated Audrey Hepburn to such great deeds as a nun. We knew it was time to leave our dream of becoming real nuns behind. Besides, I no longer believed my place in heaven had been compromised by the decision to leave the Church. According to some Lutheran friends and family members, Catholics were just another form of heathens. But I did experience a twinge of guilt at my failure to make a commitment to goodliness. I wanted to be a Good Girl. Not in the eyes of my family, but in the eyes of my good-looking and kind Savior.

My brush with religious fervor was followed by a commitment to materialism. I looked for any way possible to earn some extra nickels, dimes and quarters. I had desires and needs, and nobody was going to indulge them. I understood that it was up to me provide myself with the things I wanted.

Among my early entrepreneurial endeavors was making flower leis to be worn by the neighborhood women. I picked my mother's and the neighbor's flowers, stringing them together and selling them back to the neighborhood gardeners whose flowerbeds I had violated. I had seen these extraordinary Hawaiian adornments on television, but marigolds, petunias, and Sweet Williams would have to suffice in Sonoma County. They smelled sweet and were such a lovely accessory to any outfit.

Later, I offered my services as a hairdresser for both real hair and the wigs that sat atop the heads of the ladies on our street. I babysat their children and ironed their clothing, all at very reasonable rates. It ultimately occurred to me that I might have underpriced my services when one of my mother's friends had me spend an entire day ironing all of her family's wrinkled, sprinkled, and rolled up clothing for a quarter. I was exhausted and my arm hurt. I felt that our arrangement wasn't fair, so I refused to iron for her after that.

During these years I had little interaction with my sister, Denise. She, being sensitive and secretive, spent most of her time in her room reading books. We all attended her lessons, rehearsals, and performances in gymnastics and tap dancing. Having developed a penchant for hair styling, I would twirl her hair into a tight little bun before performances, which I enjoyed doing. We were proud of her, and I thought her courageous as she did hands-free back walk-overs.

Some years ago I was with a group of people in which we were asked to describe what kind of musical ensemble our family lives represented. I said, "A jazz band." Each person was in their own world, improvising, with little cross over to one another - little communication and little joint activity. But we did come together one day a year; Christmas Day.

## Chapter Six:
## A Primate Christmas

As my parents had left their families behind in Texas and Minnesota, we were raised without the presence of aunts, uncles, cousins and grandparents. Except on Christmas Day.

Throughout my youth, we would pile in the car early on Christmas Day and drive to San Francisco to see my grandfather, Arthur Lanahan, and his wife Mary.

Arthur's affection for drink didn't wane after his dismissal from the police force in St. Paul. In fact, it deepened.

After his arrival in San Francisco, he began working intermittently as a lithographer. The interruptions came in the form of binge drinking that would have him lying on the floor of his basement, in and out of consciousness, for four to five days at a time. This would result in his loss of employment every year or so.

Alongside his day job, he continued to look into the needs of the future and apply for one patent after another while developing his forward-thinking inventions. There was no argument that Arthur was brilliant.

Mary, meanwhile, was a tolerant woman, a woman of means who was not dependent on the financial profile of her husband. She was a well-paid executive at PG&E. In a gesture of recognition of Arthur's previous family life, every year she put on a Christmas dinner for us.

As Mary's career became more prominent in her life, her child bearing years passed. Having some instinct - or need - to care for others, however, she decided to adopt a pair of Rhesus laboratory monkeys – Cappie and Fuzzy.

When we would arrive Grandpoo's house, Denise and I would make a beeline to Cappie and Fuzzy's room where they were housed in their own cages. We would incite them into making their hysterical, deafening noises by teasing them. It didn't take much stimulation – just walking into the room was enough - as they were extremely high strung and violent.

As time went on we noticed that Cappie began featuring a pair of very large human breasts. They were pink and smooth skinned. So prominent were they that when my father entered the room, he blushed and quickly turned around and left. Unaware of her abnormality, Cappie would position herself in what looked like an alluring pose, one hand up hanging onto the grid work of her cage with the other dropped loosely by her side occasionally lifting it to scratch herself. As I recall, scientists would check in on her from time to time to chronicle her development.

After interacting with the monkeys for a bit, we would hurl ourselves butt first down the carpeted stairs in our holiday dresses. We had no other occasion to be around carpeted stairs and it was great fun sliding down on our rear ends even if rug burn was the consequence.

Perhaps the most exciting part of our day was the bounty of chocolate. Mary would place a five-pound box of See's candy on the coffee table in the living room. This was the one day during which our parents didn't preach a tale of abstinence or moderation – we could eat all we wanted.

After dinner, we would open presents. Mary always gave Denise and me an obscene amount of money – a $5.00 bill! At no other time in our young lives would we hold our own $5.00 bill than Christmas. Along with it came a Barbie or some other relevant gift of the day for girls.

Exhausted, we would load into the car at night, drowsily passing under the orange-ish neon lights of the Bay Bridge, back to Sacramento. Even if we were a little sick to our stomachs on chocolate, bottoms slightly burned from the carpets, Grandpoo drunk and telling jokes, we had had a wonderful day. We never knew it any other way and it went on like this until I was 16 when it suddenly and irrevocably ended.

Drunk, as usual, Grandpoo waited until my mother left the kitchen when he drew close to me and tried to French kiss me. I never saw him again. Just like that our Christmas tradition ended.

## Chapter Seven:

## *First Loves*

As I grew into my teens, I found that I learned best by contrasts. I discovered more about the notion of what being a Good Girl meant by observing the behavior of some of the Bad Girls at Goethe Junior High School in Sacramento. To my great relief, I realized that I wasn't in the same league as real sinners.

These girls stole things - big things like Levis and Keds tennis shoes. They used really dirty language, let boys feel them up, smoked, drank, were mean to their families, and were all around delinquent. In an odd sort of way, I envied them for daring to be so bad, though it made me cringe when faced with the reality of their behavior. I didn't feel it was right to steal or to be mean to people or animals of any kind.

Where I chose to live on the edge was in the delicate and sweet pleasure of kissing, which put me on the probation list as far as my history of sin was concerned. The pastor said you were supposed to marry before "petting." But because I was beginning to question some of his fiendishly strict interpretations of what actually constituted sin, I kept on kissing.

The more mature teenage experience brought on an obsession with clothing; I designed my clothing and my mother would sew my creations. She had become an expert seamstress out of necessity. Our family income rarely justified store-bought dresses.

My other obsession was my hair. I was an innovator among my friends as I had discovered that if you stood outside in front of the wall mounted air conditioner the backdraft would blow your hair dry with a gale force hot wind. This was my first blow dryer, albeit only functional during the summer.

I also talked on the phone, listened to the radio, went to the movies, and spent lots of time with my steady boyfriend, Geoff.

Afraid of drugs and alcohol, after a misinformed briefing by a friend who had viewed Reefer Madness, my teens were not particularly drama-filled except for a couple of breakups, during which I morphed into a skeleton. Unable to eat, sleep or concentrate, the "orphanage" abandonment issue was rearing its rather large, ugly head.

At school, I held a solid C scholastic average - A's for what I deemed worthy of study, science and art. I received Ds and F's for the rest. There were moments of mercy, however, such as the instance in which my Algebra teacher explained that he was going to give me a D in his class, rather than an F because if he had failed me, I would end up back in his class. He didn't want to see my disengaged face any longer.

I felt insulted even though I had spent the entire semester doodling, designing clothing and passing notes. The

California educational system and I were at odds on what constituted a proper education. I was not going to be a mathematician, I was going to be a clothing designer. Why, then, did I need algebra and history?

During my final year of high school, I experienced two events that profoundly impacted my life.

Though ridiculously shy, I became a cheerleader, showing a developing sense of determination to succeed in a competitive world, and I experienced the trauma of both the Martin Luther King and Robert Kennedy's assassinations. I was particularly impacted by Robert Kennedy's assassination as I had seen him just the day before during a campaign speech at the local mall in Sacramento. The emotional shock prompted me to detail my feelings in a letter to myself, perhaps the first documented instance of introspection in my life.

*Cheerleading at Kennedy High School, Sacramento, CA*

As high school graduation approached, I stayed true to my plan and moved to San Francisco to attend a fashion design school. I wanted to become a famous fashion designer and, short of that, the owner of a cool fashion boutique. The dream was short lived. Imprudence about keeping a proper schedule for a student with a full-time job led to my expulsion from both my school and my position in the millinery department of Macy's on Geary Boulevard.

I was sleeping a scant four hours a night, attending school in the mornings, working at Macy's from 1:00 to 9:00 PM, arriving at my favorite nightclub (in possession of a fake I.D.) at 10:00 PM and dancing until 2:00 AM - every night. This precipitated a rapid weight loss as my only nutrition was half an English Muffin and a small chocolate bar each day. My manager at Macy's called my mother, concerned for my health and well-being. I was sent home, back to Sacramento, with my tail between my legs and began work at a women's spa collecting overdue accounts and assisting women on the butt-jiggling machines. This did not feel like a move up in the world.

Perhaps more significant was that I had a glimpse into the world of fashion retailing via my colorful roommate, Leslie. Leslie led a tragically fast life. Her boyfriend at the time was a married man twice her age named Larry. Larry was a fashion representative and invited us to come along on some of his sales calls as we were both presentable young women. Larry frightened me as he was very old (44), had a bullet hole in his side, and was drunk most of the time. Worst of all, he and Leslie had taken over our shared bedroom in our one-bedroom apartment. It all felt so dark and clandestine to say nothing of romantically unappealing.

When I came to realize, through our connection with Larry, that the fashion business was rife with corruption and sexual favors, I soured very quickly on my Big Plan.

Back in Sacramento, I was becoming restless. The new boyfriend, Rodolfo Jose Mayer (a Jewish boy born in Buenos Aires, Argentina in post-WWII times), who I had begun seeing during my nightclub dancing days in San Francisco, suggested he could find work for me in his industry. He was a hairdresser with a light handshake, which frightened my father upon being introduced.

'Rudy' was working at the top salon in town, which was owned by Jay Sebring. I was the innocent among my new gay professional friends. About a week into my employment I arrived at work to a grizzly scene of policemen and crying co-workers. Our boss, Jay, had been found dead with a rope tied around his neck, which tethered him to the actress Sharon Tate. She was eight and a half months pregnant, the wife of film director Roman Polanski and the former girlfriend of Sebring. It was the first of the ritualistic murders carried out over two days in August, 1969 by Charles Manson's cult. The Tate-LaBianca murders would go down in history as one of the top 25 Crimes of the Century, that is, until the plethora of mass shootings in the last decade. Meanwhile, a black wreath hung on the salon door, and we all went home severely shaken by the extreme cruelty and shock of it all.

I remained at Sebring for an additional eighteen months, which provided me with a proper street education.

My closest friend was Frances V. Lee, an African-American woman who was forty-five years my senior, and called herself Black. She took me up on the roof of the salon and taught me how to do midday tokes off her hand rolled joints. This did not ultimately serve me as I couldn't focus afterward, so these forays were few. Frances also taught me how to cook, laughing at me hysterically when, after purchasing me a turkey leg, I called and asked what to do with it.

Upon occasion, Frances would invite me over to her home for dinner. At the time I didn't understand that this could have been a risky affair.

Her house was in a tenement behind a tenement built on stilts, just off Divisadero Street. In the early 1970s, this was a rough area, driven by poverty and drugs. I was blissfully unaware of this as I stepped off the bus a few blocks from her home in the dark. I was wearing my customary shiny, white vinyl mid-thigh length trench coat and knee-high shiny white vinyl platform boots and mini skirt. The guys on the corner, speaking in hushed tones and looking disbelievingly at me, never uttered a rude or coercive word to me. I was an alien among them, bouncing along with my long hair swaying, smiling with a simple greeting of "Hi!" It didn't occur to me until decades later that they may have thought I was a narc, because they certainly didn't treat me like the other likely alternative - a hooker. Anyway, I came and went in peace in a very un-peaceful environment.

I also learned about the swinging gay life in San Francisco and was shocked to learn about many of the City Fathers' double lives. As our salon was the most elite and most expensive, the hairdressers heard all the dirt and were even invited to some of the elite soirees. These men, the pillars of society, would swing on the weekend at moneyed Gay soirees. During the week, their pictures would appear on the front of the Finance and Sports sections of the newspaper for their bold, brilliant or daring deeds.

I was not exempt from titillating invitations either. One such case involved the owner of one of the most famous department stores in San Francisco in the day: I. Magnin. A client of Sebring, Cyril Magnin preferred to come in at the end of the day for his manicures with Frances. When polished, he would call for his driver.

The elderly, silver-haired Mr. Magnin had begun offering me a ride home in his limousine as I had to stay late to accommodate his after-hours appointments. Upon one occasion, I accepted. Sitting silently in the back of his luxurious car, I could think of nothing to say to the old man, so we rode quietly.

At some point after that, I was approached by the only other woman in the shop. Patricia was an outrageous woman with a husky laugh, huge fake eyelashes, platinum spikey hair and see-through shirts under which she wore no bra. Men loved her long red fingernails massaging their heads as she washed their hair before the cut. She had the lowdown on everyone who was anyone in town. In addition, her brother was lead singer of a famous rock band, which gave us access to tickets at Winterland.

Patricia asked if I had any interest in changing to a much more beautiful apartment, all expenses paid. Blinking, I was waiting for the rest of the story.

There was a catch. This upgrade in living circumstance would be paid for by Mr. Magnin in exchange for a couple of nighttime visits a month.

My mouth must have been hanging open before I uttered the words, "Are you kidding?! No!!" She said she was just the messenger. She explained, however, that it could have been beneficial for me, but understood if I wasn't interested, the implication being that I was too provincial in my thinking. In my thinking, she was acting as a pimp for Mr. Magnin. We were worlds apart. I believed in love. Patricia believed in what worked.

The co-worker I was closest to was Frank, a handsome, 28-year-old Italian man with huge brown eyes - like Omar Sharif. Frank needed constant reinforcement as to his sexual worth so cruised the famed gay bathhouses of the day. He would stay up most of the night engaging in sexual affairs, take downers at around 4:00 in the morning to sleep, followed by uppers to get to work on time.

One morning he was more shaky than usual. He came running out from his booth to the reception area where he hurriedly whispered, "Do you have any black mascara?" I handed my mascara over to him. Later I asked why he needed it. He explained that he had made a slip up with the hair shears and had taken his client's hair down to the skin in the back. The black mascara was to cover the bald spot when the obligatory spin of the chair came for the client to check out the quality of the haircut. I stared at Frank in disbelief, asking what he thought was going to happen when the man washed his hair and his wife or girlfriend or boyfriend pointed out his bald spot! Frank didn't have an answer.

I continued my street education at Sebring's for a year and a half, until Rodolfo and I split up. He challenged our relationship and my devotion to him by seeing other women. I tried to be open-minded, as was the trend toward sexual behavior in the 1970's, but I was very hurt. No longer willing to pretend that his conduct was okay with me, I left the relationship. I was ready for something more substantial, but had no idea what that might be or what man that might take form with. Since I didn't have a plan for life, men defined where I would go and what I would think and do.

What showed up next was a handsome man who worked in the television industry on the business side, advertising sales. Bob was a bit older, 27, and very sophisticated, quoting from George Bernard Shaw in letters to me. Feeling that I was uninformed and intellectually inadequate, I began reading Shaw. When I next saw Bob, I started asking probing questions as to how he felt about some of Shaw's works. He had no idea. As it turned out, Bob had only picked up a line or two from books of quotations and had no deeper interest in Shaw's work.

That was the first time in life that I had arrived over-prepared. It had never occurred to me that people overstated their interests and accomplishments to impress others. I had come from a very simple world, one in which people knew each other and thus had no need to impress one another. My parents were without guile and stated their positions, preferences, and interests plainly. I never heard them speak poorly of other people nor witnessed them attempting to charm anyone. They simply were who they were.

As it turned out, Bob was full of charms, all of them inauthentic, which took time to reveal themselves. That part of my street education took me to New York City, where Bob had been transferred by CBS. He had asked my father for my hand in marriage - a very charming move to impress parents. I packed a box of clothing, with my parent's blessing, for the move.

The first day of my new life in the Big Apple was like something out of a fairytale; kissing in the back of the cab, Staten Island Ferry, ice cream, the Empire State Building. But that was Sunday. Monday followed.

Bob asked me to find a job to help pay the bills. A temp agency placed me as the receptionist and operator at a women's fashion school. the switchboard looked like one from the famed I Love Lucy episode where Lucy was tearing cords out and plugging them into all the wrong places on the antiquated switchboard. I was no more skilled than Lucy and in way over my head. The co-workers and students there took advantage of me in every way, using me as their personal assistant. "Can you go get me a bagel with cream cheese and jam?" "Can you cover for me? I'm going shopping." "Can you work during lunch?" One week into my new life, I drew a hot bath, lowered myself in and began sobbing.

Bob had taken me to a couple of industry parties where I was out of sync with everything and everyone around me. There was a lot of fake laughter, sophisticated jokes I didn't understand and sexual innuendo between people who weren't married to one another. Including with Bob.

After three weeks I told him I was lonely for California and wanted to move back home. He paid for my one-way ticket and promised he would come and see me soon and often. Instead, he hooked up with an industry co-worker.

I was left with a broken heart fueled by my first drafts of love-inspired poetry. Though I had no means of articulating the depth of feelings that had been running through me these first nineteen years, living more or less by happenstance, poetry seemed to be a portal to the first glimpses of the mysterious subconscious mind.

## Chapter Eight:
## The Boot Camp Marriage

I wasn't entirely clear on what a modern, post-sexual revolution marriage entailed except for a couple of reports from girlfriends who were forced to marry early due to unforeseen circumstances, i.e., pregnancy. Nonetheless, marriage seemed a good, decisive thing to do since I still had no specific plans for my life other than to "see the world" by becoming an airline hostess. So, when my new boyfriend, Jackie Lee asked me to marry him, I said "Okay," even though we had known each other only a few short months following my break-up from Bob.

Jackie Lee was a San-Francisco-by-way-of-Oklahoma hippie law student.

I appreciated his irreverence, humor, and sharp intellect. His shoulder-length hair on top of a lanky 6'4" frame clad in a cobalt blue fringed leather vest and jeans added a touch of the exotic and unpredictable.

The timing of Jack's proposal was not random. I was completing my flight attendant training in Fort Worth when my soon-to-be-employer, American Airlines, offered me a coveted position as one of American Airlines' billboard girls. I was to move to New York City, bypassing the usual stop in

Buffalo reserved for those with no seniority, to be near the photographic studio and perform whatever public relations tasks were required.

Upon sharing my exciting news with Jack, he suggested an alternative - marriage. Being thirteen years older and wiser, Jack was not going to let me loose in a city that would have chewed me up and spit me out and, more importantly, taken me away from him. We married in the spring of 1971 and moved from our apartment in San Francisco across the Golden Gate Bridge to Mill Valley upon notice that he had passed the California State Bar Exam.

We quickly settled into our marital roles. I was the young, compliant wife. He was my drill sergeant. In hindsight, this arrangement was much needed, but I wasn't exactly counting my lucky stars as the reality sunk in during those early days of marriage. Perhaps I should have - no, he should have - listened to the preacher who counseled us before we took our vows when he told Jack, "She is very young and impressionable now, but she's strong inside and will rebel one day if you try to control her." Jack paid no attention to the warning, as I was his dream girl for the time being. Soon enough he was to learn that truer words were never spoken.

During the eight years we were under the same roof, I learned all of the disciplines that I had not cultivated as a child and teenager. Among my lessons was how to eat and cook properly. Up until then, a box of Junior Mints constituted a tasty and satisfying meal. So, at Jack's insistence and with what would show itself to be a bit of an obsessive streak, I launched headlong into the study of nutrition.

Protein was the word of the day, and Gayelord Hauser and

Adele Davis were my new gurus, inspiring me to cook up my version of a healthy, balanced, protein-packed meal - chicken-fried steak and fried potatoes smothered in gravy. On special days I added homemade fresh apple pie or a berry cobbler. Jack loved my cooking. Being from Oklahoma, he felt my cooking was both healthy and tasty. I learned the southern art of cooking from his mother, Lavonna, whom I considered to be a culinary diva. She made homemade fudge, heaps of potatoes, pies, divinity, and smothered pork chops whenever we visited her in Bartlesville, Oklahoma, and she was kind enough to teach me her craft.

In addition to my burgeoning pride at learning all about healthy cooking and eating, Jack taught me about the body's need to move. He made his point by suggesting that I take a look at the dimples forming on the back of my thighs. I glimpsed myself in a mirror from behind and was horrified, vowing to do anything to make them go away before swimsuit season arrived.

The first time I jogged around the park, I finished by falling onto my back while the world swirled above. My only coherent thought was that I eventually needed to stand up again so I could go to the public restroom and throw up. God! How long had it been since I had used my body? I thought it over and realized that the most exercise I had gotten the past few years was walking to the convenience store and blow drying my hair on the backside of the house air conditioner.

With the inherent nimbleness and resilience of a twenty-year-old, it didn't take long before I was running a mile, then two. The urge to see the world had not deserted me so I applied for a job as a flight attendant with a non-scheduled military charter airline called World Airlines. I was paid

$433.00 a month and was to live in a constant state of readiness for destinations unknown. I would fly to Japan, Cambodia, Thailand, Korea, the Philippines, to deliver troops to Southeast Asia during the Vietnam War and pick them up. There were some frightening moments as the unpopular war brought bomb threats, which required a quick response while cruising at 35,000 feet.

During one such occasion, our flight was at maximum altitude after taking off from a military base in Thailand. The overhead bell began dinging. Our lead flight attendant went into, then quickly emerged from, the cockpit with a concerned look on her face. She gathered the rest of the flight attendants and told us there might be a bomb onboard. We were to take our seats while the airplane did a quick dive to an altitude where we might survive a blow out in the plane wall. I sat, facing the troops headed home, took out my little photo album of my dogs, family, and Jack, and began crying silently in front of our passengers who had already been through hell in the trenches of the Vietnam War.

When we landed at a base in Cambodia we each displayed traumatized behavior of various kinds by overeating, over-purchasing, and doing other indiscreet things - just happy to be alive. One by one, we were called into the center of a circle of armed guards with machine guns. Our bags were rifled through one at a time in the center of the ring. It was a very intense night that resulted in no bomb. It had been a false threat.

The next flight, meanwhile, might take me to Athens, Amsterdam, Paris or Jamaica. My world expanded by the minute and I was endlessly fascinated by both the differences and the core similarities of the peoples of the world.

Eight months into the marriage we moved to Lake Tahoe, where Jack could spend half his time working and the other half enjoying the sporting life. He had joined a small law firm in Tahoe City, on the California side of the lake. His new legal partner was William Newsom, father of a then freckled little seven-year-old named Gavin, who grew up to become the current Governor of the State of California. Bill Newsom became a friend and, upon a couple of occasions, I babysat Gavin when his dad had a spontaneous invitation of some kind or another.

*My first photo shoot*

I, on the other hand, was presented with an offer by Chrysler Corporation to become the new Dodge Girl as the result of a day job modeling gig in San Francisco. I had been signed by a modeling agency in San Francisco at the age of twenty with the intention of making some additional income. I didn't take modeling seriously and refused to go on "cattle calls." If a client liked my headshot, I would show up for a job, but I would not sit in a room full of contestants, each equally desperate for work.

*Dodge Girl*

I had caught the eye of the BBD&O ad executives for Chrysler. They flew me to Detroit for a meeting and test shots. I was signed as the new Dodge Girl. Instead of positioning me alongside the sleekest model of Dodge passenger car, however, I would be posing on the hoods of their big rig - The Dodge Ram. I wore the requisite white jeans, white shirt, white boots and white barrel racer hat of previous Dodge Girls to trade shows and photo shoots. We were glam versions of a cowgirl, though I had never even been on a pony ride. I felt like a phony.

'Overdrive' poster girl

Many people snapped my photo. I ultimately ended up as a featured centerfold girl of Owner-Operator magazine. At trade shows I was approached by those roadway warriors – long-haul truckers - saying I had kept them company at night in their sleeper bunk, my picture hung on the "cab-over" wall. This news left me with a queasy feeling in the pit of my stomach, but I let it be. My contract paid for our apartment and living expenses during the times Jack preferred to recreate rather than work at the law office.

In addition to running (I was up to six miles a day by this time), we skied most days during the winter, played competitive volleyball, skateboarded, played a little tennis, and negotiated rafting trips down the Truckee River in the summers with Jack barking orders from the back position all the while.

Life was good for Jack as he helped free local drug dealers from the tyranny of the criminal justice system. He enjoyed other personal challenges as well such as his one ongoing project - raising an impressionable young wife. Now that my physical fitness and culinary skills had been honed, it was time to tap my lazy mind.

Jack had become, not surprisingly, my literary advisor. I read only the books Jack authorized and believed I would enjoy or prosper by. This kept my nose buried in the pages of historical novels, biographies and the occasional well-constructed love story for the better part of the 1970's.

A couple of years into the marriage Jack informed me that I was really smart and asked what I was going to do about it. He said I needed to take life more seriously. It was posed as a challenge, which flummoxed me and precipitated a stream of tears. I had no idea what to do about it as I had never considered that I might use my intelligence for future advancement. Modeling for a few good corporations and serving travelers at an altitude of 35,000 feet had seemed ambitious enough. I was already living the dream, wasn't I? Besides, if this revelation was true, why hadn't anyone told me before? My sister was the smart and talented one, having compressed three years of learning into two because of her high aptitude scores.

Maybe I had missed the clues. Come to think of it, a teacher had once taken me aside to tell me what a shame it was that I hadn't taken English seriously because she thought I would make a fine writer one day if only I tried. Upon reflection, my piano teacher said the same thing before she dismissed me, citing that I was a poor student for playing just the pieces I wanted to play instead of my lessons. I suddenly realized I had been receiving backhanded compliments all along!

A few days after this discussion, we were watching the television news, specifically a local Sierra ski report. Jack and I were having a laugh at the generous interpretation of the ski conditions given by the weatherman. We had been on the slopes earlier that day, and the surface conditions were terrible with rocks and tree roots poking through the ice, not the sparkling "packed powder" the weatherman spoke of. It turns out he had been informed about these "ideal conditions" by the ski area's public relations department.

*KCRA ski reporter*

After we quit guffawing over the report, Jack said, "Why don't you go down there and get a job as the station's ski reporter? At least people would be getting the truth before driving all the way up from the city and wasting their money on bad skiing conditions."

I offered up every reason not to do this. Number one, I had never been on television, except for one appearance on a Baton Rouge noon news show when I was doing a public relations spot as the Dodge Girl in my white apparel and barrel racer hat.

## Chapter Nine:
# A Journalist Is Born

Jack continued to goad me, pushing me to consider my future plans. I was coming up empty, though I knew one thing I would not be doing, something that generally takes up a good portion of a woman's time and life energy - having children. I had been told fifteen years prior by the Chief of Birth Defects at Stanford University Medical Center that I would never bear children. This was due to an adrenal deficiency that interfered with proper hormonal function.

As Jack continued to push for a response, I began questioning myself. I finally shouted out of frustration "Okay! I'll go for an interview at the television station!" Jack made the phone call, posing as my talent agent under a false name - Steve Evans.

I was shocked to the bones when the news director at KCRA TV in Sacramento - a top 20 market - hired me on the spot. I had no experience whatsoever. I had lied about my on-air experience to get the old-style newsman to hire me. I was to begin that week, and I was fully aware that I was in way over my head.

When I arrived in the newsroom, everyone was bustling

around, ripping wire copy from the AP, Reuters and UPI feeds, writing scripts, editing. They all appeared so competent at what they were doing including another new reporter, Joanie Blunden, later known to the world as Joan Lundon, co-host of the Good Morning America show. Joanie was doing a little consumer report on the evening news. She had been there for a few months before my arrival so I tried to emulate her style of the news "head bob," which is a movement designed to make the anchor look sincere.

My heart was pounding in my throat at my total lack of preparation and training. I glanced over other reporter's shoulders to learn how to format my script. More terrifying was the impending deadline as I was to go on live in a couple of hours!

Objectively speaking, my first broadcast could have been worse in spite of the embarrassing fact that I was looking at the wrong camera. Since I had 'enhanced' my resume regarding previous on-air experience, it was assumed I would know about the red light, which indicates which camera is live. Worse, I burped out of nervousness early in the report. Although I didn't realize it at the time, a life-long love/hate affair with the media was born in that first frantic day in the newsroom.

Within months, I was elevated to the position of weekend sports anchor, for which I was paid a stipend of $25 per show. My duties were to write, produce, and anchor three sports shows each weekend. I took my job seriously and studied sports non-stop, adding sports biographies to my stack of books at home. I did not want to be perceived as a token of the growing women's rights movement, which, of course, I was.

After a couple of years, my boss was fired due to what I felt were underhanded office politics. I quit my job as a sports anchor and reporter in solidarity. I had developed another stream of income, which allowed me the freedom to make such a rash move.

Shortly after my start with the KCRA TV sports department, I put together (with Jack's help in sales) a syndicated radio ski report. I had engaged every major market in California and Jack had signed British Leyland as my sponsor. During the ski season, I woke up at 5:00 in the morning, wrote my report based on the previous day's skiing, and called in the report to the radio stations that were part of our syndication. I was done working by 6:30, went back to bed and then out on the slopes later in the morning. I was given a Triumph sports car as part of the deal and was paid very well for the day.

Jack wanted me back in front of the camera and found a talent agent for my budding media career. Due to some clever maneuvering by my new agent, Ed Hookstratten, along with a fateful event involving a robot, my next career move was a bit less modest.

NBC's sports division was looking for a counterpart to CBS's Jimmy the Greek - someone, or something, to give the odds on the football games. Office betting pools had formed, and bettors loved Jimmy the Greek. NBC could not fall short on the expectation of armchair quarterbacks across the country to profit from their weekend sports passion.

'Statz,' as he was named, was supposed to be a cute, waist-high R2D2 look-alike, capitalizing on the Star Wars phenomena. You'd think that, with the monstrously large budget allocated to network sports, the producers and staff would think things through a bit, in other words, prepare for the season before airtime. They hadn't.

Statz was not cute. He was more than six feet tall, dwarfing NBC's star sports anchor, Bryant Gumbel. Everyone was in a panic. They couldn't risk having Bryant's stature diminished by the behemoth, metallic odds-maker, so they had to come up with a backup plan - quickly.

I got the call on Thursday and had to be in New York at the NBC studios located at '30 Rock' by Saturday morning. By Sunday morning I was on national television alongside Bryant and Statz, live, before millions of sports fans across America. I would be Statz's media partner, interpreting the game odds, which were fed to me via an earpiece as I pretended to banter with the robot.

I was flying First Class, staying at the Park Lane Hotel in rooms overlooking the skating pond on Central Park West. I could buy any clothing I wanted and eat at any restaurant in New York City. The city was my oyster! This new status deeply impacted my life, but not in the way I might have thought.

*NBC sports with Statz, the oddsmaker robot*

First, some of my friends began treating me differently. They became less comfortable in my presence and more deferential. I was a budding star in their eyes and this type of relationship makes people question their own relative value to the friendship.

Secondly, I developed a case of greed.

A former Chicago Bears running back, Mike Adamle, joined Bryant and me two weeks into the season. He had no television experience but was being paid more than I was.

I began grumbling in my mind at the injustice of the situation, which probably had sexist underpinnings, I thought. I even considered placing a call to Ed to complain. Then something clicked. I was beginning to see an unflattering resemblance between myself and the spoiled NFL players I had come to know, or know of. During their very public contract negotiations, they complained of being undervalued in spite of making more money than 99.999999% of the rest of the world's population.

Embarrassed, I caught myself before calling Ed and thanked my lucky stars for being among the fortunate ones who had been given a chance to experience a large, some might even say exciting, life in New York City. Besides, two years at the sports desk in Sacramento did not make up for a decade and a half of playing the game as Mike had. He turned out to be a wonderful complement to the team.

Third, success doesn't equal happiness.

Once the holiday season playoffs were underway, I was sent out in between weekend sports coverage to do up-close-and-personal stories with the winning coaches and stars of the previous week's games. There were no breaks for Thanksgiving, Christmas, and New Year.

On one of the flights, sitting in the second row of the First-Class section, I saw a couple with their little child and a large bag of Christmas gifts boarding the plane, making their way to economy class. My heart was suddenly seized with sadness. They were going to share their holiday with people who loved them, and whom they loved. This might be the only flight they might take together that year, to connect with what mattered most to them. I was alone, on my way to another city, production meeting and hotel room. There would be no love, no familiar holiday feasts, which I had enjoyed with my family every year up to this point.

I was also feeling severe strains on my relationship with Jack, but there was no time to think about that. I was busy reading my own press as I was featured in such prestigious publications as the Los Angeles Times and Newsweek, in which they highlighted the changing face of sports coverage - women. There was me, the former Miss America Phyllis George at CBS, and a couple of other women at local sports desks. We were tokens touted as proof that the Women's Movement was in full swing.

In the midst of my highly managed on-air presence, I fought in favor of individuality, engaging in an argument with Ed that became a matter of public record in the movie Up Close and Personal. The discussion addressed hair length and attire. I preferred my semi-hippie long hair, jeans, and Tony Llama boots, a look that worked well for my personal life. Ed insisted on a professional look since, as he reminded me, this was my "profession!"

I ultimately listened, as Ed was one of the top television agents in the United States and was quite loud when he was upset. Ed was also the executive producer of Up Close and Personal and he based the leading lady, Michele Pfeiffer's character, in good part on my early television career, though I was not aware of Ed's involvement in the film, nor my influence on the script, for another decade when a friend called and said I should rent the video because the story sounded exactly like my own start in television.

When I finally rented Up Close and Personal, I found myself becoming flushed as the story progressed. What the hell? I flashed back to a day in Ed's office when I overheard a conversation regarding a movie script he wanted to produce about an anchorwoman, Jessica Savitch. I fast-forwarded to the credits at the end of the film, certain I would find Ed's name. There it was. The unsophisticated and stubborn beginning of the leading lady's career was my story, right down to some of our conversations. The later success of the heroine was Jessica's, as I had a way of sabotaging my good fortune as a result of my self-certain and unyielding personality. I would routinely refuse to do stories that either marginalized women or involved sports that I didn't resonate with, such as hunting. Finding me maddeningly feisty, I gave Ed plenty to write about throughout our business relationship.

Not surprisingly, I had turned out to be the least cooperative and most contentious of clients, which intrigued him because I didn't appear to understand the ramifications of my actions - or didn't care. And I didn't really. I had a good life at Lake Tahoe among the pine trees and fresh air. New York seemed so harsh. In addition, I was no match for the savvy young women who clawed their way to anywhere that resembled up. They resented my Pea Coat-Tony-Llama-Hippie-attitude. As the on-air talent, I could sit at the mahogany table during production briefings with the big boys and they couldn't, which created a great deal of resentment around the production studio.

When I explained to Ed that I didn't care for New York City, he said I was completely out of my mind for not wanting to succeed, not wanting to be famous, and not wanting to make more money than I had ever dreamed of making. By this time, NBC's patience for my "town and country" commute had run out as well. It took an entire day to fly me to Rockefeller Center via Reno and Los Angeles every weekend as well as when they needed me during the week, not to mention the cost of First Class airfares and hotels.

It hadn't seriously occurred to me that our working relationship would be compromised when I told NBC, via Ed, that I preferred to live at Lake Tahoe. For me, it was a quality of life issue. I simply wanted to live my life on my own terms. The terms ended up like this. I was fired.

I was now 27, unemployed, and on the verge of divorce.

## Chapter Ten:
# Salvation Through Ballet

Flying high one minute was followed by a quick and hard landing. I wanted something to hold onto. Something that was not as subjective as my tempestuous media career. This was when I met Madame Vala Bovie.

I was late for my first ballet class. My frustration mounted as I was driving down Hwy. 89 between Truckee and Squaw Valley, stuck behind a vintage, rusted out 1960s Oldsmobile, with the convertible top folded down. The boat on wheels was weaving across the centerline, onto the shoulder and back into the middle of the lane again. I couldn't tell whether the driver was trying to commit suicide or murder. I finally passed and sped up to make up for lost time.

When I arrived at the studio, everyone was milling around, waiting for the

*Madame Vala Bovie, ballet teacher and spiritual mentor*

famed, elderly Russian-French ballerina. A few minutes later, the old Olds pulled up and Madame straightened herself on her bad leg, lifted up her chest, which was sporting a fur coat, and made her entrance. She hobbled through the door, leaning on her cane.

Clad in fishnet stockings from her performing days in Paris several decades earlier and heavy costume jewelry, Madame's eyes locked with mine. I have never forgotten the experience. Streams of white sparks shot back and forth between our eyes, a kind of phenomena that I took to have significant meaning. I sobbed all the way home from that class, convinced there was a deeper reason for my new-found sanctuary from the demanding worlds of media and marriage - ballet; pure and refined. I had found my new path in life, I would become, albeit rather late in life, an amateur ballerina. I was prepared to lose myself in the classical music and disciplines that would demand a great deal of a mature body. I was also ready to lose myself in Madame's world of spirituality and storytelling. And she had stories to tell.

When Valentina was a small girl in Russia, the Bolsheviks moved through Odessa taking the homes of the wealthy for the rebels. Her mother, a mathematics professor, was taken away to be used as a tutor for children of the higher up revolutionary leaders. Her father, an attorney and now a soldier for the White Army, was killed. Valentina stayed in a corner of their home along with other children.

Resourcefulness was required for survival. Valentina danced in the street, begged, sold things she could find to stay alive. Ultimately, her mother returned, and a plan was made to walk to an uncle's home in Poland.

Their journey was made under cover of darkness as they

walked at night and slept during the day in barns or wherever they could go without being detected. She explained to me that, through the eyes of a young girl, it was an adventure. Occasionally they heard gunshots and knew what was transpiring in the world outside, but they continued until they reached Poland. From there they were moved to Paris, where Vala was given ballet lessons to help keep her arthritis in check. Her love affair with the dance lasted until her final days at the age of 84. To her, ballet was a metaphor for all of life - beauty, discipline, courage, passion.

As a teacher, Madame was a tyrant. "You can go lower!" she would shout, followed by her lusty laugh. And we could if only we didn't need those same legs for anything else the following day. I could barely walk when I woke the mornings following those first classes. Even so, I couldn't wait for the next opportunity to be taken through the torturous routine. The graceful movement augmented by Schumann and Greig filled the place in me that felt confused and disgraced. At least I still had control over my own body, if not my life.

In our spare time, Madame would explain the art of creating one's reality. She was a devotee of Joseph Murphy's The Power of the Subconscious Mind and thought that her beliefs would create her reality. She also had two gurus she was partial to and was convinced that she would simply shift frequencies into another dimension upon her transition and disappear. In reality, her ashes were carried back onto our faces, clothing, and shoes when a gust of wind appeared as we spread her ashes to the wind in the 'celebration of life' ceremony honoring her many years later.

Radionics was a part of her diagnostic practice using a

beautiful brass pendulum she was given by a physician in the 1940's to assist her in determining her children's food allergies. But most of all she loved Jesus Christ, the mystical version of her Savior, not the one who keeps score and demands promises in return like the one the church taught us about in Sunday school. She believed life was beautiful and so was everyone around her, including me. I was to be her new project because I was committed, somewhat flexible physically, and enamored with the mystical.

As the months passed, ballet became everything to me. I transferred the obsessive reading of sports periodicals and biographies necessary for my former job at NBC to the obsessive reading of biographies of ballet dancers. I was living a magical secret life - Baryshnikov, Nijinsky, Nureyev, Margot Fontaine - these dancers were fairy tale creatures, gods in my life. The outer world fell away to relentless hours of plies, rond de jambs, and jetés. I had found an objective world in which I could judge my accomplishments. Either I could master the move or I could not. One thing I had certainly not mastered, however, was the art of marriage.

*My escape to ballet*

The union of two people competing and defending proved to have too little tensile strength to survive the rapidly changing events of my life. To this day I consider first husband, Jackie Lee, to have been my most cherished mentor in life. I believe we had a soul contract, the end written into the script before it began, as it so often is. I consider his part to have been selfless, though subconsciously, encouraging me to greater heights while fearing I might actually reach them and soar beyond his control. I had learned physical and mental discipline while pushing myself through the challenges of a career that I originally had no intention of pursuing, yet from which I benefited greatly, and continue to benefit from to this day.

As the arguments ratcheted up and the marriage wound down, I made myself scarce, working odd jobs and acting as Madame's teaching assistant. One such job was with Fine & Funky Clothiers in Tahoe City. My momentary reality came slamming into center vision while at work one day as a sales clerk.

A man of generous proportions needed my assistance in purchasing a pair of Lee's jeans. As I was on my knees marking the alteration point on his pant legs, he craned his neck out, peeking over his paunch and said, "Hey, aren't you that TV sports lady? The one with Bryant Gumbel?" I said, "That was what I did then, this is what I do now" offering no further explanation. I could feel his discomfort and confusion at my kneeling down before him.

"Okay then, they should be ready in a few days. No charge for the alterations," I said while completing the transaction.

The oddest realization hit me. I wasn't embarrassed. I should have been by all outside criteria, but I wasn't. I had told the truth. This was when I realized that I did not find my personal worth through my exterior endeavors. 'I' was something else altogether, something that could switch roles from queen to servant with little assault to my ego. This would be tested again many years later.

Jack and I were now living separate lives. Being an attorney, I trusted him to settle our affairs and saw no need for another attorney as I felt he would treat me fairly in the end. With a sense of poetry, Jack filed the final divorce decree on what would be our tenth wedding anniversary. So, as I left my divorce in my soon to be ex-husband's hands, I danced my way into my new life as a single woman.

## Chapter Eleven:
# My Son's Father Arrives

I spent my time working between three jobs to make ends meet. By day, I sold jewelry at a fine jewelry store. I was ultimately let go for telling the customers the truth when asked about my opinion of a pair of earrings, a ring, a necklace and so forth. I had apparently talked more than one customer out of a purchase based on my subjective sense of taste.

At night, I worked as a hostess at Victoria Station, the famed Tahoe steakhouse of the day. I had a knack for the timing and strategy of seating tables on busy nights when we served more than 400 dinners.

A couple of afternoons a week, I taught children ballet in Madame Bovie's stead, while driving down to Berkeley for lessons from the elderly ballerina on weekends whenever possible.

About a year after Jack and I parted, I attended a local fashion show featuring pretty girls modeling lingerie. It would have been bizarre had the models been wearing anything less outrageous considering the milieu of the times - sex, drugs and rock and roll. Besides, how else could the men be lured to attend? Male attendance was essential to support the bar and, thus, the event.

Part way through the event a raffle was conducted. I knew the next prize was mine. I could feel it. Calmly, I waited as my number was called out. The prize was a one-hour session at the Squaw Valley Hot Tubs, owned by the future father of my child, Kurt Campbell.

Kurt Campbell and his friends were legends on the Squaw Valley ski slopes. They would jettison themselves off a ski jump under the exhilarated admiration of the onlookers passing high above in the chair lifts. These fearless young men would fly off the jump into 360-degree helicopter turns and spread eagles, seemingly with no concern for the potentially disastrous outcome of these daring moves. Jack and I, when we were still married, were among their admirers as we passed overhead on the ski lift, hooting and hollering our support.

Kurt and I did not officially meet until I attended a party two weeks after the fashion show at which I had won the door prize to his enterprise. By the end of the night, he had told his friends that he would marry me one day. It's fair to say that we were not reading from the same page. I had no intention of launching into a committed relationship having just gained my single status.

We began seeing one another the next day and every day from then on. Two months later he informed me that we would have a son together. He could feel it. Shocked by the audaciousness of such a remark, I told him he was mistaken, that I was incapable of bearing children. There was no one on record who had become pregnant with my medical background.

## Chapter Twelve:
## "You Can Have Children!"

I continued to enjoy the companionship and tutelage of Madame Bovie after Kurt and I, along with his friends Larry and Pablo, had become roommates.

Bon Vivant, a restaurant on Lake Tahoe's north shore, was the lunchtime retreat for Madame and me. She did not appreciate the lack of culture in American restaurants. She also did not appreciate the loud tone with which American women spoke, nor the fact that Americans chew gum, commenting that they all looked like cows chewing their cud. She would generally follow this comment with a live demonstration of what cows look like as they eat. She was so appalled by the lack of social grace in America that she chose to make a point one day that no one present would ever forget.

It was Russian Orthodox Easter in Berkeley, California where Madame's delicious Borscht was the center of the holiday table. Her family had gathered with spouses, girlfriends, and boyfriends. The youngest of her grandchildren descended the polished wooden staircase of the stately home wearing a "wife-beater" sleeveless T-shirt.

Madame firmly suggested he go change into something appropriate for Easter dinner. He refused. Big mistake.

Madame rose from her place at the table, reached down and lifted up her skirt above her head exposing herself from the waist down. She was wearing loosely knitted fishnet stockings and no underwear. The family gasped. Her grandson went back upstairs and put a proper shirt on. That was Madame.

During the summer days at Lake Tahoe, we usually went to French or Russian cafes for our lunch break between ballet classes. It was not uncommon for these lunches to end with Madame pushing aside the unoccupied dining tables, striking a pose, and dancing for the other patrons.

One afternoon, at one of these infamous three-hour-two-bottles-of-wine noontime repasts, Madame and I discussed family and children. She asked why I had no children and I told her it was because I was unable to conceive. She said, "We'll see." I looked at her blankly as though she was unclear on what I had just said. I didn't feel like explaining

A day or two later when we were alone at my house, she pulled out her brass pendulum. It had never failed to give her the information she needed about a myriad of conditions and she was confident her divination device would tell the tale of my reproductive challenges.

She held it over my bare belly as I lay on the floor. I was a little nervous and excited at the same time. The brass ball began moving in a circle.

"Nonsense!" she declared. "There is nothing wrong with your body. You can have children!"

I lifted my eyebrows in both amazement and amusement.

That I might be able to conceive a child was a titillating concept however impossible it appeared to be. What I hadn't shared with anyone was that baby dreams had been visiting me for more than a decade as I slept. It was always the same:

I would find myself pregnant and would painlessly give birth to a perfect baby boy. I loved him so deeply that I would pack our things and run away with him so nobody could take him away from me. Elated, experiencing all of the joy of a new mother, I would suddenly remember that I had dreamt this before. Then I would pinch myself to see if it was a dream as it had been so many times in the past. Sure enough, I could feel the pain of the pinch. Yes! It was real! I had given birth to a perfect baby boy.

Then I would wake up. Sometimes I cried softly at the cruel tease of it all.

## Chapter Thirteen:
## The Son Rises

About eighteen months into our relationship, Kurt suggested we begin thinking about marriage. I was not inclined to do this. I did not want to jump into the pressures of marriage so soon after several very disciplined and challenging years. Not wanting to offend him, I said, "One day you'll want a family, and I can't give you that." He replied, "How do you know you can't have children? Have you ever tried?" While I hadn't "tried," I assured him that more than a decade of sex without birth control told that story well enough.

Meanwhile, a friend of ours had recently been to an infertility doctor. The doctor had given her the requisite charts and protocols for conceiving. She made a duplicate set for me at Kurt's request. He felt I needed medical evidence to back up my claim that I was infertile.

One morning, I followed the recommended procedures, taking my temperature and so forth and encouraged Kurt to stay in bed a bit longer before going to work, to which he obliged.

Afterward, he hopped in the shower and got ready for the

day. I, meanwhile, had suddenly remembered something I had seen on the Mike Douglas Show many years earlier. An expert in infertility demonstrated to the women in the audience how, if they had trouble conceiving, they needed to do a shoulder-stand after sex and "bicycle" upside down. This would allow the tiny swimming sperm to work their way to the egg.

I "bicycled" like crazy for a few minutes then rested upside down for a few more minutes before getting out of bed to start my day. I was satisfied that I had done my due diligence in proving my infertility.

A couple weeks later I began experiencing lightheadedness during my ballet classes followed by ravenous eating and sore breasts. "Oh no! How could this be? I was just trying to make a point! I'm not ready to be married again!" I said to myself.

I drove the 90 miles to my mother's house and, feeling both terrified and exhilarated, purchased a home pregnancy kit at a supermarket along the way. I urinated on the stick, handed it to my mother and waited, curled up in a ball and sick to my stomach with anxiety. My mother read the results. But first I saw her smile. It was a bona fide miracle.

Six weeks later, feeling short of breath in my wedding costume, which I could no longer button up because of my expanding waistline, Kurt and I were married under the gazebo in the family orange orchard. It was a lovely, small family affair.

To help support the two, soon to be three, of us, I continued working as a ski reporter for my little radio syndication, which I had been doing each winter for the previous six years alongside my television career. I still reported on the ski conditions to about ten California and Nevada radio stations six mornings a week.

During the winter of my pregnancy, I skied until I was seven months pregnant, which forced me to wear Kurt's ski clothing from the six-month mark on. I was huge! It was no surprise to learn that no ski apparel company made clothing for very pregnant women. Other mothers looked at me like I was a baby-killer, and made snide comments in the ski lift line. What they didn't know was that I was more at ease on skis than in shoes. In fact, the only time I fell during the pregnancy was while I was walking in the snow, never on skis. What they also didn't know was that my ski report paid the bills and I had to keep skiing.

At seven months and counting, I had enjoyed a wonderful day on the slopes and felt I deserved a bowl of ice cream. While scooping up a bowl of Haagen-Dazs, I began hemorrhaging. I had been diagnosed with placenta previa, this is where a portion of the placenta is covering the cervix, and I had apparently aggravated this tenuous condition by bearing down while scooping the ice cream. The ice cream was as hard as concrete, but so was my head. I was determined to have some. After one really aggressive attempt at digging out the creamy delight, I felt something warm and sticky between my legs. I had pushed too hard, figuratively and literally.

With placenta previa, the bleeding can be severe, particularly if it goes undiagnosed and the woman goes into labor. The standard protocol was to schedule a Caesarian birth before the delivery date to avoid the chance of early labor and the potential loss of the mother and child due to hemorrhaging. This meant I had a choice: to stay in the hospital the last two months of my pregnancy or go to my mother's home as she was a Licensed Vocational Nurse (LVN).

I grew rounder by the day, sitting in the recliner my father had generously given over to me, reading book after book, following what I found to be particularly intriguing news. Princess Diana was to give birth to her first child the same day my son was due to be born (I "knew" my baby was a boy from the first day). This was made more titillating to me by the fact that Prince Charles and I also share the same birthday. What were the odds? I wondered.

So, I followed the media frenzy over the royal birth as though it were a soap opera, which I had also become addicted to during my downtime between books. As it turns out, Diana gave birth a few days early and I a few days late. There was, however, still an element of synchronicity in that our sons were born at the exact same time to the minute, one week apart - 9:03 p.m. on a Monday evening.

I don't know about Prince William, but Prince Stuart was a perfect baby boy, just like in my dreams. He did not, however, enter the world without giving everybody concerned a fright.

I was toxemic, and the baby was three days overdue. At my final prenatal visit, I told the doctor I wanted to have the baby that night. My sister had flown in from Germany for the birth and had to return soon. I wasn't going to let her leave without her having held my baby. Dr. Schiff agreed to induce labor that night as he was scheduled to be on duty and would not be on again for another week.

In anticipation of my last day as the childless woman that had been diagnosed as barren all those years before, Denise, my mother and I went out for a big lunch followed by a film.

I sniffled throughout E.T., sobbing loudly at the end. My mother suggested hormones might be to blame. Emotionally drained from the vulnerable little extraterrestrial's ordeal, we drove home and prepared for the trip to the hospital, which was about 30 minutes from home.

One the way to the hospital the contractions began. I was surprised that it wasn't painful at all, just interesting. As we settled in for the long haul in the labor room, Kurt went to the pay phone to tell the family that it would be a few hours before there would be anything to report. He picked up a sandwich at the hospital cafeteria then headed back to my birthing bed.

His face turned ashen at the sight of the activity in the room. The staff told him that he was not allowed in. Blood was everywhere and people were moving quickly to prepare me for the operating room. The placenta previa was proving every bit as dangerous as I had been warned of months before. I have since been told that I should never have been allowed to go into labor as the risk of bleeding out is too high.

As the ordeal unfolded, I was "somewhere else." My sister, who was employed as a neonatal nurse at a U.S. military hospital in Germany, had seen many emergency births. As the tension in the room escalated, she held my hand and looked into my eyes without blinking while quietly insisting to the staff that the monitors not be removed from my belly. Her eyes moved calmly between mine and the uterine monitors as she tried to conceal from me that there was a great deal of stress on the baby.

Meanwhile, the world I was experiencing was far away from the fray of the emergency at hand. All I was aware of was these great waves of motion overtaking my body, like the waves of the ocean, moving without my instruction or permission to push the baby out of my body. Amazing! I thought, inured to any pain as I had been deeply hypnotized by Denise's eyes.

When I reached maximum contractions one minute apart, with the painless power of the ocean moving through me, the flow of blood increasing, they wheeled me through the doors of the operating room.

The mask came over my nose, then something was pushed down my throat. Soon I experienced excruciating pain as the emergency C-section began. The surgeon and anesthesiologist were talking about something mundane. I was furious, wondering why they couldn't see the tears falling from my eyes. I was not "under" the influence of the anesthetic. While I could not voluntarily move my limbs, I could feel everything as there had been no time to give a local anesthetic before the surgery. They needed to get the baby out quickly.

*New mother with baby 'Casey' (Stuart)*

Let me say something here. It hurt. Having a baby cut out of your belly and having your intestines manhandled and plopped off to the side of your pelvic cavity is something best experienced while unconscious, or at least with pain killers. None the less, my son entered the world alive and healthy.

There are no words for the experience of laying eyes on him for the first time. It was just like in my dreams - he was here, for real, in my arms. I was not the freak that I had seen in my mind for the past 24 years. I was a mother.

Twenty-seven years after that day, my sister ran into Dr. Schiff, the doctor who saw me through my pregnancy and that challenging night. In making casual conversation with him, she said, "I know you've seen thousands of births since 1982, but do you by any chance remember my sister Regina Campbell and her son's birth?" He said, "How could I forget! And, do you know, we have never seen a live birth from anyone with that medical condition other than her, still, to this day!" To say nothing of never having witnessed the oddity of three placental lobes for a solo child. That one is still a mystery.

## Chapter Fourteen:
# New Mommy To News Anchor

The miracle of Stuart's birth was not lost on me. I was beginning to understand that the dreams were not a fleeting hope, rather an experience within another realm. Stuart had been preparing me for his birth from the other side for years. I later learned that it had been several lifetimes since I had had children due to exhaustion and having mishandled motherhood in a previous time.

Once home from the hospital, very pale from having lost a full liter of blood, I slowly began to integrate into a slower and gentler rhythm of life. I could not hold my baby while walking as my body was very weak. I could not drive as my body was fighting to recover from the damage done by the rushed Caesarian. About all I could do was sit, holding my beautiful little son, lovingly and admiringly. When my mother would take us for a little drive, I would tighten up, nerves on edge. The world out there was moving too quickly for us. I would try to project telepathically to the other drivers on the road "Don't you know we have a baby on board? Please! Be careful!"

The summer days with my newborn passed quietly and

softly. In the literal sense, Stuart was the baby of my dreams. He was good-natured, had developed a great little belly laugh, and slept, well, like a baby. While some of my girlfriends who were also experiencing motherhood for the first time would lament the loss of their free time with cranky babies who wouldn't sleep through the night, I would find myself "accidentally" bumping Stuart's crib about two hours into his afternoon naps to wake him. I missed him, and I wanted to see his little face and hold him. Five weeks into our new life with Stuart, we were all sleeping through the night.

I found it a seamless transition into my new status as Stuart's mother. I even experienced a twinge of unworthiness when I would hear about the pain of childbirth, colic, and the like. It felt as though I had cheated somehow, that I had been issued a pain-free pass at Stuart's conception. In truth, I was grateful.

By the time Stuart reached his first birthday, it was time to resume my media career. My naturally restless energy was returning in tandem with a need for a paycheck. I found myself driving in the fast lane once again. Just as I was energetically revving up, a friend called and told me one of the local television stations needed a female anchor for the nightly news. I made a phone call and was hired immediately.

*News Anchor for KTXL, Sacramento, CA*

If you have ever had any romantic notions about the life of a 'talking head," let me help rid your mind of such ideas forever. It's all contrived - one giant manipulation. Certain subjects will not be discussed as a matter of policy - good news, UFOs, and government cover-ups to name a few. What you will cover is anything that bleeds. Is it any surprise then that the citizenry of the United States has such an incredibly skewed notion of the world surrounding us?

That said, there were moments of satisfaction like the one where I was able to talk my news director, Don Ross, into letting me produce a special series for sweeps (ratings week). With a newly emerging interest in psychic phenomena, I chose to feature a week's worth of reports on the various ways in which this mystical skill was used, including locating missing persons, healing and spying. Little did I know when I naively trundled off to Palo Alto with my cameraman to interview Russell Targ of the Stanford Research Institute (SRI), that I was planting seeds for an unfathomable future.

Luck followed, and Targ granted me permission to run the first video shown in the American media on the highly secretive remote viewing experiments in Russia, which was a joint CIA and Soviet Academy of Sciences venture although it would be another twenty years before I learned about the CIA involvement. I was thrilled that I had scored the most intriguing video of the decade for our little newscast. This was when I loved the power of television. But those moments were few and far between.

Being the bearer of blood-drenched news before the city's collective bedtime each night took its toll on me. I don't know if it was the unnatural hours (I am a morning person), the back-stabbing newsroom politics, the lack of sunlight, the massive microwave dishes on the newsroom roof overhead or what, but I became very weak. My health declined to the point where I fainted in public upon a couple of occasions, regaining consciousness somewhere in the midst of navy blue-clad firemen who doubled as EMTs. I wrote the fainting spells off to being in a field that was intrinsically incompatible with my emotional and psychological health.

The only grace in this phase of life was that my tiny son was born such an empathic being that he would allow me to sleep until 8:30 or 9:00 in the morning. He would busy himself with toys in his crib for an hour or two before my waking, talking just loud enough to nudge me awake, never demanding, never startling. As I said earlier, I didn't have a real parenting experience, it was a fairy tale version.

While on the outside my life looked relatively successful, with a sought-after career and beautiful little son, there was still a hole, something essential that had gone unanswered. I had learned by the age of twenty-six that money and a high profile were not keys to happiness. My job in the news business only cemented that realization. I adored Stuart; still, there was something more just beyond my grasp. I could almost hear it calling, and I found it depressing that I could not put my finger on it.

In the early days with my husband Kurt, I had begun having strange visions. First, I saw him in a previous life as a Native American in the Great Plains states. He would show up when I least expected it in my peripheral vision wearing animal skins with a wolf by his side. The vision was so strong that I was tempted to commission a painting. His eyes were very direct and green just as in this lifetime.

Alternately, I would catch a glimpse of his hand graced by

lace, poking out from under the sleeve of a black cut-away coat. It looked like black velvet. It seemed to be the hand of a gentleman from the Colonial times in America.

I felt like a kid in a candy shop being given permission to sample all of the goodies that parents and society withhold from us - past life regression, color therapy, psychometry, and many more delights! I found that most of these explorations came easily to me. All I needed was an invitation and a little quiet time and I could "read" things, though, like many people on this journey, I chalked most of it up to coincidence as I had difficulty believing that I was capable of extra-sensory perception. Nevertheless, I had become passionately intrigued with the "unknown" and began to study in earnest after being exposed to the subject of color therapy. I gobbled up every book I could find on the healing modality and ultimately had an experience that showed me a much deeper connection with the practice.

I was in the midst of experiencing a past-life regression when I slipped back in time to an ancient, elegant temple with an aperture in the ceiling of a healing chamber. I was a healer and before me was a patient lying on a smooth stone table with a swath of silk, in a color deemed appropriate for his particular illness, covering his body. The sun shone through the opening in the ceiling high above at the time of day when the light was at its strongest. As the light penetrated the beautiful colored silk, I held my hands above the patient using my mind to direct the healing effects of the light and color. It was such a graceful and compassionate way to heal. It felt more real than my waking life and opened me to a deepening interest in not only color therapy but also past life regression.

In spite of these seemingly random mystical experiences, I

was still hungry for something more - something that would show me a deeper part of myself. I decided that it was time, like the children's storybook character, Patty the Caterpillar, to find my wings through the use of a mantra.

I knew of people who had received their mantras from Gurus. In fact, I had experienced a somewhat chilling event in my mid-twenties when I was first exposed to transcendental meditation by a girlfriend, Libby Cates, who had gone through the training and initiation. We were both Scorpios, and she felt the mystery of meditation would be a good match for my developing curiosity of the unknown.

Unable to share her secret mantra with me for fear of whatever happens when you reveal your personal mantra to another, we made one up. Libby set an alarm clock for twenty minutes and shut me in her spare room, which had been converted to a meditative space with an altar, candles, plants, and the like. I said my made-up mantra for a few minutes and worked on quieting my mind when something strange happened.

My vision was suddenly filled with an event unfolding in front of my "inner eyes." An eastern Indian woman wearing a red sari hurled herself off a very high cliff in an arid landscape, the fabric of the sari rippling in the wind as she fell to her death. I watched in amazement and shock. Who was she? Why had she done that? Why, of all things, did I see that?

Focusing on my mantra after that was difficult. I couldn't wait for the alarm to go off so I could share my vision with Libby and ask her what she thought had happened. As she was older than by two years and much wiser about the world's mysteries, I expected her to have the answers.

She had no idea.

I chalked it up to another figment of my imagination, though it did not feel like my imagination. I certainly wasn't making it up. I was watching it unfold. I closed that early chapter in my psychic development until many years later when my Indian friend Monica Dhinsa explained the following over samosa, dahl and vegetable curry one day.

In times past, when an Indian King would suffer the misfortune of having his land and palace overtaken by another King or aggressor, his wives would ritualistically commit suicide to avoid being taken into custody and service to another man. They would don their wedding dresses, which were red saris, and either vivisect themselves, jump off a precipice to their death, take poison, burn themselves or find some other way to leave earth life. This, according to Monica, was an accepted practice.

I began to put some pieces together. I have a phobia of cliffs and heights. On more than one occasion I've found myself clinging to the side of a mountain, either hiking or skiing, unable to think, blacking out, terrified. It took until I reached my 40's before I could drive along the Pacific Coast Highway without clinging to the seat or the driver, hyperventilating. I deduced that the woman in the red sari may have been me. I have always had an affinity for the Indian people, land and mystical elements of the culture - to say nothing of saris and curries!

My 2008 conversation with Harvard educated psychologist Paul Von Ward brought up some fascinating points as to the functional elements of our individual development that he feels may point to having had previous incarnations.

"First of all, the whole discipline of Psychology in the

1960's, 70's, 80's, 90's and up to the present has no plausible developmental theory to explain the uniqueness and the differentiation of human personalities as we experience it in our own lives, and as we observe in other people. I really spent a lot of time while I was doing other things, I mean ministry, counseling, and the Navy and the Diplomatic Service and so on. I was always involved in those professional roles with sort of another eye up here [just above crown of head] saying why is the situation the way it is? Why are people behaving the way they behave? So, my work at Harvard in the mid-70's with Psychologist David McClellan and Chris Argyris, was also driven by that urge to understand. But, people respond in unique ways that cannot be explained by their family environment, by their early childhood culture. They make decisions, they know who they are, they define themselves and a very precocious level, and I'm not talking about just prodigies who are doing symphonies at age eight, as Mozart did, or becoming mathematical geniuses as people have at age nine. I'm talking about all of us. We have those kinds of what I call precocity; we are precocious. We know things at early ages that we haven't known—no one has talked to us about them, we haven't read about them, we haven't been exposed to them, but we have beliefs in them. In research going on at Yale University right now people are looking at children who hold beliefs in the multidimensionality of the Universe, who hold beliefs about the transcendent nature of consciousness at three, very young ages. And they resist adults telling them that it is wrong. Now, where does that strength in conviction come from?"

Considering the powerful impact of my first formal meditation, I felt it was time to pursue Transcendental Meditation. By this time, I was following anything that felt right in the moment.

Thumbing through the pages of a local metaphysical journal, a picture of a man with a black beard and a turban caught my eye. I felt I was finally making progress in my search for the key to my enlightenment, my mantra.

No sooner had my eyes scanned his photo, my heart lifted with the possibilities, when I found myself almost as instantly drawn, like a moth to a flame, to the picture of a woman and man positioned just under the man wearing the turban. I fell into the woman's eyes - soft, gentle, quiet, intelligent and unassuming.

I quickly read the copy under the picture; she offered her services for something called channeling. The advertisement explained that you could learn about your past lives, soul's purpose, and much more. While I didn't believe I was looking for any of those things specifically, I knew that I had to meet this woman - immediately.

I began what became a campaign to secure a channeling. The woman said she wasn't doing any readings at the moment because she was in the middle of a move to a new house. I told her that was no problem, I would give her a week or so to settle in before calling again, which I did. Repeatedly. Still no luck. I later learned that, while listening to my phone messages, she was telling her husband "That pushy TV lady called again!" as they were accustomed to seeing me on the nightly news.

After a few weeks, she relented and scheduled a channeling session for me. My anticipation was characterized by parallel feelings of excitement and a mild dread that I would find that my life was off course, or worse yet, that I was a bad person in some way.

When the day arrived, the channeler's husband, Fred, invited me inside, whispering instructions to be very quiet. He ushered me into the meditation room where Linda reclined, seemingly unconscious, in a La -Z- Boy chair. There was an energy I had never felt before permeating that room. It felt huge, deeply penetrating, soothing, powerful, and made me feel light-headed in a good way. I didn't know it at that moment, but I was about to meet one of the most profound influences of my life.

## Chapter Fifteen:
## An Eager Seeker

I asked the channeled Being about my name, Regina, my son, my marriage, sister and family, and my adrenal condition, gobbling up every morsel of greater understanding. While the information was meted out judiciously, according to my own ability to understand the answers, I was overwhelmed with the feeling that I was hearing the truth for the first time in my life.

Among the bits and pieces that shocked me were the past life descriptions of Kurt in which he was a Native American Indian and then a banker in Colonial America. Those visions! How could anybody know these things? I had never spoken of them to anyone other than Kurt, so I was paying attention closely now.

In response to my question regarding my connection with Kurt, I was told that the two of us were married in my last incarnation. This is what was shared with me:

John and Sarah Ravenwood were married during the Colonial times in which the Declaration of Independence was being structured. There were many people involved who were not reflected in the signatures at the end of the historical document. People such as bankers whose assistance was needed to forward the agenda. John Ravenwood was one of those bankers.

As Sarah Ravenwood, I was an only child, well-heeled, barren and restless, filling my days with charity events and designing my own dresses, which I commissioned to have made.

John was busy with affairs in the city and had begun a relationship with another woman as he spent long periods away from home. I/Sarah was bitter and resentful of his absence and relationship with another woman.

Living alone now, John did the gentlemanly thing and allowed me to have an escort for the charity events that had become my primary focus in life. This move on his part was very generous and considered to be quite bold in the day.

Ultimately John died and I tired of the social scene. Having been left with some resources, I had a need to do something more meaningful than attending dress-up affairs. Having never had children, I chose to create a home for orphaned children of African slaves, of which there were many. I loved spending my days holding the children, teaching and playing with them, and helping with the administration of the facility. This became Sarah's/my passion for the remainder of that lifetime, though it threw me into the role of outcast. The townspeople did not approve of my mixing with the "negro" children.

Sara/I died elderly and alone, but deeply satisfied with the years among the children. This may well have been practice to begin child-bearing incarnations in the future as I had apparently had several lives without children.

As I drifted back to present times, I began to contemplate the notion of the "soul development", or a soul's collective experience. This is the aspect of ourselves that I believe continues the journey beyond the physical and seeks its own learning and refinement, which we could call the journey of our True Self.

I reflected on my life as Sarah Ravenwood. This connection with African Americans played itself out in this current life when I found myself fascinated with the occasional black person I would encounter growing up in my overwhelmingly white neighborhood. I wanted to know them and befriend them, which was as unpopular in the 50s and 60's as it was in colonial times. But I felt a warmth in their company that overshadowed the societal pressures of the day. Also, I was obsessed with Thomas Jefferson when I was young. It felt like something akin to a crush. It appears that was a holdover from social occasions in which he was present and I, as a younger woman, watched him admiringly from afar during the colonial incarnation.

Before the American colonial times, I had come out of the French Renaissance era. I was taken back when I found myself physically sickened in a very personal way when I saw the film Ridicule, which depicted the way of life of the French Royal classes. Laced with gossip, humiliation of outsiders, and manipulation, I could feel that this type of lifestyle had been something I had experienced in one of my French incarnations. In addition to these feelings of revulsion and guilt, I had other evidence as to this incarnation as well.

As an anecdote indicating preferences carried forward from past incarnations, the use of pearls in my fashion preferences was mentioned during a past life regression that was conducted with my husband, Kurt. He shared his remembrance of the life of John and Sarah Ravenwood in great detail including my clothing. I regularly used pearls in my designs as well as fabrics colored with special natural dyes from the West Indies.

Moving forward a few years, I was performing a past life regression (a skill I learned as a hypnotherapist) on a woman whom I had not previously met when she went back to a time in France in which she was an expert seamstress. As she found her bearings and described her surroundings, she immediately began describing a dress she was sewing on which she had sewn hundreds of pearls.

As she was relaying her experience, I was seeing the dress in full detail, as I would often enter the "mind/remembrance" of the person I was regressing. I shivered when I realized it was my dress she was sewing, possibly from the lifetime loosely represented in the film Ridicule.

I asked her if she by chance knew the woman who had commissioned the dress. She haltingly said "No... I don't think so." The statement was not convincing to either of us, but I let it go as it was not relevant to what she was looking for.

When the channeling was complete, she said, "You know when you asked about the owner of the dress with the pearls?"

"Yes," I said.

"It seemed so clichéd at the time that I thought I must have been making it up, but what I actually saw was that the dress was being made for you! Is that weird?"

I explained what I had seen while working with her, Kurt's description of my Colonial attire and of my penchant for pearls throughout my incarnations and into this lifetime. These are small observations, but there is a consistency that lends to the backdrop of personal history that has come from a variety of sources.

As another note, the woman I regressed was a professor of textile design at a university at the time. As mentioned earlier, I had planned to become a fashion designer directly out of high school to play out my obsession with clothing design.

Among the many other understandings that came from my first channeling with Linda and her Guide was the importance of learning all that I could by way of developing my intuitive forces so that I could access my past/present/future without coming to Linda and Fred. The Guide seemed to believe that I was quite capable of accessing my own information, though I had no reason to feel confident at the time.

I left the channeling a changed person, my head spinning with new perspectives on every element of my life. I felt as though something or someone had looked deeply into my soul and reflected essential truths back to me.

My next question was "Who was this being?" The answer would become a decades-long journey, but one that began the moment I walked through Fred and Linda's door.

I began showing up weekly with friends, co-workers and family members in the hopes that each one could find the clarity I had found in the experience. As the years passed, I would learn that many people's lives were deeply impacted by their time with the Being that became known to me as the Guardian.

## Chapter Sixteen:
# Past Lives Stranger Than Fiction

My days were bathed in a new kind of light, that of someone whose own mind has begun to illuminate to the possibilities of multi-dimensional existence, karma and soul progression. I had never felt more at home in my own skin. Nothing I learned intimidated me as I wanted to know everything. What is the human race? How did we begin? Who are the "others" who were said also to be here from the beginning?

I quickly gained a reputation as the one who "asked too many questions." More often than not I was told by The Guardian to look inside and see for myself. "You're quite capable of doing this," I was told from the beginning, though I didn't believe him/her/it. I generally defaulted to calling the source a He as there was a distinctly masculine feeling to the energy surrounding these experiences.

Fred helped me in the process of accessing my own knowledge. He had an uncanny skill at hypnosis, and I had more curiosity than fear as to how it all worked. Soon I found myself being taken "under," sinking into deeply placid areas of my psyche. Once I had developed enough trust in the process, Fred could simply place his fingers in the center of my forehead and instruct that I find my way to the time or place in which I was seeking information or clarification.

One of my first journeys was to go back to the earliest times of humanity, to the vast continent and civilization known as Lemuria. What I have always found about regressions is that there is no magical access to knowledge of the times, only that which was personally experienced. Also, these journeys can be quite disorienting because the viewer often has no idea who they are or where they've ended up. A good guide like Fred simply advises, "Stop thinking. Just report what you see and nothing more." Good advice for what was to follow as my left-brained mind would have choked it off before I could relay anything.

I was a young man of perhaps fourteen or so. The entire landscape was shades of brown - beige grasses, sand, beige sky, brown water and a very large brownish-purple bird. I could not see any color beyond this brownish purple, which was brown with a light infusion of the color red in it:

In this scene, I put my body to rest, sitting down with my back propped up against a stump. I looked at the massive bird, larger than a condor by quite a bit, and mentally signaled that I would like a "ride." I lifted out of my body and entered the body of the bird, and we took flight. I could feel the air under my wings and on my feathers. It was glorious! As we glided around, I saw another of the same kind of bird who was also "occupied." I mentally signaled to the other joyrider.

Fred asked how I knew that this bird was being ridden for pleasure by a human. I told him that these birds were far too large to fly just for pleasure, they preferred to conserve their energy for hunting. Thus, when spotted, they were generally sitting around on stumps and in sparse tree tops.

After a lovely ride, I found myself touching down in the same spot, exited the bird's body and thanked him for the joyful experience and merged with my own resting body.

Fred brought me back up from the hypnotic state. I began making excuses for such a bold tale. "I was probably just making it all up," I said, to which he replied, "I want you to listen to something."

Fred rifled through a large audiotape case until he found what he was looking for. He said, "This woman had the same experience as you." I listened, fascinated at the prospect that I may not have been making up such a whopper of a story, but may have been tapping into a very ancient experience.

As our sessions progressed, I learned that the woman who had ridden in birds and I had many similar experiences that one would not ordinarily conjure up. To hear her telling of her experiences offered validation to me for the inexplicable events I was experiencing.

No matter, I still needed validation as I was afraid that I might somehow be influencing what I was seeing and experiencing - it was all so previously unfathomable. I was never one to read science fiction or fantastical tales. I preferred biographies, non-fiction, historical novels, and other well-written works. Now I was riding the wind inside a massive bird. Get real.

Meanwhile, my fascination with color therapy continued. One day I read a passage from one of my color therapy books that gave Homer's account of the color blue noting that the sea was "the color of wine." I also learned that the original root word for the color blue in Chinese, Arabic, and German was "black." The author went on to explain that mankind's eyesight has evolved over a long period of time and that we could not see color as we do now until very recently in human historical terms.

While I could see nothing but shades of brown while "in Lemuria," it wasn't this way at all when I visited later civilizations, which I experienced in vivid color.

I was now beginning to see this new adventure as a giant puzzle and mystery to be solved, and I was running toward it at full speed.

## Chapter Seventeen:
# Paranormal Or Normal?

Fred and Linda found my enthusiasm invigorating and invited me to join in their weekly meditations with a few other people. We were all on the same journey into the unknown and spent our Sunday afternoons in various stages of meditation and altered states, sharing our experiences over bowls of Linda's vegetarian chili at the end of the day.

It wasn't long before I connected with my first crystal, an obligatory sort of thing when one is on "The Quest," or at least inevitable in the 1980s.

I had also been spending time with two other well-known psychics in town, Sherri, who was mentioned before, and Stephanie. We all participated in media events together as I was still anchoring the news at the time. Once again, I had talked my incredibly patient news director into allowing me to do a live interview with Linda on channeling to complement my other productions on psychic phenomena, which had featured Sherri and Stephanie. It didn't take a psychic at this point to ascertain that a pattern was developing in my career and life.

Once I forged friendships with my newly developing circle

of psychics, I was invited to join in some of their esoteric practices.

One of the rare activities I took part in was that of going to the bedside of dying people with the intent of reviving them. The group consisted of Sherri, Stephanie, Zack (Sherri's husband), and myself. Sherri referred to us as a mini coven of white witches. I didn't know anything about witches, but if you could help people by gathering around them and sending them some good energy, then I was up for it.

One winter day, late in the afternoon, I received an urgent phone call from Sherri. Mrs. Whipple was in the hospital and in critical condition. She was bleeding internally, and the medical staff didn't know if she would make it through the night. I was to meet Sherri and Stephanie at the hospital immediately.

Mrs. Whipple was a legend in Sacramento. A short and stout woman in her early 80s, she wore a starchy white nurse's uniform and sturdy white nurse's shoes to work every day at her reflexology practice. She had been a nurse in her youth, but her psychic abilities began to intrude on her patience for the clumsy and inaccurate treatment given to the patients in conventional medicine. She decided to strike out on her own and do some real good by actually healing her clients, which included injured police officers, firefighters, regular folks, and everyone in between. The police department would send her their tough cases where diagnosis had proved to be a challenge.

The first time I went to her was for fatigue, or what was more likely Chronic Fatigue Syndrome, though I didn't know it until many years later. She tersely, without any small talk, worked on my feet while her assistant, a large, quiet and sweet Mexican woman, massaged me. It was all very quick and efficient, but the speed robbed nothing from its effectiveness.

At the end of our first session, she said, "Here. Take one of these." It was a footsie roller. I asked her why. She told me that I had an adrenal defect that had to do with the shunting of a specific enzyme and that if I stimulated this (she showed me a spot in the upper center of my foot) area, my adrenals might begin working better. It took Stanford University months to figure this out all those years ago. The Whip, which was her nickname, discovered it in minutes.

I went to her every Monday before going to the newsroom. My body began feeling stronger and the lifelong stiffness and pain in my neck dissipated. Sherri and Stephanie were also among her devotees. They referred to her as the "healer's healer." I don't believe I need to explain that we all needed her and we were determined to "save" her when the call came from Mrs. Whipple's boyfriend, Joe. He asked that we come quickly to the hospital.

On the way out the door after receiving the call, my intuition told me to go back to my room and pick up my crystal. I didn't know the reason for this, but I did it nonetheless.

I was the first to arrive at her bedside. Her diminutive 80-year-old boyfriend was standing by, helpless. He didn't want to lose his dear Geraldine.

I approached her pale and seemingly unconscious body and gently picked up her hand and held it in mine. Then I spontaneously placed the crystal in her hand and waited for the others to arrive while sending her light from my mind. I had no idea as to what I should do. This was new to me.

When Sherri and Stephanie arrived, they closed the curtain

around Mrs. Whipple's bed. The hospital staff gave us free range to do whatever we wanted because the prognosis did not look very good. "What was there to lose?" was their position.

We conducted our energy work and incantations, which were led by Sherri. I projected as much light into Mrs. Whipple as I could and envisioned her alive and well. When we left, she was still unconscious, and we simply hoped for the best.

I checked in with Sherri the next morning to see if she had heard any news about Mrs. Whipple. She had indeed. Mrs. Whipple had come out of her coma during the night, the bleeding had spontaneously stopped, and she was doing fine. She was weak but otherwise fine. We were thrilled! It wasn't the first time we had experienced this, but it was the most heartwarming because we all adored Mrs. Whipple.

The Whip was back at work in no time. A couple of weeks later when I went for a reflexology session, she asked, "Was it you who dropped the crystal in my hand that night?" I told her it was. She said that she had thought so.

She explained that at the moment I dropped the crystal in her hand, she was in the process of experiencing her death. The black crows were circling her head, and she knew she had only a short time left. She said that my energy, carried by the crystal, had brought her back into her body, and she knew she would live. She went on to tell me that I had no idea of my own power yet but that one day I would, and that I was capable of much more than I could imagine.

I felt flattered but knew flattery was not her intent for sharing this. She wanted to convey this message while she could. As far as I had known, I was just along for the ride on these adventures. I never dreamed my presence was having any real impact, but I continued responding to these requests because people kept getting better. While I was excited by her revelation, it was also a secret I would keep to myself as I had no idea what she was referring to. But it did reaffirm that I had to continue my adventures in healing.

As the years progressed, I learned about Reiki, Quantum Touch, Spontaneous Healing, Vibrational Healing, and many other forms of hands-on healing. Over time, what had been a mystery in those early days of experimentation became second nature in my understanding. I no longer questioned that human beings can assist in healing people, including themselves, with their mind and energy fields.

Now that I had my training wheels on, I was open to just about anything that came into my view, the typical beginner's posture. I had no idea, however, that the strange was about to turn into the stranger.

Having spent some time studying the notion of the astral planes and the beings that inhabit this space, often called ghosts, I wanted to have an experience but had nothing specific in mind.

A few weeks later I decided to lie down for a rest before going out on a dinner date for my birthday. I was lying on my back on the bed, and within minutes an "experience" began:

As I was beginning to relax I felt a tickling feeling in my left hand. Soon I felt energy streaming through my arm and down through my hand, which by now felt like it was being massaged by some unseen force. Deciding not to overreact, I remained still and allowed the experience to continue.

Next, the energy began streaming down my leg and out my foot, literally like a vacuum sucking the life force out of me. My curiosity satisfied that it was a bona fide experience, I told whoever it was to stop it immediately. As I rolled to the edge of the bed to stand up, my legs completely gave way and I found myself feeling a mass of jelly sitting on the floor. I felt as though I had not so much as a microvolt of energy left in my body. It gave the term "draining" new meaning for me.

A short time later I had the opportunity to speak to The Guardian once again, as I did on a fairly regular basis now. I told of my "draining" experience.

The Guardian asked me if I had a problem with the experience. "Yes! It left me with no energy," I replied.

"Then why did you allow them to take your energy?" he asked.

"I suppose because I was curious to see what would happen," I replied

"Then it was taken with your permission. There was no violation here," he said.

He went on to explain that many Beings beyond the veil of the third dimension like to spend time around the living, including me. He said they find my energy uplifting and energizing. Because I give my energy freely to them and others as a matter of course, they thought nothing of enjoying a little voltage feast on my birthday. All I ever needed to do was to tell them, "No." They are not disrespectful by nature but I had simply not set any limits. And I had asked for an experience.

It should not be surprising to say that this story mirrored my earthly life too: I have few boundaries, and I'm not good at saying, "No." I had never given thought to how our experience in the third-dimensional realm would be repeated in other dimensions as well. This is what I called a lesson worth learning. As fate would have it, I would have another chance soon.

My friend Don called me in a panic. He was railing at me for having introduced him to the world of metaphysics, he said his life was falling apart. I asked him to slow down and tell me what happened:

He explained that he had been on the lawn of his home with his family and in-laws at a family gathering when he suddenly blanked out and was no longer there. Instead, he was on the East Coast of the United States in the midst of a chaotic and bloody train accident. He felt himself being tossed about the train as it overturned. He heard the screaming and watched the passenger's private belongings being flung through the air and landing everywhere. He was terrified.

When he snapped back into his body, people were staring at him and wondered what had happened. Later that night, it was reported on the evening news that there had been a terrible Amtrak train wreck just as Don's out-of-body experience was taking place. Don had inadvertently astral traveled to the site and had become entangled.

When speaking later with physicist Dean Radin about quantum entanglement, Radin explained that we have to acknowledge the new sciences to make any sense of the kind of phenomena my friend Don experienced.

> "The reason why I am interested in the physics of this is because the mystery within psychic phenomena is

all about Physics. It's about how is it that my experience can include things which are far away, and are not going to be able to make it through my ordinary senses, or at a different time? So, we are talking about mysteries of Space and Time. Well, many people who don't think about it very much say, "Well, psychic phenomena can't be true because it violates the laws of Nature." But, they are talking about the laws of nature as we knew them in the 17th Century, not now. Now, we know that time and space are relative; we know through entanglement phenomena that things are connected, even though they appear to be separate. All of the underlying physics of how we understand space, time, matter and energy, now, are completely compatible with the notion that you are mostly in here [indicating the brain], mostly brain activity in the way that Neuroscience understands it, but not all. And, it is that extra piece, which is left over, which seems to be very compatible with what people talk about as psychic experience and mystical experience."

Meanwhile, Don was furious at me for putting him in such a vulnerable position by turning him on to the world of the unseen. I told him I understood and tried to soothe him but my body was becoming more and more over-amped energetically as I listened. I was buzzing.

The conversation finished with no resolution. Meanwhile, I was late in preparing dinner for a friend, and I had yet to go to the store to purchase the ingredients. I rushed over to Safeway and picked up the things I needed to make vegetarian tacos, including an onion.

I am very particular about my produce and food in general. I always want the freshest and best produce. I say this as background to suggest that the following event wasn't merely a matter of oversight on my part.

When I arrived back at our apartment from Safeway, I emptied the contents of the bag on the kitchen counter to begin prepping the meal. I picked up the onion to start chopping. What was this?! The onion had grown a sprout about an inch and a half long in ten minutes. How could anyone miss this? The grocer would surely notice before putting it out on the stand. I definitely would have noticed as I always roll the produce around in my hand checking for spoiled spots.

Freaked out, I had no one to consult as to what I should do with this mutant onion, so I ran downstairs to the back garden with a large soup spoon and began digging up earth to bury it. I didn't own gardening tools. When my friend arrived for dinner, I was huffing and puffing, running up the back steps trying to tell him that I needed to go to the store to buy an onion. "You're never going to believe what happened." I told him about my experience, but he didn't believe it.

As the evening progressed, I thought he was closed-minded, and he thought I was a nut. "Oh well," I sighed to myself, nuttier things were to come. I might as well start getting comfortable with the fact that I had opened Pandora's Box, and there is no way to know what's going to pop out next.

It was becoming clear to me that the most productive path to intuitive guidance was to do it myself. While the channelings with Linda were profound beyond measure, The Guardian was increasingly instructing me to "find out yourself." I envied the newbies who were granted the answers to anything they desired, except their futures, which they were held responsible for creating. I felt like I was being cast out into the cold, foraging for my soul's food alone, though, as a mother, I knew this is what a good teacher does.

I started in all of the obvious places by going to the local Toys R Us to pick up a Ouija board. I decided I would get my information one letter at a time.

As a backdrop, I had begun what would become a lifelong habit of inviting stray people into our home for a respite from their challenges. At this point, Stuart and I were sharing our apartment with a seventeen-year-old girl from France, Charlotte Peltier, who was in her gap year between high school and university. She was the friend of my niece Kelly, and her living arrangements had fallen through for what was to be a year of adventure and English classes in California.

We split Stuart's two red bunk beds apart, putting them on opposite sides of his room. There, he and Charlotte shared stories, songs, and toys. Being the good sport that she was, she was equally agreeable to placing her hands opposite mine on my new Ouija board.

We had barely placed our fingers on the little plastic divining plate when it began circling the board as though it was on methamphetamines. We laughed nervously wondering what, or who, we had tapped into.

Once the plate settled, we began asking questions, mostly of a mundane nature. Charlotte wanted to know about her future with her new American boyfriend. I wanted to know who we were talking to. We had some fun with this for a couple of weeks when Charlotte discovered that the board was equally lively when she operated it alone. I quickly tried going solo too with the same results. We both liked the fact that we could ask our questions in private and were no longer reliant on a second party.

One morning, with the intention of playing with the Ouija board a little later, I went for a run around McKinley Park. As I was running, I had many questions on my mind. The desire for answers was so strong that I decided to cut my run short. Some unseen "force" had other plans.

As I approached the corner I would normally run pass in my three-mile jog, I decided to turn right to take the shortcut home. Something bizarre happened. I could not make my body turn right. It was as though someone was pushing against me, hard, to keep me going straight ahead on the running path. By this time, I had learned that there are some things one simply doesn't fight, so I kept running straight ahead.

By the time I arrived home I was suitably fatigued from my run and immediately sat down at the Ouija board. The board told me to get a pen and paper. I did as I was told. I assumed something unusual was about to happen, and I didn't want to influence it, so I relaxed my body and mind completely as though I was preparing to take a nap. As I rested with my chin in my hand, eyes closed, my writing hand began to move seemingly of its own accord.

I looked the other way as my hand moved, slowly at first. It picked up speed and began creating circles on the piece of paper while I continued to face the opposite direction, eyes closed. Soon I could feel the pattern change to what felt like vertical loops followed by a sequence of straight lines. Once my hand settled down, I peeked at what had transpired and was shocked to see absolutely perfect circles and loops, identical to the one beneath it. I doubt I could have done this with my eyes open!

I felt as though I was being prepared to do automatic writing, which I had heard of before. Ruth Montgomery had written her book A World Beyond from information given to her by a deceased friend, Arthur Ford. She channeled the information via automatic writing - or typewriting in her case. Was I about to become a medium?

I found it difficult to relax at the beginning as I was now under the impression that I was in direct contact with an unseen entity. But soon enough the words were flowing from my pen, large and loopy. Within minutes it was indicated that I should go to my typewriter to speed the process of taking down the information. I did as was suggested.

After a few moments, my hands began feeling as light as air and virtually floated up to the keyboard. My head nodded, eyes closed again, and I started typing. While I cannot say the process was effortless or that I was a brilliant medium, I was able to download some very intriguing esoteric information of which I had no prior knowledge. Still, I was fighting my doubts and fears of being wrong, or worse yet, delusional. I was convinced, however, that I had connected to something beyond my conscious awareness.

Being the communicator that I am, I couldn't keep this to myself and began telling my open-minded friends of my experience with what appeared to be automatic writing. I was soon contacted by the local newspaper, the Sacramento Bee, to be featured in a special Sunday report on psychic phenomena. This was my moment of truth. Was I willing to "out" myself in one of the largest newspapers in the country? It took only seconds to decide. If by having been in a position usually given a degree of credibility - the news media – I could help others become comfortable with an intrinsically uncomfortable subject, then it would serve some higher purpose. I agreed to the interview.

The article featured as a full-color two-page spread in the Sunday paper. The Bee handled it in a fair way, and the reaction was generally positive. I believe it was as a result of that article that our station's new radio host Rush Limbaugh became aware of my fascination with metaphysics.

When he was new to the field, I would introduce his television segment on our news show from time to time though I never really knew him.  Years later, after he had become a neo-conservative media phenomenon, he was asked what Shirley MacLaine, myself, and one other woman whose name I don't recall have in common. He just replied, with no diatribe or insult, "They each have an interest in the occult." I was a bit surprised that he treated us respectfully and offered no further titillating commentary. In short, if Rush Limbaugh was accepting of this in my nature, I shouldn't have been surprised that others were as well.

## Chapter Eighteen:
# The Tiny Mystic

My not yet four-year-old son, Stuart, known by his nickname of Casey at the time, was beginning to have his own experiences.

Kurt and I had divorced by this time. It was beginning to appear that I was a bit of a handful for the men in my life. In addition, it was becoming clear that I had a low tolerance for any extended unhappiness. I had not yet discovered that I was the common denominator in my seemingly "failed" relationships. It would be a decade or two more before I would identify my own core issue of not asking for what I wanted, nor stating my needs. Something I still struggle with.

That aside, in the spirit of goodwill, Kurt and I agreed to share custody of our little boy whom we both loved deeply. We each lived for our time with Stuart, which suited our son just fine - open arms were always waiting for him on Monday afternoons, the switch day. Any sins of the past week were absolved as the parent passing him to the other said goodbye with a heavy heart until we would reunite the following Monday.

One evening, I was feeling a bit lost and blue while the now nearly four-year-old Stuart and I were relaxing in our home. My mind was preoccupied with life, divorce, and my future career path. My contract as a news anchor had not been renewed due to budgetary shortfalls that left the news director to make a hard decision - to choose between the more skilled news anchor, which would mean having a solo woman anchor. "We can't have a woman up there alone," he explained to me, as women weren't perceived as having the credibility of a man. With most of the other female news anchors I knew, that would have been an invitation to a lawsuit. But I am not litigious, so I viewed it as a hidden blessing, a blessing that left me with no income and a child to support.

*Happy mom and happy son*

As I pondered these things, I said to Stuart, "Honey, I want you to know that just because I'm not much fun at times does not mean I don't love you. There was a time when I didn't treat you as well as I could have and I would never want to do that to you again." I will get to that in a moment.

Completely unaffected by my soul-baring comments, Stuart continued making a fort from the cushions on the sofa and love seat. After a minute or so he said "Don't worry about it mom. We all do it sometimes. I did it to you too."

Shocked, I said, "What are you talking about, honey?" My

pint-sized, sandy-haired son went on to tell me the following story.

"A long time ago I lived in a place called England. I was a daddy, and the mommy was dead. We had a bunch of kids, and you were the oldest one. I was so sad that I used to beat you up."

As I gently asked questions about his surroundings, he described the terrain and common style of low brick buildings. He said he was wearing a red shirt and black pants with a big, round metal "thing" around his neck, which sounded like a medallion.

I asked him how he knew about all of this and he said he saw it one day when he was supposed to be taking a nap at Busy Bee, his pre-school.

As he spoke, I had thought I was a boy in that lifetime, an assumption on my part. Many years later he told me that I was a girl. I apparently reminded him of his dead wife whom he missed terribly, to say nothing of being overburdened with his brood of kids.

I don't need to tell you what a flight of inquiry this information inspired. In addition to the past incarnation when Kurt and I were John and Sarah Ravenwood, I had also been told in my first channeling with The Guardian that I was here in part to re-balance my relationship with the entity who was now my son after having been an unfit parent long ago.

In my previous incarnation with Stuart, I was told that I had given birth to one too many children and, exhausted, had refused to care for him. His siblings and others took over that role as I was beyond caring, giving him literally nothing of myself - abject neglect. No surprise that I sat out the childbearing experience for a few lifetimes until I had recovered and could take it on again, but properly. This was to be my make-up time with Stuart, which is more commonly referred to as karma rebalancing.

Of course, I began to wonder about the cycles of karma - who had started this whole destructive cycle between the two of us? Did it even matter? What's done is done and now we had the chance to make it all good again. I seized every opportunity to do just that.

Meanwhile, we shared our new rental duplex with an apparition that began making regular appearances. From time to time, I saw the large, dark shadow of a Being moving across my sliding glass door at night. Our ornamental silk tree in the living room would often be knocked over when we woke in the morning. Stuart, meanwhile, was none too happy to have the large, shadowy entity pay a visit to him while he was on the toilet. He came out into the hallway to find me with his pants down around his ankles so he could tell on the "bad ghost."

Shortly after the apparition event, Stuart brought his blow-up globe to me. With his growing ability to articulate what was in his own psyche now, he approached me with a concerned look on his face. Being terribly dyslexic, and thus not prone to reading, he typically used the crude beach ball that featured a map of the world for kicking around.

Purposefully and meticulously he turned the "globe" a little bit at a time until he spotted a tiny dot on the ball that represented the country of Afghanistan. He said, "Mommy, are people being killed here?" I looked at the tiny country under his little finger and said, "Yes, there's a war going on there between these people and the Soviets." He trundled off looking concerned.

About two days later he was sitting next to me at the table while I was thumbing through a copy of Newsweek. On one of the pages, there was a small black and white photo of a soldier, a Soviet soldier. He quickly tapped the page and asked if this was one of the people that were being killed in the war. Neither his father nor I watched much television news now that I was out of the horrible business, nor did we discuss this war. It appeared he was hooked into it from some other source.

I asked him what he knew of the war, and he said he remembered "whirlybirds and big guns." "Whirlybirds" was what he and his father called helicopters. I calculated the years, and realized that it was entirely possible that he had died in the early days of the conflict and had done a quick turnaround. In addition, I had been told in one channeling that my son was not to be exposed to any sort of violent sport or activity, "because his being has seen too much of this."

After having read many books about life beyond life, one of the stories that came up repeatedly is that men who die violently in war often incarnate again very quickly. They do this because they had barely begun their life's journey as a young soldier when they were killed. No need to rest due to the fatigue of old age and long life. No desire for contemplation when life was cut short.

Was it possible that Stuart was still recovering from a violent act of war? I'll never know, but I listened to The Guardian's advice, which led to the decision to put Stuart in the Waldorf School. No violent sports, games, and the like were allowed in this pastoral setting. Instead, there were fifteen acres of heaven covered by orchards, gardens, a barnyard, soccer field, play yards with sand, and various school buildings. If Stuart wasn't in heaven, I was. As the years went on, the value of keeping him out of the harsher realities became clear. His gentle soul found a place of peace to call his daytime home.

## Chapter Nineteen:
# The Baptist Who Loves Kwan

During this transition away from news anchor and deeper into motherhood, I was drawn more deeply into a desire for esoteric knowledge. Perhaps the most exciting part of this mystical journey was the information that I became aware of as a result of my participation in the Sunday meditation group.

Linda and Fred had authored a book of some of their original channelings titled The Guardian: The Answers. Naturally, after my first channeling, I snapped up a copy of the book having no idea as to its contents. As I read this life changing text, I wanted to know more about how Fred and Linda came by this information. Little did I know at the time that Linda and I would become meditation and journeying partners for decades to come.

In the 1950's and 60's, Linda's family had always been relatively open to the greater mysteries as her uncle Jerry had started the only metaphysical school in the Midwest. The School of Metaphysics ultimately spread to 32 cities with its home base in Springfield, Missouri.

But Linda's own intrigue with the mystical began as a young

girl far apart from her Uncle Jerry's tutelage.

She stood mesmerized at the foot of the Guan Yin (Kwan Yin) statue housed in the Nelson-Atkins Museum of Art in Kansas City. The gilded, ornately painted wooden deity rose twelve feet above her little head. At seven years of age, she had never felt the presence of the divine before this moment.

While the other kids on the school field trip to the Nelson-Atkins Museum of Art left with pictures of Monet's Water Lily, and the works of other modern impressionists, Linda pressed postcards of the famed Goddess of Compassion, Kwan Yin, and the Dancing Shiva to her chest on the bus ride home. As her world melted away to the deeply intriguing and mysterious wooden entity she had just experienced, the notion of "home" was taking on an entirely new meaning. Linda secretly felt that she was adopted and that her true family lineage was Egyptian, Peruvian, and Chinese. Thus, there was a "coming home" when she laid eyes on one of "her people" in the form of this magnificent statue.

As the years progressed, Linda's heart continued to pour forth love and adoration for Kwan Yin. She found this very concerning as she felt no emotion at all for the Jesus statue hanging in the Southern Baptist church she attended twice every Sunday. She feared she was surely going to some form of hell because of her feelings for the Asian deity. In the spirit of self-preservation, she kept these feelings to herself as a youngster growing up in in the "Show Me" State of Missouri.

As a 23-year-old mother, Linda nearly leaped out of her skin when she came across a statue of Kwan Yin in the form of a small statue. She took her wallet out and bought it without even thinking, not like the frugal young woman she usually was. It was the first time Linda had seen the secret object of her affection since her encounter almost sixteen years earlier. As in her childhood years, she continued to keep her curious love for Kwan Yin buried safe inside. She was savvy enough to know that Baptists didn't care to hear about false gods.

With her tiny statue as her lifeline to the spiritual realms and a rocky start to the institution of marriage, as illustrated by two divorces, Linda began dating Fred. As with most of us, it was a state of grace that shielded her mind from what was to transpire in the years ahead. Ignorance was indeed bliss at times in each of our lives.

A one-legged, four times divorced father of five children, one of Fred's commitments to his kids was taking them to Judo class twice a week. When Linda learned of this, she was thrilled. At long last, an Asian activity she could participate in. She was filled with a desire to gain the strength and discipline of the Japanese masters in this martial art form that is known as "the gentle way." Here was something she could actually touch and feel that was from the Far East, a solid addition to the local Chinese buffet.

Linda was crushed when she realized that she would not be participating in what she thought was to be a life-changing experience. It turned out that Fred's ex-wife had found an evening job. Ordinarily, this meant that Fred's eldest daughter would babysit the younger ones, but she was among the kids taking Judo lessons. Linda would have to babysit the ex-wife's baby. Somebody had to do it, and Linda always did what she was expected to do.

Crestfallen, she was driving to work about a week later when a disembodied male "voice" said the word "Yoga." Again, and again, "Yoga." Whose voice was this? And, what is "Yoga?" She had never heard this word before as Kansas

City was not a hot spot for the exotic in the mid-60s. In Kansas City, Blues and BBQ were the height of culture.

She went to the library and looked up the word "Yoga" and found there was a book on the subject by Jess Stern called Yoga, Youth and Reincarnation. She gobbled up every part of the book except the part on reincarnation because, as a Southern Baptist girl, she knew reincarnation was nonsense - just superstition. But the rest of the book....

She immediately began doing the exercises shown in the book and was fascinated by the characters talking about such intriguing and exciting new concepts. Initially, she had suspected that the book was a work of fiction because she had never imagined such things could be true.

After the third reading of the book, she located the only yoga teacher in the entire metropolitan area who happened to be conducting a class at the YMCA. Mildred Jensen was a student of Vivekananda, a direct disciple of Yogananda.

A new world opened up to Linda. She was willing to put up with the ridicule by family and friends for the discipline and new understandings she was gaining. To push it even further, she decided to go back and read the forbidden chapters of Sterns' book explaining reincarnation.

All of the unanswered questions she had pondered throughout her life began to fall into place. Her life was on a new trajectory now. A part of her being was hearing truths that had been hidden from her, which created an opening that she later understood as a "remembrance" of what she had already known. But all of this was a tiny droplet of the mystery she would open up to under the hypnotic influence of her husband.

Always ahead of the times, Linda had learned hypnosis for childbirth, which she used to birth her son Tony. As often happens to new mothers, Linda had gained some weight with the pregnancy and her new life as a stepmother of five. This made her unhappy, and she wanted to shed it. Since the hypnosis had worked so well for the delivery of her son, Linda wanted someone to hypnotize her to help melt the unwanted fat from her body. She talked Fred into learning about this mysterious pathway to the subconscious mind.

Innocent enough at first glance, as Fred began mucking around in the deeper recesses of Linda's mind, he began to feel the true power of this tool and became frightened. He told her adamantly he would not work with her any further. She was on her own with her weight loss issue.

After a time, Fred's insatiable curiosity began to stir. He decided to revisit the subject of hypnotism due to a proliferation of self-help tapes entering the market offering transformation for a variety of personal development issues. Fred bought a handful, and at some point, he was introduced to the notion of past lives, an idea that set his mind on fire with questions.

Not one to waste time, Fred offered to hypnotize a woman and peek into her past at a holiday party. Surprised and intrigued, she agreed to the adventure.

Once the party guest was suitably under Fred's spell, he began asking questions of her past. Suddenly an entirely different voice and persona started answering him. He was flummoxed. What was happening? Where did "she" go?

Though startled, he remained calm and began asking questions as to what was transpiring, which is when he learned about channeling. Now here was something truly useful: to talk to unseen beings about the mysteries of the universe.

Linda spent months laid back in the La-Z-Boy recliner under Fred's hypnotic influence. There was no stopping him now. It was nothing more than a riotous adventure for both of them, and Linda proved to be a very amenable subject. She could go with ease from one experience to the next, but invariably she kept going back to the times that were termed "Atlantean," which meant the earliest days of Atlantis.

In her regressions into ancient times, Linda was a girl under the tutelage of her master teacher in the temple. That teacher was none other than her present husband, Fred. As a young priestess in training, she was learning about the protocols for going to her Master Guide who was referred to as "The Guardian" by other beings she encountered within her hypnotic adventures.

Day after day Fred would hypnotize Linda. He would gain her cooperation by dropping her a bone with some weight loss suggestions. His sole motive, however, was to satisfy his desire to learn the keys to contacting higher sources of information. Each session would provide a piece of the puzzle; a key or a symbol. They recorded and kept notes on each new discovery until they had what they felt was the full protocol for summoning the great teacher - The Guardian. They soon learned that Linda had spent many lives in contact with this Being throughout ancient incarnations.

The day had come to put it to the test. Linda was guided through each phase of the protocols meticulously, stepping through one symbol after another, waiting for instructions for the opening to the next. Little did she know that just beyond the veil between the physical world and dimensions beyond was her ancient teacher, The Guardian.

Fred had struck gold! He was as ecstatic as any treasure hunter who had located the hidden booty to find that the Being who was revealed to Linda as her Guide and Teacher was alive and well and could still connect with her after what appeared to be tens of thousands of years, from a time and place long forgotten.

With Fred, every appetite was big. Now that he had been hooked up, he wanted to know everything and pronto. Linda was weary of this new obsession of Fred's, knowing his desires always superseded her own. She knew her life was about to be enlisted into duty to her husband's seemingly unending curiosity.

## Chapter Twenty:
# The Messy Origins Of Humankind

I too was devouring the new information and lived for my Sunday afternoons at Fred's and Linda's house. My entire reality had been turned upside down, while at the same time validating something deeper inside. This was sped along as I read their book, The Guardian: The Answers. What caught my curiosity the most was the story I was exposed to of the origins of humankind. Instinctively, it made sense to me from the first moment.

In the intervening thirty-some years I have been exposed to a wide variety of creation stories, but this account still permits me to look at the origins of our species through a lens that allows for all of the other stories to be true. It requires an open mind, however, in the understanding of the duality that is the tragedy of being human.

A few years ago, I interviewed Michael Cremo, author of Forbidden Archeology. In reviewing his work, I was surprised to find that the science he quotes views the origins of humankind in a very similar way to what I had been exposed to through the Guardian writings more than thirty years earlier. The only significant difference was the motivation for the souls to take physical form, whom, according to Cremo, came into physical density from a parallel reality. He writes that human beings have been on earth throughout its history, simultaneously with other species which were previously thought to have existed before the appearance of homo sapiens. In Michael Cremo's research and the teachings of The Guardian, there is no missing link. Each "ape-man" lineage was its own development. Humans did not evolve from apes. Even scientist Gregg Braden acknowledges that there seems to have been a highly intelligent hand in the creation of the modern human. Both Cremo and Braden state that, while we may not have proof of the forces involved with the development of the human vehicle, we should not rule out intervention from outside intelligent species. This does not diminish the fact that each species undergoes its own process of evolution throughout time.

Cremo and I also spoke at length about the Darwinian agenda. He stated that a great deal is at stake to keep that bad science alive. A human who is aware of his or her "source" and true nature is an empowered human, which is not necessarily desired in a materialistic worldview where consuming and asking few questions is necessary to maintain control of the species. This is why the Darwinian theory has been subsidized by the state in western cultures. Meanwhile, those who operate at the highest levels of power politically, economically, and spiritually are fully aware of the mysteries of humankind and our potential for making quantum leaps in our mental, spiritual, and physical progress as a species.

The understanding that we are infinite Beings that give life, electricity, energy, and animation to the animal body we possess became my truth. Still, we live within a power struggle between the true self, or pure consciousness, and the animal/physical being. This struggle leaves humans with a deep sense of separation from "source" - the "source" being us! We carry the divinity of the cosmos, God Being, within and between each and every cell of our being. But we have been led to believe that we are somehow less than that, separate from the great creative force, and in need of forgiveness and grace. We are only in need of these things from ourselves.

Linda and I edited together a short essay on the information regarding Human Origins. It's available on my website – reginameredith.com - as a PDF and is well worth taking the time to read as it gives the context of extremely high levels of creativity and intelligence as the essential nature of our species as well as articulating our multi-dimensional nature. Some of the information is heart-wrenching in understanding the challenge of a non-physical being merging with a physical body. To me, it is still the most fascinating and compelling story I have come across.

If we are a species which has virtually lost all connection with both our essential self and our previous body of knowledge and abilities, then we must all feel this yearning for connection. This also means our greatest collective fear is the fear of abandonment. This has put us in a vulnerable position from the outset of this earthly journey by allowing us to be open to many forms of manipulation. I have a sense that a significant turning point for humankind and our loss of "memory" came from the Atlantean period of history, which is still shrouded in mystery.

As with most people, I too have spent much time feeling disconnected on a heart level, yearning to feel that special connection with something beyond. Why did my heart feel so bare and alone? I would ask this question for years, from my days in Fred and Linda's living room until sixteen years later when I chose to dig deeper into the archives of my own subconscious to solve this lingering human mystery. To identify what may have separated me from that feeling of all-pervasive love, I sought out a skilled regressionist.

In the year 2001, I met with the hypnotist Dolores Cannon at a conference at which she was presenting new information on her contacts with extraterrestrials. Like many lecturers of her kind, she generally created time around her lectures for personal sessions. I inquired as to her availability for private regressions. She had one slot open so, without hesitation, I snatched it up.

When we met in her hotel room, she asked me what I wanted to work on. I told her I wanted to go back to the time when my heart was damaged and began to feel restricted and closed. I could feel a tightness in my heart region and did not feel free to express myself with others. I didn't understand why. My assumption was rather mundane. I thought I might have had a love affair that ended disastrously at one time in my past and if I could identify it, the spell over me would be broken. I couldn't have been more wrong in my assumption.

As the regression began, I found myself walking up alabaster or white marble steps into a beautiful building. I entered a circular chamber where twelve other women were standing silently in a circle. As I tuned into my surroundings, I realized that this was a temple in the Atlantean times. I discovered that I was part of the middle generation of temple workers, whose duty it was to hold the energies of the region stable. There was also an older generation of women who had completed their time in the temple and whose energies were conserved for times of great emergencies and grand ceremonies. There were also the Young ones; students who were still learning, who worked alongside us on more straightforward tasks. But as the middle generation, we were the ones responsible for the duties of the temple. When I say middle generation, I perceived my body as being somewhere in the 30s or 40s by our standards, but I told Dolores I was more than 200 years old. We apparently had much longer lifespans at that time.

Moving further into the experience, I understood that we would stand, often for 24 hours at a time, focusing our intent on keeping the earth's energies stable. We had, in fact, been attempting to subdue this increasingly destabilizing earth energy for many years, generations even, and I realized that this was a somber day because we were losing the battle. Meanwhile, outside the temple, those who worked with our energy supply systems had also been experimenting with subduing the building energy by ramping up the outputs of their crystal technologies. I was distressed by this as I felt that our lives were already very satisfying with access to everything we needed and more. Why did they have to keep ramping up the energy?

As the regression unfolded, I became aware of a feeling of death in our temple circle. We were preparing for our own ends by holding one final silent vigil. There were symbolic objects in our hands, which I can no longer recall, and then there was a great and quiet aura of despair. We were going to blow apart at the seams because nothing could stop what had happened to the energies. I began crying with despair and told Dolores repeatedly that "we have ruined our relationship with the sun...it took many years to develop the delicate matrix between the sun and earth to allow everything here to survive and thrive, and they've gone and ruined it! Why?!! We already had everything!"

As I looked at what was happening outside the temple, I saw spaceships hovering just above the city. I realized they were friendly and were also trying to stop this disaster from playing out by using their energy to stabilize what was transpiring. I was horrified, however, when I saw that one of the primary technology workers had made a deal to get himself out before the explosion. He was in one of the craft and was going to survive while the rest of us would be suffering irreparable harm for a very long time. I couldn't understand how he could have done this.

Suddenly I was out of my body, and I saw the water in the rivers turn gold and begin to boil. The fish were all dying, and the crops were scorched. I was now surveying from above. We had lost everything. I told Dolores, crying, "We are going to go to sleep now." She wasn't clear what I was speaking of and asked me what I meant; did I mean we were going to bed? I told her, "No, all of us are going to go to sleep for a very long time now. We have to forget everything." She asked why. I told her that to remember what we had just lost would lead to such deep despair that we would have no incentive to incarnate further nor try to rebuild. It would be best for all to forget and learn again. The journey would be impossibly long and it would be very difficult to re-discover and recreate what we had just lost.

And it has been.

When I later shared the experience with Linda, she said, "Yes, it was like that," and went on to add details. Surprised, I asked how she knew. She told me that she had been taken back to the same lifetime and that same day, in the same temple, some years prior in a regression. Also, another man Fred had performed a regression with had remembered the same event from his perspective as an extraterrestrial in one of the UFO craft I had "witnessed" hovering above us, as he worked to stabilize the energies of the Atlantean area.

As an aside, it was not until later that I came to realize that my experience was tainted by my own lack of knowledge at the time in being isolated as a temple worker. I had thought the people working with the energy technologies were creating the problem, rather than attempting to control an energy dynamic that was rapidly spiraling out of control. My prejudices came through in the regression as I placed blame on them. I was learning, in those early days of journeying into other times, that we are not suddenly awakened just because we have glimpsed into another time. As I've mentioned before, if we are genuinely exploring or remembering another lifetime, we have access to no more knowledge or understanding than we did then. What I saw was merely my experience - not a vast, clear overview that stretched beyond my experience of that time.

In these early days of opening my aperture to my own consciousness, I came to believe that we each have a rich history living in the shadows of our very controlling conscious mind. The task would be to break through to our true self, beyond the control of an adaptive mind that feels it will lose power and control if it allows our essential self to come into our own awareness. To merge with Self is to lose the personality's identity. This is a theme I have come up against again and again.

Along with this little group - Linda, Fred, Nichole, Jon, and Kayla - I was learning about the complexity of being human, and it was in these grace-filled days of exploration that I learned to be patient and forgiving with myself. The realization that all of us have been on unfathomably long and mostly forgotten, journeys has given rise to feelings of appreciation for those of us who still choose to show up. As one dear friend used to say, we should kiss ourselves on the shoulder for being so brave!

## Chapter Twenty-One:
# Changing Perspectives

In the early days of these explorations, I was still working in the newsroom. My world-view was expanded to a cosmic view, and I could no longer see the world of news that came across the UPI or Associated Press wire and video feeds with the same sheltered eyes.

One afternoon, news came of a man slaying his wife and children before killing himself. I sat at my desk lost in thought. Was it the karma of the husband or the wife that created this horrible situation? Had the children incarnated into this family with the understanding of what was to happen? What could have been in need of balance to have agreed to such a harsh experience? I could no longer take life at face value.

Still, I would become emotional when particularly heinous events transpired such as a drunk driver killing an entire family in a head-on collision. Little shoes and stuffed toys were strewn about the road while news crews captured footage of the driver weaving under his own weight as he was taken to the California Highway Patrol car and placed under arrest. When I reported the incident on the evening news, I left out the official news speak disclaimer language of "allegedly" drunk. He could hardly walk to the police car in the video footage for God's sake!

The news director called me into his office to inform me, very loudly, that teams of attorneys would likely swarm the station's legal department and that the case could be thrown out because of my "prejudicial commentary." I felt like Mary Tyler Moore being upbraided by Lou Grant, but this was a good lesson in Journalism 101. This is why you will never hear it straight while watching the nightly news.

As the weeks and months passed, my mind seemed to create a never-ending stream of questions. I wanted to know about everything including the new disease called AIDS, sex in the human species, emotions, other dimensions, extraterrestrial species, and who exactly was the Being to whom I had been speaking for the past year.

The Guardian explained, "I am so far away that you cannot comprehend this, yet I am right here where you are." This was before I had begun to contemplate the vastly confusing topic of multi-dimensionality. When I would ask for an identity, he would simply say, "This is not important." But others continued to put a name to it.

As people showed up for regressions, Fred found that a few of them were also bringing through entities. Those entities, without exception, deferred to Linda's connection, calling it/him/her as "The one who knows all", and more intimidating, "The Guardian for our Universes." Universes?! There's more than one?!

When I insisted on taking the question as to "its/his/her" identity to a more personal level, The Guardian would say "This will not be given at this time."

I found this statement annoying and frustrating. "Why not?" was my response on many occasions. I ultimately learned over the years and decades that there was always a good reason for this answer, but I wanted it handed to me on a silver platter - all of it. The Guardian wanted me to go through the process of discovery, analysis, and learning the art of original thinking. In truth, I would generally find the answer to my question by putting pieces together over a period of time, sometimes years. Then would come the day when the lights would explode in my head: Oh my God! That's it! and I would be overjoyed at having discovered it for myself.

As I continued attempting to quench my thirst for knowledge, The Guardian was downright terse with me at times, while showing unbelievable softness and compassion for others. This was generally the case with people who had no idea of whom or where they were in their incarnation paths, those who had resorted to suicide in previous incarnations or were working off some difficult karma. The Guardian showed such deep kindness and compassion for people who were deeply suffering, while I was the one who asked too many questions and pushed for answers. Little did I know that I was also one of those people he would demand more of because I was, unbeknownst to me, capable of the task of remembering and possibly even awakening again one day. He was not going to encourage me to become lazy and coddled, though I would have much preferred it most days, especially as the challenges kept coming.

Recently divorced from Kurt and having lost my news anchor job, I became fearful around the issue of money once again. There are only a handful of these jobs in any given city, and I had already occupied a couple of them. Also, I had to deal with the issue of being a working single mother.

At first, I was relieved when I was offered a job anchoring the nightly news at another station in town. Then the reality of my single status sunk in. I realized that I no longer had someone to watch my little son while I worked now that I was divorced. I felt Stuart deserved better than to have an absentee and stressed out mother, so I declined the job.

My life could have become extremely difficult at this time as there was nowhere else to go within my profession due to the custody arrangement between Kurt and me in which we had agreed to stay in Sacramento to co-raise our son.

As fate would have it, I was given a period of grace to get it together when my parents offered to help me financially until I could put my life back together. I was grateful beyond imagination. My parents had never had any extra money when we were growing up, but my father's business was doing well, and they said they wanted to extend the help they weren't able to provide when I was college age and before. I accepted. There was no time for pride, as I genuinely didn't know what lies ahead.

I began checking in with my heart as to what I would like to do with my life. I had been learning about energy, dowsing, hypnotherapy, alternative medicine, and many other esoteric subjects. What had particularly caught my fancy was the subject of color therapy. I had picked up a copy of a little book, The Seven Keys to Color Healing while on a Hawaiian vacation with Kurt some months before. I sat on the beach wholly engrossed in the magic of color, unaware of the waves crashing on the shore, children playing and screaming at the cold water or anything else going on around me My focus was so great, I could have been swept away by a tsunami and barely noticed.

I was clear that I did not want to go back into the world of media as I had known it. If I was going to place myself in that kind of mental and emotional pressure cooker, I wanted to use the medium for spreading information of a more healing nature.

Inspired by my newfound love of color therapy, I decided to use my (also newly acquired) first credit card to subsidize a budget trip to Europe to interview all of the authorities on the subject. At that time, I did not understand that when it comes to energy healing, you could not isolate one modality from another, so my interviewee list became more diverse by the minute.

I shared the vision with my friend Clint, who had done some production work for a cable television station and owned a professional video camera. Raised in the military, Clint had traveled the world as a child, and he was filled with fond memories of Germany. Without blinking, he volunteered to come along to capture my interviews on tape.

We met with Dr. Jean Claude Darras, the first Westerner to use low dosage radioactive isotopes to prove the existence of acupuncture meridians in the human body. He had become a hero in Asia for his work.

Dr. Darras guided me to a meeting with Dr. Bernard Meuschlein, who was working with Kurt Olbrecht with the Ergonom 400 microscope. Their experiments were showing that cancer cells can mutate from mold to bacteria to virus. This was groundbreaking work in that it was the only existing microscope to have the capability of observing living objects magnified 50,000X.

Royal Raymond Rife's famed Universal Microscope, which could also magnify living objects to near 50,000X, had long disappeared. In the mid 1980s, the electron microscope was the most progressive tool used in research facilities and labs, but it killed the organisms, which limited researchers to witnessing only dead, non-dynamic organisms. I found this fascinating and was the first journalist to interview Olbrecht and videotape the super-scope. My story eventually aired in short format as a CNN news segment.

In England, we met with Vicky Wall, a blind woman who could differentiate colors by feel. She had developed a system using colors suspended in water as a means of divination, a method called Aurosoma, which is popular to this day.

Our Swiss contacts took us to the Geotheanum, the headquarters of Rudolph Steiner's body of work in Anthroposophical medicine, education, spiritual development, and agriculture. In this Hobbit-like habitat, there were a series of education out-buildings including a Color Therapy Laboratory. I was fascinated by the knowledge of the master color teacher who explained basics such as why the sky is blue.

Our contacts at the Geotheanum pointed us to the Wegeman Clinic in Ascona, Switzerland, where patients were being treated with a combination of western allopathic medicine and Rudolph Steiner's Anthroposophical healing practices, which nurtures the entire being. This was an eye opener for me as the patients were in sunny rooms looking out onto gardens. Each patient had a full schedule of painting, sculpture, color therapy and eurythmy dancing. With both my mother and sister working as nurses, the hospitals I knew were gray or dull green antiseptic spaces of illness. This was a splendid place for the weak to heal!

The trip was a smash success with each person leading us to another piece of the healing puzzle. Once home, we created a short feature pilot series of the subjects I had covered. I called my old friend Ed Hookstratten, the attorney who had represented me in my NBC sports days. I was hoping he might see the value in an avant-garde series on alternative medical practices, which I had titled 'A Second Opinion'. He was intrigued and told me to come to Los Angeles. Meanwhile, he would arrange a meeting or two.

One of the meetings was with the president of the news division of Lorimar Productions. They produced short features that could be inserted into the nation's news programs to help cut the station production costs and offer diversified information. He loved the idea, which thrilled me. It was, after all, 1987, and only a comparative handful of people had heard of these holistic healing practices in the United States.

We signed a contract that would have taken me off the family dole with money to spare, and we began production. But no sooner had we begun videotaping new features when we received word that Time Inc. had purchased Lorimar and all projects were frozen.

Months passed. I worked selling leather clothing (repugnant to a vegetarian) at my friend's clothing store and teaching my color therapy classes as I waited for word about the fate of 'A Second Opinion'.

Finally we were given the green light and began to gear up into production. "Halt!" came word from the big guys at Time, Inc. A deal was being negotiated to create a mega media entity by marrying Timer, who had absorbed Lorimar, with the mega media giant of Warner Bros. Thus Time-Warner was born. Warner wanted to go through all programming and budgets and no new programming would take to the air waves until the final analysis had been completed.

A year and a half had now passed since my European journalistic adventure. The good news was that I had overcome the sickening feeling I got when I entered the leather store each morning and had become the top salesperson most weeks, which netted me something like $500 a month as a part-time employee. The bad news was that my dream had just gone up in smoke. There would be no 'A Second Opinion' debuting on the new Time-Warner mega media company as the Lorimar division had become defunct during the Time-Warner merger.

At this juncture in my life, another option laid itself before me. Ed Hookstratten had let it be known that he was fond of me. He liked that I was stubborn, opinionated, and focused, though he found my propensity to shoot myself in the foot by turning my back on opportunity somewhat disconcerting. This, he said, was a rare commodity in Los Angeles where the women he knew - including high profile actresses and TV personalities - were out to secure a high profile, or wealthy, mate. This did not appear to be my agenda, and it wasn't. He liked this. He also found me amusing and appeared to genuinely care for me.

One day during my business dealings with Lorimar, Ed sat me down and asked if I would like to join him in Bel Air and become his partner. Stuart was seven years old at the time.

Ed continued by saying that he would provide my son with everything he was capable of as he had done with his own two children. Having had the pleasure of meeting his children, this was a lovely offer. In spite of having a high profile and wealthy father and a lovely actress as a mother, Ed's children were well balanced, family oriented and had found success in their own right. As Ed said, "I'm great at my job serving my clients, good as a father and lousy at being a husband. I didn't give the marriage enough of my attention, but I gave the kids the best I could." And it showed. And now he was older and wiser and would make time for a relationship.

I, meanwhile, could not bear taking Stuart away from his father, who had equal rights to our child. I also could not bear the projection of others that I had married for money and position. Nor could I bear the thought that I might find myself unfaithful to Ed someday in the future as he was eighteen years older than I. I chose to keep up the good fight on my own and rejected Ed's offer.

Soon after I had told Ed of my feelings, the decision began haunting me. He and I got along wonderfully, it was an easy and light-hearted rapport. He genuinely cared for me and had shown his willingness to be there for me over the previous thirteen years. He had never crossed the line of propriety because I had been married, and so had he. Now we were both free. He had made me his best offer, and I had refused. I did what I felt was correct, but my life would be destined to remain a struggle.

As we consider the notion of free will, had I made a decision in alignment with my soul's plan or had I deviated from my script? Something told me I had deviated from this wonderful opportunity to be with a kind and loving man who could open any door for me that I wished and provide warm companionship. But I believed in romantic love and hadn't developed any sense of how this fit or didn't fit with a larger soul purpose.

I reached out to Ed a while later, but the door was closed. He had made his offer, and I had refused. He didn't see any reason for putting himself back in a vulnerable position with me.

He ultimately met a wonderful woman and married for which I am glad. But to this day I am left with the feeling that I shut a door that was intended to be opened to me so I could land on my path in the media at a much earlier time in my life to share conscious programming with a mass audience. In addition, my son had needed the guidance of a mature, wise and loving man. Instead, he would struggle along with his stubborn mother.

Sometimes our path may not look like what we would expect, and it's only the wisest ones who can see through the illusions to choose their destiny. While filled with perceptions of ethics and moral standards, I was lacking larger wisdom at this stage of my life.

Back in Sacramento, there was a growing awareness of the environment bubbling up in mass awareness. As a tree and earth lover, protecting the environment was a sentiment I could put myself behind. Perhaps I could be the first to introduce this type of consciousness to the U.S. television news market.

I titled my new idea 'The Envireport' and approached the News Director at the CBS affiliate in Sacramento to introduce myself. She sounded mildly intrigued and said she would give me a call when she had the time. Weeks passed with no call. I called her again. Still, no response.

I had begun having challenging dreams, which are very rare for me. In one of these dreams, everyone with whom I had ever worked in the television industry was successful, bustling about on stories and making a good living. I watched them feeling that I had been shut out, nose to the window, like an orphan of the news industry.

One morning I was in total despair, feeling I had exhausted every avenue in this relatively large, but sleepy, media city. Though Sacramento was the 20th largest market in size, that still boiled down to five television stations with whom to negotiate.

I went back to bed after taking Stuart to school and cried. Then a little voice inside said, "Stop it! Get up and do something about it!" So, I showered, put my make-up on, combed my hair, and drove down to the CBS affiliate. I marched up to the receptionist and asked to see the news director, Judy, who I had spoken to all those weeks ago. The receptionist called Judy's office. Judy had the receptionist tell me she would be happy to see me in a little while. I waited in the lobby.

To her credit, Judy did emerge from her office and agreed to hear me out. Within thirty minutes I had a new job, was out of the leather apparel jungle and off of parental subsidy.

In the following year, I produced more than one hundred mini features on the environment designed to inform the average consumer of the earth-friendly choices they could make in their lives. The Envireport was the first regularly featured segment on environmental awareness in a nightly news program in the United States. I was loving my job and the excitement of field reporting while maintaining my anchoring skills at the live news desk.

My time with Fred and Linda remained precious throughout all of my personal and professional challenges. One day, at the request of my friend Susan, I took her to their home for a channeling.

I sat at the back of the room as Susan asked her questions of the Guardian, listening somewhat passively. Suddenly

Linda's hand floated up and, with finger extended, pointed right at my face and said: "And YOU do something about the trees!" I blinked and looked around, which was silly as I was the only other person in the room. "Are you talking to me?" I asked. "Yes, to you." Just as suddenly the Guardian went back to attending to Susan's questions.

My mind was spinning. "Do something about the trees?" What was I supposed to DO? I didn't know much about them other than that I loved them and hated to see them cut down, which perpetuated some pretty unruly backyards over the years as I didn't like having my trees mutilated. I felt pruning resembled an amputation.

Soon enough I was given an opportunity to pursue this "tree" thing.

The 1991 recession had begun, and news departments across the country were cutting budgets. Judy called me in and explained that there had been a drop in news revenues and that, while viewers could not get along without medical features and movie reviews, environmental news was dispensable. Suspecting that interest in the environment may be just a fad, my segment was canceled. My job was being eliminated, but "thank you, it's been a great little segment while it lasted." The next day, my misfortune was at the bottom of the front page of the newspaper - no hiding from one's humiliation in this line of work. I spent the next few days feeling sorry for myself.

Around this time a special news series in the Sacramento Bee titled 'Sierra in Peril' won a Pulitzer Prize. Tom Knudsen had spent a year traveling throughout the vast Sierra Mountain range chronicling all of the environmental challenges. It was brilliantly written and very compelling to an activist mind, which I had been developing.

Simultaneously, I had become a featured writer for the Sacramento Bee's Food and Wine section with weekly articles on vegetarian cuisine, which put me in close enough proximity to approach Tom with my plan; to make a documentary version of his journey with updates that had occurred since he finished the project. Tom loved the idea and agreed to be a consulting producer.

I was able to secure a meeting with the program director at the local PBS station, KVIE. While she too thought American interest in the environment to be a passing trend, something in her intuited that this project was the right thing to do. The only small detail left was funding - in a recession.

Months passed as the station sought backing for a documentary that most outside experts said wasn't a "sexy" enough topic - "trees, air, rivers, and watersheds, where's the juice?" they said.

Meanwhile, I needed to generate some income while waiting for the documentary funding. I reverted to my usual pattern of doing menial work so as not to bind myself to anything requiring a serious commitment. This would allow me to free myself and act quickly when my project secured funding.

Toward this end, I approached my friend Jim, who had opened a lovely, world beat restaurant in Sacramento at Broadway and 15th St. called the Tower Café. The Cafe was opened on the first Earth Day and named after the original Tower movie theater, which was across the street from the original Tower Records store also named after the movie theater.

I asked if he would let me make espresso drinks behind the

bar as I had no experience waiting tables. He reluctantly agreed. He did not think I was a good fit for the job, overqualified and clearly not committed to climbing up the company management ladder.

So much trauma struck in the months that lay ahead that I was deeply grateful to have this sunny, lively place as my refuge four days a week. It taught me some beautiful lessons of friendship, a sense of belonging, and humility. As I once again joined the fallen of my media profession, I was to have a repeat of the Fine & Funky Clothiers' experience selling jeans.

The Tower Café was located just down the street from my former workplace, the CBS station from which I had just been freed from the bonds of employment. It was a favorite place for reporters and news anchors to have lunch. It was only a matter of time before one of my former colleagues would stumble across me while putting in an order for a latte to go.

The embarrassment on their part was palpable; I could hear their thoughts - How humiliating. God, could this happen to me?! I made small talk with them as they fumbled for change and, as in my jeans-selling days, felt only a little uncomfortableness with the situation. This is what I was doing now. And it was fun. And I was making new friends. And it gave me a place to go between hospital visits while my mother lay in a coma, struggling for her next breath.

## Chapter Twenty-Two:
# Loss Of The Elder Woman

Owing to my days appearing before the public on the television, I would receive the occasional bothersome or obscene phone call.

One such call made it to Stuart's ears first. He was about 10 years old at the time. Stuart picked up the phone and listened politely to God knows what, then calmly said: "Mom, I think it's for you." When I answered, a breathy male voice told me all about the things he would like to do to me, the same things he must have just said to my son. After I listened for a few seconds, I uttered something mundane and hung up the phone, more focused on the absurdity of my son not only hearing the obscenities, but calmly discerning that such a phone call must be for me. We laughed until our sides nearly split over that one.

What happened next wasn't funny.

In addition to the odd prank calls and hang-ups, my phone would ring two or three times every day at 4:00 a.m. then stop. It rang long enough to wake me up, leave my heart pounding and send me lurching for the receiver. Every time the caller would hang up either before I got to it, or right after. I had made reports to the phone company to have it traced, but the problem persisted. I was becoming very frustrated at being awakened from a deep sleep every night.

At 4:00 a.m. on January 9, 1993, the phone rang at the usual time. For the first time, I decided not to answer it. As it turned out, it was not a "crank" call, it was my sister, Denise, calling to tell me our mother was being rushed to the hospital, she had suffered a massive stroke.

Mom was 62, "healthy as an ox," as she would say, a volunteer to every organization imaginable and supporter of another twenty or so through monthly and annual donations. She was a whirling dervish of activity, particularly focusing on her grandchildren, spending as much time as she could with Stuart and his cousins Kelly, Alexandra, and Lucas, Denise's children.

Mom had been having headaches for a couple of years. The doctors said it might be the shape of her pillow. She began a search through every kind of high tech pillow to find the one that would put her head at the perfect angle to stop the pain. Still, the headaches persisted.

On the morning of January 8th, over breakfast, she had told my father that she wouldn't mind "going" (dying). She mused that she was happy she had never suffered the loss of anyone dear to her. She continued, saying that she was not happy with the way the country was going (Clinton had just been elected). In fact, she had stated upon a few occasions that she'd rather die than see Clinton take office, as she had become a born-again Christian and conservative. Her values were of a pragmatic nature. A decade before she had switched from her lifelong status as a Democrat to Republican. Surprised, I asked why. "Because you can be a Democrat when you have nothing to lose, but when you have made money you need to be a Republican to protect it."

I was stunned at the directness and lack of guile in her response. She and my father had worked hard, and she felt they deserved to protect what they had accumulated. A simple and understandable philosophy for two Depression-era people.

While at work the afternoon of January 8th, my father was overwhelmed with sentimental feelings for my mother. His heart was so full that he called her from the office inviting her for a dinner date, which was a rare occurrence. At the restaurant, they had another of those life-has-been-good-to-me" conversations.

By two o'clock in the morning my mother, stumbling, woke my father. Something was wrong, she said. Dad jumped out of bed to help her change from her nightgown and take her to the hospital. During those intervening moments. she began losing her sight. By the time she arrived at the Emergency Room entrance, she was mumbling and mostly unconscious. That was when my sister called me, and I didn't answer.

Mom went into emergency surgery to stop the hemorrhaging in her brain. My sister called again, at about 7:00 in the morning. That time I answered. I went pale, and my mind went sideways as Denise told me what had happened. Denise said they were waiting for word from the surgeon, the best neurological surgeon in the region as luck would have it.

I arrived just as the surgeon emerged from the operating room. His face was grim. My father began crying. The prognosis was not good. Mom was brain dead. Just like that.

Having dinner one moment, and brain dead the next. Her brain had been hosting a growing aneurysm he told us, one that generally takes the person's life between the ages of ten and forty. She had made it to 62.

Mom didn't die immediately. For ten days Denise and I would hold her hands, hearts leaping with hope every time her body made what we later learned were involuntary movements. Her arms would roll inward, as would her legs. It gave the appearance of stretching before waking up. For those few moments, those first days, we had hope that this feisty and hearty mother of ours had pulled herself through her dark night.

Denise was a godsend as she was a cardiac nurse at the same hospital, which allowed us a little favor here and there during the ten days beside Mom's comatose body.

It was odd watching my mother's face change as the days passed. Each day she became younger. The frown lines and grimace lines were disappearing as her face lay in a state of quiet repose, save for the occasional frown that would accompany the involuntary arm and leg rolls.

After eight or nine days she began struggling for breath. Everyone knew this was an indication of the end of her journey. The doctors asked us if we were ready to take her off life support. They were now certain there was no chance that her brain would recover.

Though I had no practical understanding of what would follow, Denise and I said "Yes." Our mother was drowning in her own fluids. We had never imagined that our mother would die young. We were preparing for her ornery old age, where we would tiptoe around her diatribes about this bit of news or that. But here she was, helpless, growing younger and prettier and more peaceful by the moment.

On the tenth day of her coma, the decision was made. She would be removed from life support as her brain showed no signs of life beyond brain stem function.

I asked Denise to take our mother's hand while I held the opposite one on the other side of the bed. I asked permission of my mother's soul to allow me to see her and intuitively tuned into where our mother was now living. We had not been able to feel her essence in the room the previous couple of days, which indicated to me that she was loosening herself from the physical plane.

She "showed" herself to me as a young woman wearing a green tee shirt and khaki pants. Behind her was a semi-circle of pale blue beings of light. She quietly and peacefully looked at me and telepathically said she was fine now. It was okay to let her go.

In the background, Dionne Warwick was singing "Do You Know the Way to San Jose?" on the hospital speaker system. It stung. Did I know the way back home without my mom as a touchstone in my life? I told Denise each scene and the telepathic words Mom expressed during the meditation.

Exhausted, Denise needed some rest and, assuming it would be a long night to our mother's transition, went home for a couple of hours. I decided to stay a while longer. As her body would cough and gag uncontrollably, I would panic, tears streaming, ringing the button to the nurse's station and calling out for someone to please help her. I had not yet witnessed the process of death, an everyday event for the nurses in this ward. Yes, I knew about the soul and could even speak to various aspects of a being, but this was my mother, whose life was so inextricably intertwined with ours. She was the leader of the tribe in her elder status.

Helpless, I sat on the floor, and wrote a poem. She had asked me so many times over the years to write something for her. Here I was at the 11th hour and 59th minute of her life, finally inspired to write for her. Before that I hadn't known what to say. Now I wrote about her huge, sometimes angry, overly-generous, noisy and demanding heart. It was called "Bad Tempered Angel."

*A complicated woman*
*this bad- tempered angel,*
*her clipped and angry manner*
*cloaking a pristine heart.*

*Words rolled from her tongue*
*like a school bell ending recess.*
*"That child needs meat?"*
*"Bill, you're driving too fast!"*
*Words, years' worth, a familiar barometer*
*to the workings of her mind.*

*Victimized house robes,*
*pockets torn against inanimate objects*
*defying her will.*
*A maelstrom of fury left their existences untouched*
*her toe bloody and swollen.*

*Then there was frosting,*
*gooey and rich*
*dripping from our lives,*
*spread by our mother*
*generously, gregariously, unrelentingly.*
*The tide of the sweet stuff never ebbed.*

*Through our cumulative toothaches, bellyaches,*

*heartaches and finally, headaches*
*the heart that fed us all never faltered.*
*Lying still now, breaths hard fought*
*her heart the last force standing*
*unfaltering*
*even*
*now.*

At 7:00 p.m. I left the hospital to get a little rest. The morphine was dripping to comfort Mom's body and relax all of the muscles, including her heart. The nurse had assured Denise and me that the transition would take time and that, when the time drew near, she would phone us so we could be with her at the moment of transition. My nerves were shattered.

As I left the hospital and walked through the dark and wet parking lot, my awareness was suddenly transported to a forest:

I saw the largest tree in a stand of redwoods falling. As it fell, the sun streamed in and shone on the tops of the smaller trees, giving them light for the first time. It would be their turn to grow to great heights. The fallen giant would create nourishment for the saplings and other flora. This was the cycle of life and death. The sun was now on me, the eldest female of our family, and my sister. I couldn't feel my body, I seemed to be floating across the pavement during this experience. Suddenly I was shocked back to reality and became aware, once again, of my surroundings. A black, wet parking lot. I walked numbly to my car.

The nurse did not call us on time. Denise chose to go to the morgue but suggested I stay behind. She had seen many people to the other side and felt she had enough energy left in her to handle it. She later said to me, "That was the first time I could see where you came from. As her face grew younger and softened I saw your cheeks and jaw; I saw you." I wept softly, then loudly.

As it transpired, when I learned of my mother's transition, I found myself walking in circles, alone, in the middle of my living room, one hand clutching my hair and the other my shirt - exactly as I had done at age two in the Children's receiving home when my parents had walked away that day.

The next morning, we met with Dad to begin arrangements and suddenly, as if being startled out of a coma ourselves, we realized that Clinton was being sworn in that morning. We couldn't help laughing. She did it! She had said she would rather die than see Clinton take office and she died fifteen minutes before midnight, the day of his inauguration. Mom had the last laugh, she never saw Clinton take the oath and never had to witness the loss of anyone dear to her.

Tower Cafe had become my sanctuary with global rhythms, caring friends, and mocha lattes to my heart's content. I had found a safe home in which to process an increasing amount of loss.

Three months after my mother's passing, I had a dream:

I was driving my car into a large warehouse parking lot. It was a store like Costco, but everything was pure white. As I approached the building, the sides of the building pulled up so I could drive my car inside and park. As I took my keys from the ignition and prepared to leave the car I heard a voice speaking to me from the car radio. I thought This is impossible. I have the keys in my hand and the car is off. The male voice continued: "We know you have been through loss and pain, but there is more to come. We will be with you."

I spoke with Dr. Larry Dossey about his research for his book The Power of Premonition. He had spent much of his life as a skeptic of such phenomena, but certain cases had struck him deeply enough to re-examine his beliefs about precognition. One such example was the precognitive dream of a young nurse.

> "This one nurse - she was a young nurse just fresh out of training - she had a dream one night that the phone rang and she answered it, and someone on the phone said 'I want you to go down and help a little boy in the lobby get admitted. He is really sick, and you will recognize him because he has blue, pink, and white pajamas on.' So, she did. She goes down, and this child runs into her arms as if the boy knows her. He is a little three-year-old. And, she helps him get admitted, but unfortunately in the dream, the boy dies within 24 hours. She, at the time, records that this is the most vivid dream she has ever had in her life."

I said to Larry "This seems to be a hallmark of these experiences."

He replied, "Yes, there is a—this is a rule of thumb about which ones to take seriously…If they really feel realer than real, pay attention to them."

> "So, she goes to work the next morning and this has so impressed her that she tells her nursing supervisor about her dream. While she is in the process of telling the nursing supervisor her dream, the phone rings and someone tells her to go down to the lobby to get this little boy admitted. She goes down; the blue and pink, and white pajamas and the whole thing is repeated as

in the dream. And, as in the dream, unfortunately, within 24 hours this little boy dies. So, I couldn't get away from these premonitions. You know they kept coming at me from not just my experience, but my patients' experience, and the experience of nurses, and on and on."

My dream was "realer than real," as Dr. Dossey had said. I woke with a start. Such a cryptic message! I began running everyone I loved through my mind to see if anyone was in danger. Stuart was going to go on a small airplane tour over Yosemite with my father the next day. I had to stop it.

I called my father and told him about my dream. He said he was going anyway, but I kept Stuart on the ground. As it turned out, my father had a marvelous flight, and I felt silly for spoiling the potential adventure for Stuart.

Five days later I got a call from Madame's son, Guy Bovie. His voice sounded weak. He told me that his mother had passed away a few days before (just after I received the message in the dream). She had suffered a stroke in the middle of the night, was in a coma for a few days and had died peacefully.

Madame had become my second mother, grandmother, mentor, and friend rolled into one. My heart sank into my stomach, and I felt ill. I had just talked to her a couple of days prior. Her infamous 1968 Oldsmobile, which she named "Pandora" because she never knew what kind of surprise it might offer, had been stolen and stripped. She was now without wheels. She told me that life was not worth living if she could not drive herself around town freely anymore - life without her Pandora was not worth living.

In truth, she was 84 years of age, and her legs had begun failing her decades before, forcing her to live on red wine and codeine to dampen the pain. She should have been taken off the road long ago, but sometimes life provides small mercies for us all. She never killed anyone while behind the wheel, though I'm sure she left a string of heart palpitations in her wake.

She only had to live without Pandora for a few days before leaving this earth plane to be with her deceased daughter Monique. Her desire to be reunited with Monique had been even greater than the pleasure of driving Pandora with the top down, sun beating down on her olive skin and white, white hair.

There are times when I am grateful that my intuition is sometimes non-operational. Three months before Madame's death, the day after New Year's, my mother had invited her dear friend Geri, Madame Bovie and me for a women's luncheon with lace, crystal and finger sandwiches. It was as though we were girls of all ages playing grown-up. Everything was lovely with the dappled light coming through the curtains illuminating our time together. This beautiful setting of women talking about their lives would be the last time I would see both my mother or Madame alive.

I joined Madame's family in scattering her ashes to the wind at her beloved Berkeley Marina. There were a few surprised faces when the wind turned, her ashes blown over our faces and shoes. She would likely have been laughing uproariously.

I was completely numb by the time I got the call from my Aunt Shirley a few weeks after Madame's death telling us that my mother's mother, my grandmother, Henrietta, had aggressive stomach cancer and had little time left to live. My sister and I left immediately for Minnesota to see Grandma one last time, passing the time playing cards with her and visiting other relatives.

In June, she was released from her body. I had lost every Elder woman in my life within five months. I had also lost my job at the television station and had to move from my home. Stuart and I packed our things, again.

In psychological terms, there are a few critical stressors in life that can put a person in a precarious state of balance: the death of a loved one, job loss, moving, and relationship breakup. If ever there was a time in which I would have fallen apart, it would have been the year 1993. Instead, I wrote poetry to put some order to my emotions, and I put one foot in front of the other with no idea where they would take me next. My future was a complete unknown.

## Chapter Twenty-Three:
# The Funding Arrives

Unlike what happens with many producers in the television business, the phone did ring. The funding was in, at least enough to begin the documentary Sierra in Peril. Me and my co-producer, Lori Lane, who was assigned by the television station to keep me from going over budget and to keep an eye on me, began a wonderful friendship and adventure.

I began digging into the research behind the Sierra's environmental damage, it's causes and solutions. Everyone with whom I sought an interview said "Yes." We were where we should be all the time, every step of the way in the creation of this video that "no one would be interested in." It was as though the path for success had been greased.

Hmmm, it's almost too perfect, I thought. Then I reflected back to the channeling in which the finger pointed at me, and the voice said: "And YOU do something about the trees!" I laughed. My invisible friends were helping once again.

One day we were at the top of Mammoth Ski Area getting a wide shot of the terrain when I had a flashback to my youth in which I had watched the French film A Man and A

Woman. At one point in the movie, the Woman found herself directing a film, wearing her big car coat, in the snow. She was laughing with the crew.

Meanwhile, my crew and I were laughing over my secret habit of warming strands of red licorice in my bra for a few minutes before chewing off a piece. This was a practical solution in sub-freezing weather as red licorice was the crew's comfort food on the road. Suddenly my awareness was elsewhere.

As my mind carried me back to my seat in the movie theater all those years before, I remembered thinking, Wow, a woman director! I've never seen a woman direct a film; does that actually happen in real life? I had been well on my way to becoming a housewife, married to my first boyfriend at that moment in my personal matrix. A woman director! How neat is that! I had thought back then.

Here I was, laughing in the snow with my crew, directing my first documentary. The feelings I had watching A Man and a Woman revealed a great new possibility, even though I acknowledged the limitations of the day. Was I merely glimpsing into the future that lay ahead, or was I creating my path through my emotions and desire? Or are both an aspect driven by the intention of the soul?

As I knuckled down to complete the job at hand, I had to dust off every hat I had worn throughout my patchwork career. It was my project, and I was responsible for carrying out the vision, so I was the researcher, director, producer, and scriptwriter. This was also a necessity due to the minuscule budget with which we had to work. I had little choice but to wear all of those hats.

As we waded in threatened streams, surveyed patchy clearcuts of forests from helicopters, conducted fly-overs above polluted copper mines and sat in on State Water Board hearings, or worked with our composer, Roger Voudouris, to get just the right soundtrack for the video, everything we needed fell into our laps effortlessly - except one thing.

We had been searching for months for a narrator because the station program director was star struck and felt the documentary would be an easier sell to the PBS stations if there was some star appeal. She believed that trees and water simply weren't compelling (sexy) enough. We talked with Richard Chamberlain and Graham Greene in particular, but no one wanted to work for what we could afford to pay. The time to record the narration was upon us.

Personally, I could never see a narrator other than myself doing the job, but I never shared this feeling. I had narrated many programs in the past, but, more importantly, I knew the content of the documentary like nobody else did. I knew where the trees were suffering and the water suffocating. I had trod the land and heard the stories, why shouldn't I tell the story on behalf of the mountains?

At the last minute. I was asked to do the job. Not, of course, for the same amount of money that was budgeted for a star, but for a part of it. I was thrilled.

I loved every minute of the research, shooting, writing, editing, post-production, audio production - I was present for every minute of it. When Sierra in Peril was finished, the station was surprised by the quality of the production, especially considering the paltry budget, and chose to enter it in a number of competitions for television production.

When the dust settled, we had four Emmy nominations - producing, scriptwriting, video and audio - and won an

Emmy for the sound. I won an award from the Columbia School of Journalism for writing, the Silver Apple award for second place in top educational documentaries in the PBS system, Best Documentary from the Sierra Club, and a few others.

The documentary was also selected to be distributed as part of the educational curriculum through institutions ranging from middle schools to UC Berkeley's public policy department.

As icing on the cake, an "anonymous grant" came from a major logging company, which shocked all of us as Sierra in Peril was not particularly friendly to the logging interests. They wanted the money tagged to create a fully packaged educational course with an accompanying study guide as they felt the time had come to take a more comprehensive view of our earth's resources.

Perhaps the most satisfying part of this project, however, was that I was invited to community town hall meetings in Sierra Nevada to moderate a showing of the film and the following discussion that would take place between the State Resources Board, logging families who were losing their jobs, environmentalists, and timber interests. People began talking to each other - without yelling. New legislation was introduced. The trees were being spoken for!

I was trying to take it all in. My first documentary was a piece of cake in every sense of the word, not the usual nightmare I had heard tales of in which the producer waits 5-10 years for funding alone. I had reached for my dream and had achieved it. I reveled in the moment.

Once the euphoria wore off, I was left as flat as a pancake. Now what? I had no further vision for my future. I requested a conversation with the Guardian and Linda obliged. I felt lost and deflated, like post-vacation blues, only worse. The Guardian commented:

"You have done an excellent job in helping the trees." I had actually forgotten all about this by now. Much good had been done he reassured me.

"But what do I do now?!" I asked. He replied in a matter of fact tone "This is only the beginning. Much more will follow."

More followed all right. After having become the darling of the television station and having my pick of documentary projects, hosting regularly featured shows, reporting, and producing special projects, it all abruptly came to an end - with no explanation. The following is what I believe happened, though I will never fully know.

Right after Sierra in Peril had been aired, our station became the guinea pig of the PBS affiliates. A legendary news figure named Van Gordon Sauter would be taking over the position as station manager.

Van Gordon Sauter was a man with a past. He had been the president of CBS Evening news and had power over the careers of such people as Walter Cronkite and Diane Sawyer. He had been featured in books written about network news such as Who Killed CBS. Uh, oh. Now he was coming to our modest sized PBS station? Why?

His mission, it turned out, was to prove that PBS stations could become profitable by forging tighter relations with the business community for underwriting purposes.

On his second day on the job, one of the "problems" that ended up on his desk was Sierra in Peril. One of the station's

Board members complained that the documentary was not friendly to developers, that it was too oriented toward conservation and environmentalism. Well, yes, it was. It was called Sierra in Peril! What was he expecting? The environment is seldom improved by development and stripping of natural resources, particularly when it impacts delicate watersheds such as those surrounding Lake Tahoe. The Board member, who was also in charge of developing new superstores for a large grocery chain in our region, demanded that we change the documentary to include a more "open stance" on development.

Along with Lori and Chris Cochran, the production department's executive director, I was called into Van's newly appointed game room/office. It wasn't looking good for our environmental documentary as he had animal pelts covering the industrial carpet to create a homey touch along with a mounted elk head on the wall.

He started by complimenting us, saying that he was astounded to hear we had done this project on $90,000 plus some in-house production time, and that such a production would have cost ten times that at CBS. "Well done!" he said.

Then he told us of his predicament. He agreed that the developer's demand was not particularly reasonable, but he needed that company's "support." Could we do something to alter the script, just slightly?

Throughout the entire meeting, Van never looked at me directly, instead, addressing Chris or Lori, who were sitting on either side of me, despite needing my editorial agreement as the producer and writer.

I began having some strange feelings and tuned out of my surroundings and the conversation when I had an awareness that I knew this man from long ago. I immediately understood that this was the source of his discomfort, but I didn't know what the story was, at least not at that moment. Disconcertingly, I felt that I somehow had an 'upper hand' in all of this. How was that possible?

As I tuned back into the conversation, I was madder than a wet hen at the notion of compromising my journalistic honor to please a land developer. But I did. It was a small token and looked exactly like what it was, and I had just learned another lesson of Tele-Journalism 101: He who pays for the productions can poke their fingers in the stew. I had thought PBS was somehow exempt from all of that, the last bastion of journalistic integrity and all.

Meanwhile, I went on with my various duties about the station when word began leaking that Van was referring to me behind my back as the Ice Queen. Most everyone who was present when he made these comments scrunched their nose, raised their eyebrows and said, "Her?" I was actually quite friendly around the workplace as I was happy with my work and co-workers.

I found Van's Ice Queen comments odd, but amusing. One day I decided to "check in" on the situation intuitively. By now I had become relatively skilled and comfortable with relaxing and allowing whatever popped onto the "viewing screen" to be there without judgment or conjuring. What I saw relating to in my past connection with Van was immediate and startling:

As I tuned into the scene, I found myself in bed with a very large man who was at the top of the pecking order in our society. We were in France, and he was apparently a King, as everybody was frightened of his temper and would scurry around trying to please him. I was married to him. We were involved in a conjugal visit.

I lay there perfectly disinterested, literally glancing off to the side, bored. I was doing this intentionally to show him my disdain for his unkind treatment of myself and others. I was determined to show no feelings toward him, which angered him to the point of screaming at me out of frustration at having no control over me. I was hoping that he would permanently take up with one of his consorts and leave me alone.

"Ice Queen," he had called me. Well, I was indeed icy in the scene I had just "experienced." This type of vision comes very quickly, and just as quickly disappears, leaving me with only a snapshot of a situation with no room to analyze or ask questions.

A few weeks later I was at an afternoon party at the television station when Van came up to me and awkwardly confessed, "You may have heard that I have been known upon occasion to call you an Ice Queen behind your back. But I just want you to know that this is actually a compliment. There is something intimidating about you, and the only other woman I have felt that way around is Diane Sawyer, so you're in good company." I just smiled and gently teased him about the backhanded "compliment."

Shortly after his confession, he requested me to be his producer for a mini-series on the Donner Party as the sesquicentennial (150th anniversary) of this grisly piece of American history was approaching. I said I would be happy to produce it, but I needed to know who was the boss, he or I. I was very serious about this because it always gets a little unnerving out in the field when quick decisions have to be made. I am a pragmatic producer and try not to wander from agreed upon timelines and budgets. Van was notoriously spontaneous, so I needed to know if I was going to be given that power or not. He said, "Of course, you would be the boss." I looked at him with level eyes, knowing this was a pretty generous agreement for a man accustomed to having his way. "Okay then," I said.

We loaded our gear into the jeep with our cameraman, John, and headed up the mountain to recreate what was one of the most gripping nightmares in U.S. history - a party of lost pioneers trapped under a deluge of 30 feet of snow, unfortunate souls who resorted to eating one another for survival as those among them died. It was the most depressing research I've ever done, often leaving me in tears at the end of the day.

Van, on the other hand, considered himself a frontiersman of sorts and wanted to speak for the dead a century and a half after the chilling, history-making events.

The adventure started off well. I was a woman and, ironically, a vegetarian, so it was my job to pack the snacks and lunches for the road.

Teasingly, I tossed Van a small package of raw meat for a snack to honor his intrigue with cannibalism. I thought it might be a good way to lighten up a heavy assignment. We all had a laugh and a fruitful day of videotaping. The second day, however, brought a different flavor to what I had come to suspect might be a karmically-challenged relationship.

The proof is in the pudding, as they say, and the time had arrived for me to play Boss. Van, as it turns out, didn't actually mean that I could tell him what to do. I was to be a token boss, not a real one. Unfortunately, we were on a tight schedule and budget, and someone had to rein in his extemporaneous requests that we add new elements to the production. "We can't, Van. We don't have the time or money to do that." I reminded him that I was The Boss.

We didn't speak the remainder of the trip other than to alert him when we had arrived at a particular videotaping site. He lumbered off, mumbling, like a big pouty bear. Unbeknownst to Van, he had left his wireless microphone on, and John could hear everything he was griping about as he walked to the location, reporting all of it back to me for our mutual amusement. I could not afford to let Van get to me. I had a budget and schedule to keep.

He eventually got over it, or so I heard when a fellow employee mentioned that Van told them that the Donner project was the most fun he had had on a production trip in a long time.

Really? Good. It was helped by the fact that the series was very flattering to Van as an on-air personality. He did look the part of the frontiersman and used his robust voice and colorful vocabulary to their best. He was a natural on camera and a charismatic orator.

Meanwhile, I needed a vacation to recover from the gruesome imagery of cannibalism and from working with Van, not quite sure which was worse. I had the perfect excuse for a trip to France, which was where I fled at every possible opportunity. My past lives of decadence were pulling on me - croissants, chocolate, and coffee, lovely cheeses and crepes from street vendors. We had French friends and free accommodations, so I made a quick decision: Stuart and I would go to France for our friend, Charlotte's, wedding.

## Chapter Twenty-Four:
# The Missed Metro And Retribution

We arrived in France amidst some tension. There were the usual ongoing train and garbage strikes and the threat of terrorist attacks. But we were in Paris and not going to waste a minute worrying about that sort of thing.

We were staying in Charlotte Peltier's family's apartment in the Latin Quarter. Our day started at the corner bakery with buttery croissants, crisp on the outside, soft and moist on the inside, the kind with which you can still peel the layers away one by one. Heaven! After that, we were off to the Egyptian wing of the Louvre.

At the end of the day, exhausted, we headed back to the apartment. I was skilled at using the Metro as I had been in Europe many times and enjoyed public transit. The maps were very clear and easy to follow, and I stayed in the familiar Quartier Latin most of the time.

So on this day I followed the usual signs and ran to the platform to catch the next train. One metro stop into our ride home I noticed that we were going in the wrong direction. How was that possible? I had never taken the wrong train in my life!

I grabbed Stuart's hand and quickly jumped off at the next stop and ran across the upper passageway to connect to the train going the opposite direction to get back to where we had started.

When we arrived back at the original station, I went to the platform going in the proper direction, still flummoxed at my mistake as we trotted toward the train. Out of breath, we arrived just as the train closed its doors.

"Daschdt!" as Madame used to say. It was hot and the metro was crowded with commuters. It became hotter and more crowded as we all waited and waited for the next train. A voice came over the speaker system and made an announcement. There were small gasps among the crowd and concerned looks. I couldn't understand what the lady on the loudspeaker had said as her French was too fast for my very basic level of comprehension.

Someone who spoke English told us that there had been an explosion in the train that had just left, the one Stuart and I had missed by a heartbeat or two.

We were all told to leave the station. We walked above ground, and the scene began to unfold before us.

Police and undercover cars screaming around the corners, helicopters and ambulances were everywhere. The Pont Notre Dame, the bridge over the Seine, and the route back to our neighborhood had been cordoned off. Television news trucks were swarming the scene.

We watched the news that night, thanking our lucky stars at my "confusion" as to the metro platform, but shaken at the tragedy. We learned that a gas bottle had exploded in the Saint-Michel Notre-Dame station on line B of the RER (Paris regional train network). Eight people were killed and 80 wounded. This act was part of a series of terrorist attacks reportedly carried out by the Armed Islamic Group who were extending the Algerian Civil War to France.

I could have sworn that I had followed the signs correctly. Maybe I did. But perhaps what I saw wasn't what was printed on the signs. Sometimes my "intuitive forces" have to trick me and hit me over the head to get me where I need to be. This phenomenon was portrayed nicely in the film The Adjustment Bureau in which caseworkers in another dimension of reality would find ways to prevent us from altering our life plans by placing obstacles in our paths. To have been on that train may well have irrevocably altered our life plans.

I said to myself, and whatever other force was looking out for us, Thank you, thank you, thank you. My son and I were safe.

The wedding was a lovely salve on our shaken nerves. Ice sculptures, long tables of desserts and cheeses, I was in French heaven! Dancing under a gazebo until dawn with a handsome Frenchman named Emile, wonderful champagne and puffs on Charlotte's uncle Fred's Cuban cigar. I don't smoke, but something felt soft and grounding in this. Stuart and I, years later, would occasionally share a cigar and thank Uncle Fred for introducing us to the oddly soothing, but guilty and smoky pleasure.

We were enjoying the best France had to offer. Little did I know that there would be a "quarantine" on my visits to France years later. It appeared that I was spending too much of my energy returning to the scene of my previous past life crimes of pettiness and insensitivity. New ground needed to be forged.

Meanwhile, it appeared it was time to pay the piper for my slights against Van in what I had come to believe as our former incarnation together. Not that this was conscious on either his part or mine.

When we returned home from France, I was hit by a big surprise. As karma would have it, Van was an ardent Francophile as well, no surprise considering what I had seen in my vision. No sooner had I returned the Paris Access guidebook that Van had loaned me for my trip than I was informed that I was no longer anchoring the twice-weekly television program I had been hosting. The producer didn't know why just that word had come from Van.

The same thing happened with every other department I was involved with - "Sorry, I don't know what happened, but Van said you're off the job." I was utterly dumbfounded and a little frightened. This was my only income and Stuart was attending the Sacramento Waldorf School, which was a substantial obligation for someone who earned a relatively meager production salary.

No one could, or would, tell me what had happened, including Van. I packed my things, tears streaming from my eyes as I tried to fight them back. I loaded my videotapes, photos, files, and other odds and ends into my car and drove off to an unknown future once again.

## Chapter Twenty-Five:
# Vegetables Take Center Stage

One of the projects on the burner before my untimely departure from KVIE was a joint venture to produce a vegetarian cooking series, which we had titled Regina's Vegetarian Table.

The world of vegetarianism was still pretty lonely at this time. I had been writing a weekly column of recipes for the Sacramento Bee's Food and Wine section for a year or two and had a cookbook well under way. The program director at KVIE had agreed to raise the funding for the project. I, meanwhile, had busied myself with everything that struck my fancy in the production department as I waited for the funding to arrive.

Before being fired, rumors began to circulate that Van had other plans for the development of new series and that my program wasn't part of the plan. Months had ticked by, nothing. Then I was ousted empty-handed and behind schedule on my plans to take the vegetarian show national.

Fortunately, my work with Sierra in Peril and another documentary I had written and produced about the life of artist Wayne Thiebaud, titled Heart Cakes to Bow Ties, had already come to the attention of the programming department at PBS in Alexandria, VA. Dick Hanratty and Alan Foster agreed that the trends in American consumer habits had changed and that a vegetarian show could draw an audience.

I wanted to produce the show for an entirely different reason. Through my spiritual contemplations, I had been exposed to the concept that eating the bodies of other animals kept our consciousness at a lower level. Since I had access to the airwaves I felt I should do my part in both raising consciousness and freshening up the American diet. I wanted to do it in a way that was inviting, fun and non-pedantic. It was nobody's business why I was a vegetarian, only that it would do us all some good to add more fresh vegetables to the diet.

*On my Regina's Vegetarian Table set with guest chef*

The only challenge was that I had no funds for production. KVIE was to have taken care of that uncomfortable business. I would have to raise the funding on my own, not a strong suit.

I busied myself with errands of every color for about two weeks after my departure from KVIE, licking my wounds from the public humiliation of another job loss.

Monday morning rolled around. I was still busying myself and had resorted to polishing the chrome on the sink faucet, anything to avoid the promise I had made to myself to begin the daunting task of finding money for my project. I had a sudden overwhelming urge to sit down and meditate to gain some clarity on my strategy.

As my behind sank into the chair, I heard a very impatient and loud male voice say: "Just begin, and all the help will be there!"

"Okay!!" I replied, agitated. By this time, I didn't think anything of talking back to the voices that attempted to give me guidance - wherever they came from. In other times I would have been "put away" for this.

Several years later, I had a one-hour conversation with Dr. Susan Shumsky, author of Divine Revelation in which she explained her methods of connecting with our own inner guidance, or as some people call it, God. She was adamant that all of us have the ability, with a little practice, to develop this deep dialogue for our daily use. I hadn't followed any particular protocols, but I was nonetheless confident in this blossoming relationship that seemed never to fail me.

Coming out of this lightning speed meditation, I sighed, not at all able to see where all this "help" was going to come from. I got up from my chair and walked listlessly across the street to the supermarket. I planned to pick up some copies of vegetarian food magazines and inquire as to advertising rates via the magazines' marketing departments. What relevance this had to PBS underwriting I don't know. It was a hair-brained idea, but it's all that popped into my mind.

I opened Veggie Life magazine, thumbed through the pages to a display ad for advertising rates and placed a call. "Just begin, and all the help will be there!" Yeah, right! I thought, dreading having to speak with someone on the other end.

Bill Ruha answered the phone. He was the head of sales and advertising for Veggie Life.

After I introduced myself, I began telling him why I was calling, though I had planned to be a bit more covert in my motives for obtaining advertising rates. I'm not very good at lying, however, so I just explained what I was looking for and, to my surprise, he told me that his magazine was, in fact, looking for a television show affiliation to boost circulation. PBS would be a perfect alliance.

Once we determined I was only a ninety-minute drive from Veggie Life's headquarters, he asked if I could come down to Concord the following day to meet with him and the publisher.

I think the term in British slang is gobsmacked. In other words, my mouth was hanging open with the words "Just begin, and all the help will be there!" tumbling through my head. My God! Can it really be that easy? Just one phone call when it takes people months, even years, to find such a business relationship, if ever?

It was that simple. Bill and I bonded like super glue on our common intention to bring Regina's Vegetarian Table to the American viewing audience. He rolled up his sleeves during his evening hours and created all of the publicity materials, gathering demographic information and analyzing the market.

Bill turned out to be a marketing genius saddled with a disastrous private life that kept him hopelessly broke and desperate for new business opportunities. He is also one of the funniest and most brilliant human beings I have ever met - from Elvis impersonations (he sounds like E did on a good day!) to reciting the speeches of JFK in a perfect Bostonian accent to writing sci-fi thrillers. Such a mind is rare, and now he was using it to help me put my show on the national airwaves.

Once the funding was in, my old friend and Sierra in Peril co-producer Lori Lane rallied the boys. "The boys" are my beloved and trusted videographers from past assignments. John Davis shot the entire Sierra in Peril documentary, for which he was nominated for an Emmy Award. Kit Tyler, also an Emmy Award winner, was my favorite videographer from my days in the news business. We had a crack team, but more so, we had four years of fun to say nothing of absolutely fabulous food!

Because I'm essentially shy about being on camera, I don't like to have all of the focus and pressure on me. To ease the job, I made sure I had a constant stream of guests on my programs. We featured an organic gardener, Joe Patitucci, who has since passed on; Dr. John McDougall, an M.D. who focused on the benefits of a plant-based diet; our wine pairing expert and friend David Berkeley and a host of top chefs from across the country.

During the nightly crew dinners, we would laugh until our sides hurt. On particularly challenging days of videotaping, the boys would choose to drink by themselves and grumble about the Boss, which was me. By morning we would all love each other again. The show was alive with color and healthy cuisine, and remains the only cooking program that features what I call Healthy Fats Cooking.

By a stroke of luck, I had become good friends with Udo Erasmus, the author of Fats That Heal, Fats That Kill. He gave me an excellent education into the damaging effects of cooking with fresh oils at high temperatures as well as the devastating health effects of using highly processed supermarket oils. I wove this information into each show in which I was the chef, teaching the viewer useful cooking methods to avoid using and creating trans-fats in the diet. It would be several years before the US government would come clean about the health effects of trans-fats. Surprisingly, no one else is teaching people how to cook without creating trans-fats.

My editor, Kip, and I put a considerable amount of creativity and energy into our shows. Regina's Vegetarian Table was the first to insert mini features within the body of the cooking show and use music in the production. I hired my son Stuart and my friend, recording artist Roger Voudouris, to record the original music for the shows; his music brought so much life to the colors and flavors of the food. Roger was a brilliant musician and I was broken hearted when I learned of his death after a long struggle with alcohol and his own emotions. If someone plays one of the shows in our house, I hear the music in the background and my heart leaps, conditioned to a wonderful half hour of food, fresh produce and sunshine! But what was perhaps the most satisfying part to me were the emails from viewers.

One that stuck with me was from a low-income woman from Appalachia, an economically depressed region in the South. She said her husband and kids were not well and that the doctor had told her they were eating poorly. This had come to weigh heavily on her. She happened to stumble on my cooking show on PBS, a station you could still access via "bunny ears," a small antenna.

She said she began to learn about vegetables and was now making some fresh food for her family and was so grateful to have had someone teach her these things because she had been afraid for her husband's health. She just wanted to share her appreciation for our work.

I was in tears to think that people were having these private experiences across the country and that I would never know the impact this show had on their lives. This is the sad part, but also the incredible beauty of the medium - it's vast reach.

Ultimately, Regina's Vegetarian Table aired in all but one of PBS's 300+ markets as well as on Canadian and Australian cable television. It's total run, including reruns, was five years. Along the way I wrote two vegetarian healthy-fats cookbooks - Regina's Vegetarian Table and Regina's International Vegetarian Favorites - a good effort for never having taken a cooking class past my junior high school lesson on making croutons.

## Chapter Twenty-Six:
## A Boy Grows Up

Regina's Vegetarian Table was solidly up and running, with Bill Ruha remaining in the position of Development Director, or fund-raiser, throughout its entire run of 72 episodes. This allowed me some freedom as Stuart was now of driving age and had some control over his own comings and goings. He was still at the Sacramento Waldorf School, playing in a band, on a soccer team, and doing all of the usual things a teenager does. I had been a soccer and basketball mom, music mom, camping mom, and commuter mom, which was the stable background of my life's canvas. This was a marvelous balance to the total unpredictability of my professional life and my love life, which I participated in during the time Stuart spent at his father's home.

Stuart was a perpetual delight to me, partly because of the kind and intelligent being he is, and partly due to his impeccable instincts as to when to keep me in the dark about his teenage activities.

I had some basic rules. If my son went out in his car to an event in the evening, he was never to come home late. I knew all of his friends at the Waldorf School, a school that was not known for hard drugs and partying, but instead for pot smoking overnighters. Because he and his classmates had known each other for their entire post-kindergarten life, there wasn't much romantic intrigue between them. But they were a very close lot and loved to go on trips and have weekend sleepover parties together. Their relationships with one another were reminiscent of the television show Friends. They were friends first, on rare occasion boyfriend or girlfriend.

Because Stuart was wired so sensitively, I knew he would not handle alcohol easily. I attempted to de-mystify the elixir by holding to the European custom that it's best to allow your child to taste alcohol with good food for special occasions, so they do not see it as a forbidden activity, just another beverage on the table.

On New Year's Eve of Stuart's fourteenth year, we had a group over to make our annual vision boards, which I had been doing since the mid-80s. I had found this very useful throughout the years, and the images generally materialized into real experiences in my life with increasing speed as the years went on. I would barely get the thing glued together when the pictures seemed to jump to life.

In fact, my first visioning board, which is a collage, featured a woman scuba diving, a woman on horseback, and a piano, among other images. My boyfriend at the time gave me a course in scuba diving as a birthday gift. Another friend allowed me free access to his polo pony to ride any time I liked. And, finally, my mother told me to go into my room and cover my ears for fifteen minutes while she surprised me as a crew of men delivered a piano to my home for Stuart and me.

I had not told anyone that I was wishing for these things to appear in my life, yet here they were. Needless to say, I thought this was a great alternative to becoming intoxicated at a New Year's Eve party and driving home amidst the drunk drivers. Still, it was New Year's so I would have bottles of Champagne for my friends along with some good food. As we sipped and ate, we would dive into our magazines, tearing out images for our vision boards in a spontaneous frenzy.

On this particular New Year's Eve, Stuart was quietly watching us paste our collages together, taking regular sips of champagne. I hadn't noticed that he had filled his glass several times until he turned around and walked into the wall in his attempt to climb the stairs to his bedroom.

The next morning, I went up to his room to check on him. There was vomit running down one cheek and flowing over his bed, down to the floor. At first, I was frightened and checked his breathing. He was fine, drunk as a skunk, but otherwise alive and well. I thought about how best to handle the situation and ultimately tiptoed downstairs to fetch a bucket, carpet cleaner, and a scrub brush.

I was placing these cleaning items beside his bed when he woke up. I looked at him and couldn't help but smile at his unfortunate circumstance. He smiled and groaned in return as I pointed to the bucket. He saw, and undoubtedly tasted, the gastronomical remnants of the evening before and started laughing and groaning with pain and embarrassment.

At around dinnertime that same day, Stuart was still lying on the living room floor, trying to get his equilibrium when he sheepishly asked how long the hangover would last. I told him he would likely feel better the next day. He groaned and giggled again. This was his lesson in overconsumption of alcohol and it has, with a couple of exceptions, stood the test of time as he takes it easy with alcohol to this day.

Because hard drugs were not part of the Waldorf scene and because Stuart didn't drink, I trusted him to use some judgment and arrive home on time, which he did. It was years later when I found out that he had done the requisite stupid-teenage-boy-things such as driving down the road at high speed on the wrong side of the road for kicks with his friends.

I was horrified but deeply grateful not only that he survived his teenage years, but that he had neglected to share these experiences with his parents. Ignorance can be a good thing. Kids are going to do some stupid stuff, and we can't always be there to stop them. So we have no choice but to explain the consequences, love them and trust them, even if we know that they will at some time or another break that trust because they are kids. In the end, we both have been there for one another and have made sacrifices for each other at pivotal times throughout our lives.

## Chapter Twenty-Seven:
# An Old Man Dies

Linda and Fred came over to our house one afternoon for tea and cookies. Fred was going away on a business trip with his sons to fulfill a construction contract in Oklahoma. I was suddenly overwhelmed with the feeling that I would never see him again and was feeling tender and sentimental at saying goodbye to him. He suddenly looked soft, like an old man rather than the impish, bad boy tiger that he had been his whole life, and it made me sad.

Though I was busy with my various projects - Envireport, Sierra in Peril, and Regina's Vegetarian Table - which limited my time with Linda and Fred, the connection between Linda and I continued to strengthen.

One day she asked me if I would do an intuitive reading for her, which was a switch in roles for us, but I somewhat self-consciously agreed. She was curious about something that was to take place in her future. As I "looked into" her near future I saw that she was alone. I was surprised at this and chose not to tell her this part of the reading, focusing instead on another specific thing she wanted to know about.

Around this time, she told me that she had been having

visions. She repeatedly saw herself driving through the desert of the southwest to her home, which was a little home behind a big house. She wanted to know what I thought of that. Still not wanting to share what I had been shown, I told her I had no idea, other than that there was apparently a significant change ahead since she was driving alone, Soon enough I would understand the significance of Linda's visions.

Linda called a short while later, her voice badly shaken. She had to leave for Oklahoma City immediately. Fred was in a coma, after having suffered a severe stroke the night before. The prognosis was not good. I understood what this meant from my days at Mom's bedside, which all came rushing back.

I told her I would clear my schedule and join her in Oklahoma City. Together we might be able to help "bring Fred back around," or so we thought. The truth is that when a soul has chosen to leave the body behind there is little anyone can do to change that fate.

I arrived in Oklahoma City a couple of days later dreading seeing Fred in a catatonic state.

When I was left alone with him in the hospital room, I would connect with him telepathically to learn what he wanted to do. He was clear in his communication: he was finished with this life. He liked the attention, but he was done.

Linda, however, was not, as she pumped his feeding tube full of fresh vegetable juices, which his body liked. His mind seemed to wake up for a second or two here and there, and his eyes would open briefly. One day he seemed to notice me and tried to smile, then his face went back to that blank canvas of those who are spending their time in another dimension while their body lives on - the comatose.

Fred was ultimately flown back to California and died after lying unconscious for three months. All of our intentions to save him failed. Or, I should say Linda's intentions as I had stopped in the effort to "save" him long before. I was there to support Linda now, not Fred.

A couple of days after Fred's transition I startled myself with the thought that Fred had left Linda nothing. No will. No life insurance. No money. I also knew that he had a penchant for hiding cash because he had told me so. At one time he said he was carrying $10,000 in the trunk of his car because he didn't trust banks, Linda or anyone else. Fred only trusted Fred, and apparently me, a bit. He asked me not to tell Linda about the money. Now that's awkward. She was scraping to put food on the table thinking they were flat broke. I didn't tell her while he was alive, but he was dead now and had left her nothing. I realized that I had to "speak with" Fred.

I went into a deep meditation beside the pyramid he had built for our group meditations years earlier. It had been moved into my living room for Fred's "going away" party, i.e., his funeral, wake, or celebration of life in the more common parlance.

Maybe because Fred could see the absurdity of the situation, it wasn't difficult to reach him on the "other side."

I started with the proper niceties such as "I hope you're enjoying your time over there" and quickly moved to "Where did you hide the money? Linda's broke!" I heard his familiar cackle of laughter, and my field of vision was taken to a place in his attic, specifically behind panels of insulation between the beams. I thanked him then asked where the safe deposit boxes were, but I was shown nothing.

Having had my previous experience "speaking" with my mother as she lay unconscious, I felt comfortable "speaking" with Fred. This is a relatively common experience between the living and deceased and is within each of our abilities to do. Still, skepticism runs deep.

Harvard trained psychology Professor Dr. Gary Schwartz has done exhaustive studies on communication with the deceased. One of his seers in his academic experiments was Alison DuBois upon whom the TV drama Medium was based. We've met with Gary a few times, and on one occasion he told me of the lengths to which he had to go to gain scientific credibility in this field of research.

> "I'm trained as a mainstream scientist, and so I apply the methods of science, and I approach it from sort of a skeptical, certainly agnostic, if not skeptical perspective. And, so, consequently, if you're going to do research in the area, you have to control for a whole host of things, including the possibility of fraud, the possibility of what's called cold reading, which are techniques that mental magicians use. By the way, I have actually taken classes on how to be a fake medium... and, I'm pretty good at it. So, I know what it is, what cheating is involved. You have to address the question of whether the people who are the sitters, the people who want to hear from their loved ones, to what extent they are biased, grabbing for information or accepting information that really doesn't apply to them. You have to be sensitive to possible experimenter errors or experimenter biases. So, all these things you have to take into account if you're going to address whether the mediums are for real.

Now, we were very sensitive to that right from the beginning. And, I began working with one research medium, one by the name of Laurie Campbell, and we did what are called both single blind, and double-blind experiments where the medium didn't know who the sitter was; the medium couldn't even talk to the sitter, so they could have no information. And, also, the sitter [the person wanting to reach out to a deceased person] wasn't present, or the rater wasn't present at the time that the reading was taking place.

> ...we began with one medium, and much to my amazement, we continued to get positive results, ruling out these things like fraud, and cold reading, and rater bias, and experimenter error.
> 
> Then, through the good fortune of Lisa Jackson, doing a documentary called "Life After Life," for an HBO special, in 1998, she was in contact with multiple mediums, including John Edward, George Anderson, Suzanne Northrop, and Anne Gammon, and others. And, she was interested in the idea of science addressing this question. We had the scientific methods and the expertise; she had the access to the mediums and the funding. So, we put our efforts together and we did the first ever controlled multi-medium, multi-sitter experiment. It was actually videotaped as a real experiment, and then, ultimately, the special, Life After Life, and that enabled me to then develop a solid working relationship with John Edward, for example. And, he participated in three experiments in the laboratory before he became famous before he had his television show.

Once the work became public, then other mediums started

hearing about this, and so, the way we would discover mediums is that they would come to us. And the second wave of mediums included a woman by the name of Janet Mayer, and also by the name of Allison DuBois. And Allison participated in the lab for four years. Based on her remarkable experience as a medium, coupled with our research in the laboratory, a television program was ultimately made, and inspired by her life, which is called, Medium..."

Another of our interviewees, Terri Daniel, lost her severely disabled teenage son to a debilitating disease. Her book, A Swan in Heaven, details the rich and very personal communication between her and her son after his passage. She told me of her profound and heartwarming experience with him.

> "Thirty minutes after he died, I was holding his body in my arms, and I said, 'Where are you? Can you show me where you are?' And he sent me this ridiculous vision. It was a picture of him standing in about two inches of water kicking his feet and laughing, and he was wearing a T-shirt with rolled-up sleeves and pants with rolled-up cuffs, and he looked like James Dean in Rebel Without a Cause.
>
> And I laughed my head off. I just thought that was so funny and I said, 'Why are you showing me this?' And he said, 'Because I want you to laugh. I want you to see how much fun this is.'
>
> I was totally hearing him, and this was thirty minutes after he died. But, the hearing isn't like you're hearing me right now. It's not sound in your ears; it's thoughts in your head. And they were so clear and so articulate, and he was very articulate when he could

talk, and he turned out to be extremely articulate on the other side, as well. And, he said, 'Well, here we are. We've planned this; we worked on this; now the fun and games can begin. This is what we're really here to do, so let's get started. We've got work to do.'"

I had also been intrigued by the works of Ruth Montgomery and her relationship with her deceased friend Arthur Ford. So, it did not feel a stretch to enter into dialogue with those beyond the veil for me. It's important to know of their presence regardless of whether or not we choose to communicate directly with them because they are there and often feel powerless to get through to us. To acknowledge their presence and treat them with respect is a compassionate thing to do and may help smooth their transition to their new vibratory state.

My conversations with Dr. Raymond Moody, author of Life After Life, deepened my understanding of the relationship between the living and those beyond the veil as he had documented thousands of near-death experiences.

Back at Fred and Linda's house, Fred's sons climbed into the attic and recovered a few thousand dollars from behind the insulation. I learned many years later that Fred had told them about his hiding place. The rest was still in bank deposit boxes at undisclosed locations and would never be recovered.

A couple of weeks after Fred's goodbye party Linda called. She was feeling pretty good. In fact, she said she was sleeping better than she had in years. "Funny," I said, "I have been sleeping horribly." At once we both thought, It's the energy in the pyramid! She was in no hurry to have it come back home, and I was in no position to argue the point, I was too tired from a lack of sleep.

The pyramid was built out of copper, plumbed for a waterfall that trickled down through a garden of crystals below. It mystified Christians and Pagans alike. For some who could see energy, it inspired awe and even fear. What looked like streams of smoke rose up the edges and flowed out the top, which is very attractive to some beings who live just beyond the veil, including those we call spirit guides. The house was teeming with life! Once my sleep settled down, I was fine with this shared living arrangement.

Soon Jon, from our original meditation group years before, joined Linda and me for meditation. One evening we were relaxed and sitting around the pyramid together when I found myself somewhere else, no longer aware of Linda and Jon or my surroundings.

Jon asked where I was. I told him I was in the sky above the clouds. "Where?" he asked. I looked through the clouds and saw the red rocks of Sedona and, upon closer examination, an arched rock that I had passed beneath on a hike a year or so before. Linda was with me at the time and knew the archway too. Suddenly Linda and I heard a male voice tell us "You need to be here." Chills began running through us. "Did you hear that?" I asked. She had heard the same thing.

Linda was shocked when I called her the next morning and told her I had purchased tickets to go to Sedona. "Are you crazy? Just because of a voice in our meditation?"

"No. I'm not crazy," I replied. "Why would some Being tell us both to go to Sedona only to have us ignore it?"

During the two weeks between the meditation and our trip, I noticed a couple of pictures on my New Year's collage, which featured a jeep driving over the red rocks of Sedona! I didn't know why I had chosen that image because I did not like the desert. But part of the picture selection process was to be totally spontaneous without any judgment or thought about the images.

When we arrived in Sedona, on January 7th, 2000, we headed directly for the site I had seen at the pyramid during meditation with Linda and Jon. It was at Palatka, which was once home the Anasazi, Yavapai (and Navajo) Indians. As we walked along the path toward the archway, we kept our 'feelers' alert to any special kind of energy.

When we reached the archway, we stopped to feel the energy. Nothing. We kept walking. At the end of the path was the grotto that the native Americans had used for rituals and ceremonies for centuries. We entered, and when we reached about halfway toward the back, we both felt this strange plasma kind of energy, like the special effects in movies when people pass through stargates or wormholes. It was a bizarre sensation.

We took a seat along the natural rock ledge that had been used to sit on during ceremonies. As we closed our eyes we tuned into the energy. Quickly we each heard the male voice again, first Linda then me. Linda heard, "All change begins here." Then I heard, "Do what you can, and do what you must, but be here."

Linda and I both got the shivers like little girls on an adventure and excitedly exchanged ideas about what this all meant.

Since we had another day to kill, still pondering our experience at Palatki the day before, we decided to have a realtor show us around for an afternoon - just for fun. There was no way I could move to this place because Stuart was only halfway through his Junior year in high school. I would have to wait until after his graduation to seriously consider a move if that was indeed what was shaping up.

The realtor took us to several places, none of which I liked. After an hour or so I asked her if she would take us over near the Chapel of the Holy Cross, the small Frank Lloyd Wright-style church embedded in the red rocks. I had been there on a previous vacation to Sedona a couple of years earlier and thought the area was beautiful.

As we entered the neighborhood, I had an instinct and asked her to turn right here and left there. We started down one road when the realtor's own intuition kicked in, and she made a spontaneous U-turn. Instead, she took us down the road that led to, as he would confirm some years later, the home of James Redfield, author of The Celestine Prophecy. We were all flying on instinct now.

We pulled up in front of one home when I got this excited feeling and said, "See that one? If I were ever going to move to Sedona, that would be the kind of home I would be looking for."

Linda said, haltingly, as she strained to see something, "Regina. There's a 'For Sale by Owner' sign knocked over on the ground. Would you like the phone number?"

A tingle of excitement moved through me, I said, "Sure. Why not?"

## Chapter Twenty-Eight:
# Red Rock Seduction

The owner of the house answered the phone and told us that we should drive around to the front of the house if we wanted to take a look inside. I understood immediately why our intuition took us around the back. I would have had no interest in the house if I had first seen it from the front. It was the large bay windows and elevations on the backside that I found beautiful, while the front was more an ordinary modern Southwest style home. Once inside, however, I felt the excitement of new possibilities.

I was frozen in the entry hallway or vestibule. Eight Moroccan style archways rimmed an octagonal foyer just ahead. The ceiling looked like those in the smaller Duomos of Italy, rising to a dome about 20 feet overhead. I immediately imagined Fred's pyramid in the center of the room. What possibilities might exist here for traveling through the cosmos and to dimensions beyond!

Having advanced only a few yards into the octagonal foyer, I viewed the great room. There were very few right angles to be found. Curves, octagonal vaulted ceilings and graceful, soft angles - A Rudolph Steiner dream. My attention was now focused on the fact that I needed to use the bathroom. This bit of information may seem mundane but is actually a critical point.

Throughout my life my body has had a direct communication link to my intuitive process - at least when it comes to buying or renting homes. When it's the right house, I have to dart to the toilet immediately. My body can't contain the energetic excitement. As a result, I have been very fortunate in this area, always choosing places that serve me and mine for the time intended. On occasion, a family member in the midst of house shopping has asked me to come and "validate" their choice. They're thrilled when I make a beeline for the bathroom.

This day was no different. Honestly, I don't remember if I even walked through the entire house. There was no question - this was my dream home, though I had no idea how I could possibly manage such a purchase financially.

When Linda came back from touring the house, I, still standing in the foyer, asked her what she thought. She said: "I don't think it matters what I think or you think, it's already a done deal." She explained that the master bathroom was exactly like one I had described to her years before as my dream bathroom complete with large windows to the outside, trees, and skylights with no peering eyes from the outside.

I should point out again that eighteen months were remaining before Stuart's graduation with a class he had known since the age of five. Moving was out of the question. Yet, Linda and I finished up the weekend speaking of nothing other than how I could make this happen, let alone afford the house. We kept referring back to our experience in the grotto – "All change begins here." And "Do what you can, and do what you must, but be here."

My heart was racing with the challenge of what lay before me. How could I possibly buy this house yet remain in Sacramento with Stuart until his high school graduation?

After a restless night of sleep, I made an offer on the house on a wing and a prayer that it would all somehow work out. I knew it was complete insanity to stretch myself this far. I would never consider taking Stuart out of the school that had been his second home, pulling him away from classmates that were like family to him. Was I completely delusional? Why was I even considering this scheme?

When the owner of the Sedona house accepted my offer, I was caught between wild enthusiasm and nerve-wrenching fear. What would I do with the house for eighteen months until Stuart graduated from high school? I most certainly could not afford two mortgages. Though Regina's Vegetarian Table television series on PBS was going well at the time, I wasn't making excessive amounts of money by any means. This is when the hand of fate, or a heart-rending sacrifice, came into play.

The day after my offer was accepted on the Sedona house, I received a call from the Waldorf school. The school wanted to speak to me about Stuart. He was being expelled from school. He had until the end of the week to pack his things and say good-bye.

I was completely dumb-founded and shocked.

Typically, a student must be found in a drunken stupor, carrying a gun, or have created some other such offense to be kicked out of a Waldorf school. Stuart proved a different kind of challenge to the new headmistress, a former Catholic nun. I had raised him to stand up for himself and told him that, while he had to play by the rules to keep his life moving forward, a person, even a teacher, had to earn one's respect. It appears he took these words to heart.

He had had three disruptive events of speaking back to a teacher and hijinks with classmates—three strikes. After eleven years he was ejected from the tribe in which he was the class's social leader. I didn't know how I was going to tell him. My heart was broken.

Stuart had been out of town for the weekend competing in a fencing tournament at Notre Dame University in Indiana, a sport he had been invited to participate in by a friend who owned a respected fencing club. It was now early Monday morning, and Stuart was still en route home having been delayed by snowstorms in the Midwest. My stomach was knotted with grief.

He was exhausted when he dragged himself and his fencing gear through the front door, but was determined not to miss school. I sat him down on the edge of my bed and told him about the phone call. He stared ahead blankly, also in shock. A tear rolled down his cheek. A moment or two later he wiped it off and said, "Mama, we're going to Arizona! Let's find a school so I can start next week."

What happened next will stay with me forever. I learned about this from Stuart's class sponsor and one of his teachers, both of whom were present for this event.

Stuart went to school that day and the rest of the week. He asked to speak publicly to his classmates on Friday, his final day at Waldorf. He stood before his peers and told them that everything in life happens for a reason. He said that, while it may not seem fair at face value, something in his soul created his participation in the disturbances that had led to his expulsion. He continued by saying that perhaps his soul was trying to nudge him from his safety zone and into new territory for his own growth.

He blamed no one but himself for creating what were, in truth, relatively silly and innocuous events. The class sponsor was in tears as were many of the students, who insisted Stuart got a raw deal.

After Stuart's departure, a grief counselor was called in because of the gap left where Stuart had been. He was Mr. Sunshine, even if he had a little devil in him too at times.

A meeting of the staff was called because of the rare nature of this event. Stuart had not actually broken any acknowledged rules. Some serious soul searching began among the Waldorf faculty. In the end, the substitute teacher who had accused Stuart of raising his voice to her was fired along with the principal. Meanwhile, Stuart and I were about to begin a grand adventure.

To finish this chapter in Stuart's life, eighteen months later Stuart and I returned to Waldorf to attend the graduation ceremony of his classmates. He was upbeat and supportive, while my emotions were still raw. Traditionally, during the graduation ceremony, anyone in attendance who was previously a part of the graduating class is acknowledged with a round of applause.

The tradition held, except for Stuart. His exclusion was the pink elephant in the middle of the room. He ignored the snub, while my heart sank into my stomach feeling as wounded as the day he was asked to leave. Even writing this brings tears to my eyes because of the grace he exhibited, and still does, most of all when he is under fire.

That said, it was clear to me that every minute of these unfolding events was orchestrated by a larger hand than mine or Stuart's. I kept reflecting back to the Genie in the ceremonial cave at Palatki—"Do what you can, do what you must..."

I believe Stuart's soul made this decision, perhaps even sacrifice, for the higher good of each of us. He needed to stretch his wings and venture beyond the educational womb of Waldorf, and Sedona was calling me. My son's transgressions had freed us to follow.

Parallel to these shifts in our lives I was beginning to have shifts in dreamtime. In one such epic dream, which occurred just before the Sedona move, I saw an essential truth that would become a touchstone for me. It went as follows:

I found myself on the streets while people were panicking around me. I looked up and saw a large black cloud coming toward us and knew that we had reached the final hour of our lives.

As I moved through the turmoil surrounding the scene, I came upon a motorcycle with a fitted cover over it. Under the cover was a large lump. I was concerned that someone was hurt so I reached out and touched what I thought might be an injured person. A man leaped out from under the cover, pointing a gun and threatening to kill me. I told him it was okay, I didn't want anything from him, I was just concerned about him. I could feel the panic in him as he was trying to protect the only thing he valued until the very end. This motorcycle was his most precious possession and represented freedom.

I continued walking, knowing I would be caught by the "event" that was bearing down on us soon and sought shelter. I looked up into the window of an apartment building about fifteen feet above the street level. There was a large, extended family of African American people. I telepathically asked them if I could join them for safety. They laughed at me and refused, sending back the telepathic message "Are you kidding? After all your people have done to us, you want us to help you?!"

I telepathically told them that I had never harmed them in any way, and was, in fact, an ally, but they did not budge in their denial of my request. They felt it was payback time and I was part of a demographic that had caused them pain.

Soon I came upon a very tall, reflective, cylindrical building. It would have looked like a donut from above. I entered through a passageway and immediately understood that this was a place that housed people of a more enlightened viewpoint, people of all races, creeds, and colors. At the center of the complex was a grassy knoll. People quietly began gathering in the central courtyard garden with concerned looks on their faces. They knew that a great threat loomed. I looked at them and began delivering a speech in which I told them that the final moments were nearing, and that there was time for one thing only - to forgive and love one another. The speech was eloquent and continued to explain how love was the only lesson worth pursuing with the small amount of time left.

I noticed that among those in the crowd were Presidents Nixon and Clinton. Nixon began telling the crowd to listen to me because I was speaking the truth. Clinton started to cry. He then telepathically sent me the message that he was so sorry that they could not take me with them. They would be going to an underground place in which they (the privileged and powerful) would all be safe. He was sad that

I could not be among them, for if he were to take me underground, it would cause a riot among the others on the street.

I telepathically replied that he should not be sorry. I had not chosen a life of power such as his and was aware that I would not be allowed to go with them. He and Nixon got into their respective black cars, looked at me and drove off toward the bunkers. I stayed behind with the people, peaceful.

Little did I know that this kind of thinking and relating was waiting for me in Sedona.

## Chapter Twenty-Nine:
# Settling into Camelot

In a full-time state of expectation now, with Sedona beckoning, I began "feeling" my way through life more than ever. I listened to some "Sedona music" that I had picked up from one of the metaphysical shops crammed with crystals, healing rods, divination cards, books, and jewelry before returning to California.

The vibe of the music disconnected me further and further from my reality in California. With our move to the Southwest imminent, I stopped at the East West metaphysical center in Sacramento for energetic reinforcements. I needed more music to propel me into my new life. For me, music is what helps me make a leap from one chapter of life to another. It serves as a vibrational bridge, holding my hand and heart until I reach the safe ground on the other side - like a lullaby.

Searching for my newest musical ally, a man's face on the cover of a CD jumped out at me. I flipped the CD over to learn more about the contents and noticed that the recording company was in Sedona. A chill went through me and I instantly knew that this man was somehow fated to cross my path. I was filled with a sense of foolhardy excitement, the kind in which one hasn't quite learned the lessons from past mistakes and knows it, but rushes in anyway.

I later learned that seemingly half the women who moved to Sedona had been seduced into leaving their lives behind by this same artist's face and music. I suddenly felt like a cliché. Still, there was a deeper impulse, let's call it hope, that persisted - maybe I'm not the cliché, perhaps I'm the exception I told myself. This is the burden of the optimist. History can tell its story all it wants, but it doesn't apply to the optimist.

As I headed home, I ejected my original moving-to-Sedona music from the player to insert my new moving-to-Sedona-and-I'm-likely-to-have-my-heart-broken music. In making the swap, I noticed that the artist on both CDs was one and the same. What were the odds? No escaping my fate I thought as this delicious, but slightly dangerous, feeling slid over me. So, I lost myself to the music – and to my 'fate.'

I did not look back as Linda (who had decided to start her desert life as my roommate) and I pulled out of the driveway of my gingerbread, turn-of-the-century home in East Sacramento. I could only see what was ahead of me, as though my past had already been relegated to another lifetime.

We crossed the Arizona border as we were listening to a book on tape of a fictionalized account of the life of Cleopatra. It was oddly appropriate as these were to be the power years for me. While Cleopatra may not have been the best role model, per se, she was free-thinking, stubborn and adventurous, the traits I was relating to in myself at that moment.

A few hours later the snow-capped Twin Peaks of Flagstaff appeared after which we wound our way down the Oak Creek Canyon toward Sedona. The canyon route that stretches 26 miles between Flagstaff and Sedona has been rated by National Geographic as one of the ten most beautiful drives in the United States. I would agree. My heart leaped, as it still does, at the sight of the first monolithic rock formations. If rocks could talk, they certainly had our names on their dry, red lips whispering "Welcome, your life is about to begin."

My new home was a dream. It was located on Lynx Drive. The lynx, in the lore of animal divination, means the keeper of the secrets of lost magical systems and occult knowledge. It would seem, in hindsight, that I couldn't have chosen a better animal totem for the journey that lie ahead.

*Sending Stuart off to Verde Valley High School in Sedona, AZ*

Stuart settled in the Verde Valley School, which was an international boarding school, just on the other side of Cathedral rock from our new home. While escrow was closing, I spent my final weeks in Sacramento carefully furnishing my new home in white furniture mixed with rustic woods and soft earthy accents. My brief encounter with my new home left me feeling as though I was in a modern temple as I walked, softly and quietly from one room to another.

Beyond the front windows were the rocks nicknamed the Three Nuns that sit behind the Chapel of the Holy Cross. Out the other side was a clear view of Cathedral Rock, the most photographed rock formation in Arizona.

On our first day out, Linda and I went to Basha's supermarket to stock up on some basics to put in the empty refrigerator. The experience was almost surreal. I sensed that nothing would be the same again for me as I walked down the aisles. There were so many secrets and mysteries about to be discovered, but I couldn't see or touch them yet. I would have to wait, to be patient for this new life to reveal itself to me. I was pregnant with expectation.

As I was standing in line to pay for our food, someone behind me started up a conversation and invited us to a party that night. I was incredulous. I hadn't been invited to a party by anyone other than my family and a couple of close friends for years. And, here, in the grocery store in the checkout line, a total stranger invites us to a party, a Sedona party.

Linda and I arrived at a party reminiscent of the 1970s with flowing skirts and hair, but this time they belonged to grownups. People seemed to shine, freely expressing friendship, sensuality, and love for one another. The men hugged men and women stroked the hair of other women in a gesture of nurturing and friendship. In the 70s, this kind of thing had frightened me a bit because it was propelled by massive drug use. There was a sloppiness and crushing of any boundaries that I had found invasive and disconcerting. But now I was drawn to it like a moth to a flame. Perhaps because I was ready to let my own hair down and my heart out of its gilded cage where it had been protecting itself from the potential disappointments of life.

The propelling force here was the music - exotic, emotional, driven by the tabla and other primal percussion, yet ethereal. There was the requisite use of ecstasy and pot, as was the fashion in the year 2000, but the behavior the drugs inspired in those who were taking them was not disquieting nor threatening to me.

Over the first couple of months, as we settled into local life, I slipped back into my work producing Regina's Vegetarian Table, which had been running three years at that point. I was in the middle of a four-month break from production to heal the top section of my right ring finger, which had been severed from its lower half in an apartment in Buenos Aires several months before while on a tango holiday.

As Stuart had gained his freedom by way of a driver's license, my time opened up, and the first item on my list was to start dancing again. That is when I began dancing the Argentine Tango. I had become obsessed with the sensual but highly disciplined dance and joined a group of tango students on a trip to Buenos Aires. The first day of the tour was the obligatory stop at a tango shoe operation at which they custom made the sexy shoes.

*Severed finger emergency in Buenos Aires*

After my feet were measured and I had chosen the colors and styles of my new shoes I milled around the building and chatted with others. At one point my hand was reached up above my head and resting on the backside of a door jamb.

Not noticing my hand, a woman tried to close the door – crack! I nearly fainted with pain. Meanwhile, unable to close the door all the way, she slammed it again. Her second attempt severed my finger. Mute and going into shock, I did ultimately faint once I saw the digit dangling by a thread of skin from the lower half of my finger.

I was taken to the people's hospital where, with a cat on the adjacent gurney and a bare light bulb dangling above me, a doctor did a rudimentary job of stitching my finger back on over a bucket placed on the floor, under my hand, to catch the blood. The disappointing part was that this was the first day of my once-in-a-lifetime tango vacation. So, I did not call home, but instead stayed out until 4:00 a.m. dancing the Argentine tango every night with a black sock covering the bandages on my right hand, which was held high above my heart for pain management. I did not let this dampen my tango holiday, and I became known as the woman with the black glove as I danced every night until roughly 3:00 in the morning.

If I were to step into self-analysis, I would have seriously pondered the symbolism of this as it was the third major accident to fingers on my right hand, having already lost the top of my baby finger and the pad off the front of my middle finger, which was sewn back on.

When I arrived back in the United States, I sent a whimsical little postcard to the PBS station programmers featuring me staring, shocked, at my missing finger saying Regina's Vegetarian Table would be back when the finger grows back. This was a perfectly-timed break in that it allowed time for our move and transition to Sedona life.

I was beginning to venture out to the cafes, most specifically a local cafe called Osho's. The Bhagwan Shree Rajneesh

(Osho), with whom the media had a frolic after outing he and his followers on their ranch in Oregon, still had a robust following in Sedona. They owned some of the local businesses, and I noticed how they were operated with high, clean standards. I also grew to appreciate their ethics and kindness. But, most of all, I appreciated the role the Osho Cafe would play in my social life.

One morning in early June 2000, I felt an urge for a psychic reading of some kind. I still hadn't found my Sedona groove and was too impatient to let it play itself out. As I left the Osho café, a man with longish, wavy gray hair made a passing salutation to me.

I turned and asked him if he knew of a good psychic in Sedona. Had I only known that this is like asking if there are any good horse trainers in Kentucky. Everyone seems to be a psychic, or at least believes they are, in Sedona. My soon-to-be new friend, Paul "Lawrence" Curtis, was no exception as he replied, "Well, if I do say so, I am."

"Really?" I asked.

We arranged for a reading, which included one of his "angel" paintings, later that afternoon. These were representations of the energies he perceived around his clients as he was doing the reading. Painting was his meditation as he was a professional artist, so it wasn't a stretch for him to paint as he did intuitive readings. During the reading, he asked at one point if I would mind his painting me. I thought that was a flattering offer to do a portrait of me only to find that he meant to paint ME.

I left his house with a spiral on my forehead, some little hearts on my cheek and an intuitively divined angel painting filled with bright colors, rainbows, and blue hearts.

I also had an invitation to a business mixer, the kind of event from which I usually recoil. But this was a Sedona business mixer. Everyone gathered on the flat rocks at Red Rock Crossing near Oak Creek at dusk and opened the mixer with a group meditation. It was beautiful, even intoxicating. This month's guide was Peter Sterling the harpist and recording artist. He led a beautiful, heartfelt meditation in a large circle on the red rocks.

After the meditation, we ate and socialized. I was not aware that by wearing the "mark of Lawrence" (the spiral on my forehead), I was being sized up as Lawrence's new "friend." Lawrence had had lots of "friends," particularly women that were new to Sedona.

At the end of the mixer, Lawrence invited me to meet him the next day, and the day after, and the day after that. Within a few weeks he had become my new best friend in Sedona, meeting for coffee in the morning, attending outdoor music performances and parties, taking drives up the canyon to Flagstaff for shopping, and whatever else sounded interesting.

One Sunday in July, I was invited to join my cousin Lilli, an extraordinary body worker and healer who had moved to Sedona a few years prior, for an outdoor musical concert. Lawrence was to join Linda, Stuart, Lilli and me. After milling around for a bit, Lilli came up to me and asked, "Would you like to meet Chris Spheeris, a friend of mine, the musician?" as she gestured in his direction. This was the face on the CD I had seen while I was still dreaming my new life into existence back in California. "Yes," I replied.

## Chapter Thirty:
## *Argentina Tango*

Barbara Marx Hubbard once privately told me that, as a strong and self-sufficient woman, love has never been easy. The same held true for me. While the men I had spent time with throughout my adult life were attracted to what appeared to be a successful media woman, they were not prepared to take on the extended implications of my strength, nor of my weaknesses. I have opinions and thoughts about a myriad of topics and have never played the "subservient" role well. When I offered up my thoughts on this topic or that, their faces generally either glazed over or appeared to feel threatened, often both at the same time. I suppose it's to be expected. Who, after all, wants to talk of remote viewing, quantum healing, FEMA camps or ETs over their morning croissant?

At the same time, I am a pleaser and am uncomfortable if the people around me are not happy. So I would twist and turn and morph myself into any kind of pretzel that I felt would make the other person happy. Then, when I perceived my partner as taking me for granted, I would step back and tell myself it was time to go, time to reclaim myself. But this has the effect of never truly relaxing into a relationship and knowing the sublime feeling of trust on the deepest levels. So I found a form of sublimation in the Argentine Tango.

This seemingly macho, South American form of expression has rules. Men lead, and women follow. Women like me either become addicted to it, or stomp off the floor after their first couple of milongas (tango gatherings), never to return. I would have guessed that I was a candidate for the latter.

With Argentine tango, there is an objective element that supersedes popularity, physical appearance, and even friendship at times. If you can do the dance well, you will have plenty of partners. If you do not, you will sit on the sidelines all night long, alone. This is in part because of the tradition that men must ask the woman to dance. In nouveau tango circles, this has since changed, where women dance together and people just play, but I had entered the traditional tango scene, and I had to play by the rules or quit.

*Tango with Greg Getner*

By my third milonga/practica session I was ready to quit. The man I was dancing with had had no real feel for the dance nor the music and I felt as though I was being tortured through the entire panda (set of three - four tangos.) I would subtly try to back-lead, to no avail. He was insistent that he lead, as he well should have. At the same time, I wasn't skilled enough to dance with the more fluid and advanced men.

I sat down after the set of dances, agitated, and realized that I could either learn a little grace and humility and learn to follow another human being's cue, or I could walk out and never return.

I stayed. And I learned patience, humility and the beauty of surrender. I also learned about give and take and how a truly empowered man gives the woman free reign of expression. This was exemplified in the dances and performances of the mature dance couples in which all eyes were on the woman, though the man was creating the impeccable leads that allowed her to shine.

While I cannot say this is the perfect simile for intimate relationships, it gave me a glimpse into surrender from a safe distance. As I danced or practiced three to four nights a week, I became a decent follower and dance partner. As I further developed my skills, the more comfortable I felt closing my eyes and melting into the dance. I became addicted to the surrender. This was one place I could go and not have to make all of the decisions, not be responsible for anything except my own body moving with another body to the music.

There was one caveat: I could only do this with the better dancers. When a man was not sure of himself and gave either unclear or overbearing leads, I would keep my eyes open, alert for danger. But when a man was confident, relaxed, and skilled, I would surrender completely, eyes shut, head against his cheek, one hundred percent present and "in the moment" to respond to his next improvised lead as the entire dance is improvised and led by the man, and responded to in kind, by the woman. She brings to the dance whatever she chooses to create in response to the lead at the moment.

I had left this spell-binding activity behind in California upon my move to Sedona and needed a tango fix badly. There was only one option: I would have to start a tango community in Sedona.

My new friend Paul Lawrence was my first volunteer student and helped solicit other potential tango dancers. Soon we had a lovely little tango community. I watched insecure and physically awkward men and women blossom into confident, sensual, beautiful dancers. There was heartfelt gratitude flowing both ways. As a bonus, I had created a couple of dance partners for myself, so I could have my Sedona life and tango too.

Soon my fascination with surrender would be put to the test in my life off the dance floor.

## Chapter Thirty-One:
# UFO Hunting

Life took on an easy rhythm of meeting friends, which mostly meant Paul Lawrence, for coffee at Osho's in the morning and work on television projects in the afternoon.

I was becoming restless with my television production, Regina's Vegetarian Table. My mind was expanding in new directions and paranormal experiences were growing more commonplace. I found this the juiciest terrain of all for exploration and I had an insatiable curiosity. Restricting my on-air presentation to the value of fresh produce in the diet was feeling like a shirt I had outgrown, I couldn't quite button it across my breasts any longer. That familiar draw to the unknown was peeking above my plane of consciousness. I could feel a change coming.

Not surprisingly, once I had identified this feeling of discontent, my business partner Bill began finding it more and more difficult to procure funding for the program. This brought on waves of guilt because I understood that in spite of his genuinely valiant efforts to raise funds, my need to expand into new territory was impeding his progress in what science calls "the quantum field" of creation - but we both needed the paycheck. So, I allowed the production to go on until the money ran out.

While I loved being with my production crew, I had begun to move into other circles, pursuing a more controversial subject matter. This was at a time when the first large conferences on mind-body-conspiracy-spirituality had started to surface. Perhaps the best known at the time were the Prophet's Conferences. I signed up.

My first experience of mass numbers of like-minded people happened in 2001 in Palm Springs.

Among the presenters were Drunvalo, Jean Houston, the late Dr. John Mack, Hank Wesselman, Gregg Braden, Steven Greer, and Doreen Virtue. I made it a point to introduce myself to all of them because, unbeknownst to my RVT production crew, I had been working on a treatment to present to PBS titled Rebels With A Cause. At this Prophets Conference, I had hit the jackpot of wildly diverse presenters, concepts, and experiences, which helped me plug in the names and subjects to the treatment I would present to PBS.

While I was interested in all of it and had been studying many of these subjects privately for fifteen years at this point, I found myself particularly drawn to Steven Greer's Disclosure Project. I checked into the dates of his next CSETI expedition and slotted it into my budget and calendar. I had no idea what to expect, but I was committed to finding out.

About two months after the Prophet's Conference in Palm Springs, I was at the signup desk registering for Greer's conference in Twenty Nine Palms, California, just outside of Joshua Tree National Forest. The group of approximately thirty UFO hunters was diverse, ranging in age from twenty to seventy, all of whom held an expectation of seeing UFOs, if not extraterrestrial life itself, first hand. Among the people I met was a man named Antonio, a kind man of Italian descent with a long, dark ponytail. He was a veteran of Greer's workshops and clued me in on the rhythm of the week.

Daytimes were spent in a conference room where Greer gave us inside information on secret government programs that were involved both directly and indirectly with ETs, his own encounters with beings from 'off-planet-cultures,' and his long-awaited Disclosure event. Greer had spent the better part of ten years gathering testimony from both military and civilian aeronautics and military personnel who had witnessed or had experienced close encounters with UFOs and extraterrestrials.

Inevitably, the question surfaced, "If that many people have had direct experience, then why don't we know anything about this?" We spent the remainder of the week exploring the answer to this question. The reasons spanned from an unwillingness to give up the Cold War mentality to the aggressive military actions of the US government toward uninvited ET guests to a race for advanced technologies and who would ultimately control them.

You have to know that once you drop down the UFO community rabbit hole, you truly enter another world. As with all esoteric communities, there are legends within this community who are entirely unknown to anyone outside this circle. Each of them offers stories that are unfathomable, ranging from the frightening to the bizarre and even inspiring. But one of the surprising traits of these people, almost exclusively men, is the amount of angst and fear they have carried inside themselves since the "event" of their lives.

I have met a great number of these men and was deeply touched to see tears of relief, mingled with fear, trickling from the corner of their eyes as they publicly told their stories. Secrecy had been, for them, a matter of life and death, or at least a matter of maintaining their livelihood so they could care for their families. National security oaths are not a matter a military man takes lightly. It takes a great deal of conviction and courage to break one and risk suffering the consequences, even if he is long beyond retirement age. Yet Steven had convinced dozens of them to do just that for his Disclosure Project.

For most of us, the exciting part of the workshop was being out in the field at nighttime. Once the sky was inky black, we would gather in a circle snuggled into blankets and sleeping bags on our fold-out chairs.

The evening began with a group meditation. Steven always had among his attendees a few people who were known to be remote viewers.

We started by setting our intention to attract an "experience" of some kind. This was followed by remote viewing in which we were asked to look into the evening ahead and see when and where a craft would become visible.

I have found throughout life that as long as the focus of a group supports using intuitive abilities, I seem to blossom. I feel safe, as though the information will be treated respectfully, unlike society at large where intuitive 'hits' are more often than not viewed as just another strange musing from myself and others like me.

Out in the desert, under the cloak of darkness, we couldn't

see each other's faces and often had no idea who was speaking. I felt safe. And I could easily and accurately "see" this particular week.

One of the first visions I had was of an elliptical blue spacecraft, sitting on a flat rock at the edge of a high rocky crag. Another vision was of a vector point and time for spotting a UFO, which turned out to be accurate in yielding a suspiciously other-worldly looking craft above. Steven was very clear to point out which vehicles and lights were of terrestrial origins as they had particular patterns of movement and colors. We also learned to tell the difference between a satellite and what is called a Fast Walker, or UFO tracking quickly across the sky. Satellites tend to move much slower.

As for the blue elliptical craft, it never showed that first night, nor the second, nor the third, though I kept "seeing" it at the outset of each night's viewing.

Along with spotting some Fast Walkers, crafts with uncharacteristically jerky and quick movements and so forth, we also viewed other events. During the daytime program one day we were asked to meditate and "view" the evening ahead. I saw that we were going to run into trouble with some authorities and be asked to leave the land. Because I was new to the group, I hesitated to speak up about this, but later caught up with Steven to share this vision with him privately. He dismissed my "vision" saying there was nothing to worry about. He had been bringing groups to this spot for years and they had never encountered any such trouble.

About 45 minutes into the evening's events, a ranger came around and asked for the group permit. Steven didn't have one, so we were asked to leave - immediately. We stumbled around in the dark to gather our things and moved onto another more remote location, one where we wouldn't be discovered.

As the days and remote viewing progressed, I "saw" a small abandoned church with a rectory next to it. It was down a dirt road and appeared long forgotten. I shared my vision this time, though it had no particular relevance to UFO viewing.

The next day a woman said she had been out in her truck exploring the surrounding lands and came across this abandoned small church with an outbuilding exactly as I had described. I was feeling more confident by the moment, but I couldn't understand why there was no sight of the blue elliptical craft.

The second-to-last day of our workshop, we took a field trip to Joshua Tree National Forest. The Joshua tree, or yucca palm, was named by Mormons crossing the Mojave in the mid-1800s. The sparse little trees have bayonet-shaped leaves and are not an inviting refuge to turn to for shade. Still, they have their kind of desert allure and give a little dusty green punctuation to the arid land and rock formations.

Our group meditated in a little cave, though I think many of us were there more for the cool stone interior. As we walked through the scorching hot desert amidst the rocky crags, some of the group were taking photos as this would be our only daylight field trip outside the classroom.

For the most part, our time in the desert was uneventful under the night sky with a few distant sightings, but considerably more interesting by day listening to Steven's research into the government cover-ups of the phenomena.

I was ready to take the subject to mainstream television and was in a position to do so with my PBS distribution connections. I began to put a documentary concept together. It would be called UFOs: Hard Evidence. Much of the documentary was to be based on Greer's upcoming Disclosure event at the National Press Club in Washington D.C., which was to take place a few months after the conference in the desert.

The final day together in Joshua Tree, the room was all atwitter as I was walking in. Everyone was gathered around a television screen, which was being used to show someone's digital photos. There it was, a semi-transparent blue elliptical craft sitting on a flat rock at the base of the crags! What the human eye could not see the digital camera could! The craft I had been seeing in my remote viewing those first nights was there all along, but we just couldn't see it. It was slightly "off-phase" in its density.

Just to further this a bit, when I went out with Steven's group one more time that summer, I was aware of quite a few spacecraft around us in this other dimensional field of density. We never caught one on camera, however. This blue craft was an incredible validation for me in understanding that the UFO phenomenon is far more pervasive than we would ever believe simply from witnessing UFOs and expert testimony. And it also validated that my intuition was still in working order. Because I wasn't using my intuition in any systematic or regular way, I tended to wonder at times if my "bunny ears" were still intact. In truth, our intuition is always there running in the background of our lives, but it may not have a place to express itself so dramatically during the everyday events of life.

I would challenge myself in a more clinical setting years

later when I attended a remote viewing workshop being conducted by Tom Campbell. Among the attendees was the renowned Dr. Russell Targ, former director of the Stanford Research Institute whom I had interviewed all those years before.

We were instructed to view the contents of a box sitting on the podium. Within thirty seconds or so, a dim image started appearing, ultimately taking on more density of form. I saw an American Indian arrowhead. Fearing that I would be proved wrong, the box was opened. Tom took out a small Indian arrowhead.

After returning to Sedona, I made plans to be in D.C. to videotape the Disclosure event at the National Press Club, contracting the video crew that worked on PBS' McNeill-Lehrer PBS evening news.

The day before the event, I approached Steven to tell him that I had been successful in engaging the crew when he abruptly stated that I would not be allowed to videotape anything. I was shocked, as workers were scurrying about the room in preparation for hundreds of media from around the world. I was the only journalist being excluded.

I don't know that he had the right to do such a thing, but I was so shaken at his behavior that I just froze and didn't pursue it any further. I canceled the television crew, joined the audience and listened as one pilot, Captain, General, journalist, and G.I after another told their story. A couple of them broke down during their testimony, including a man who spoke to my heart, Lt. Clifford Stone of the U.S. Army UFO Retrieval Unit. He had been selected for his ability to communicate with beings from other dimensions. He stated that he had been face-to-face with extraterrestrials and was forever changed, split open with compassion for a little being that he perceived to be frightened after its craft had crashed.

In a later conversation with Clifford, he explained to me that the natural human response to the inexplicable is to behave with aggression or violence.

> "We respond with fear to anything that is unknown. If we have that fear, then our conduct toward that of the unknown has always been with hostility. What we need to do is get to the point where we overcome our fear of the unknown, face it head on and try to understand, logically, why that unknown stimulus is occurring. For example, I personally believe, I personally know their agenda here is purely scientific; it is not for world conquest. Should it be for world conquest, they could have taken us over many millennia ago, and we would be worshiping them today as gods. If you were to go face-to-face with an E. T., they would tell you that they are not gods; they are as mortal as you and I. Now, their lifespan is much longer than ours. But, here again, we someday will achieve that, also."

I asked him: "When they [the Army UFO Retrieval unit] took you to the staging ground, or wherever you were taken [crash site], what was the purpose of your being there?" Clifford replied:

> "You were going out to a site either to recover debris of a UFO, recover a craft that had crashed. My job was to psychically interface with any survivors. When you went ahead and you did the interfacing, they would talk directly to you. When they would talk directly to you it would be like you were hearing

it, not only in your head but in your ears, also. But nobody else could hear it. The end result is, even more than that, you could feel the emotions they were feeling. I would want to rush through that because sometimes you could feel the fear or the pain; you could feel the loss; you could feel their fear of never seeing their loved-ones again. You see, we see them as cartoon characters. They have societies; they have families; they are more human than we give them credit for. I know that sounds crazy, but they are.

Once that open contact takes place, if we can look at the similarities between them and us it will make that first contact much easier."

I was open to all of it. What do we know anyway? If life has taught me one thing, it's that we know but a grain of sand worth of what is actually available for our understanding. I believed Sgt. Clifford Stone and I wanted to know more about what was being hidden from the people of this planet.

I learned of a young man named John Greenwald who was a highly skilled computer geek. As a teenager, he holed up in his bedroom uncovering newly declassified documents on the military cover-up of UFOs and extraterrestrial contact. He created a website called The Black Vault where he posted the original documents, generally with large portions redacted (blacked out) by the agencies in question. It was becoming clear to me that the scale of the effort to keep U.S. citizens in the dark was massive and had many arms.

A respected, mature UFO researcher, the late Command Sergeant Major Robert Dean, had long come to accept the presence of extraterrestrials when I met with him. His world was irrevocably changed in the 1960's when he became aware of a study being conducted as the result of a UFO incident that was seen as a threat to national security.

"An incident occurred in 1961 before I got there. On February 2, 1961, a massive flotilla of these objects [Bob pointed up to the sky with his hand] flew over the Warsaw Pact area, over the Western Alliance that divided Europe, in formation, very high, very fast. As I say, they circled over the southern coast of England, went north and disappeared over the Norwegian Sea. That almost triggered World War III.

> An Air Marshal by the name of Sir Thomas Pike insisted on having a study to figure out what the hell is going on. Now, I worked for a General by the name of Lyman Lemnitzer, a Four-Star American General who was SACEUR (Supreme Allied Commander, Europe). Air Marshal Pike was Deputy SACEUR; he was a British Air Marshal, Five-Star rank, who was the deputy to Lemnitzer. In '61 he determined we've got to find out what's going on here. And he created a military committee to make this analysis, this study. They published it in June of '64. They called it an assessment. Subtitle: An Evaluation of a Possible Military Threat to Allied Powers in Europe. Strictly military, no-nonsense; what the hell is going on? What's happening? And it was a detailed analysis by experts from all over Western Europe. They had an annex on history; they had an annex on the scientific aspects, atmospheric physics, all of it. There was an annex on the theological implications, and that one really grabbed me because I had been a student of History.

Well, after the three-year study they concluded that the planet had been under observation, survey, analysis continually for centuries by, apparently, an advanced technology from somewhere else. That, in itself, grabbed the hell out of me; I mean think about what that would mean to you. You know, a normal, no-nonsense kind of person."

Bob went on to explain to me the findings of the report and how this would shape the military and public interface on the subject.

> "The Brookings Report is available; you can get a copy of it… [it's] about the implications of contact with extraterrestrial intelligence that was a thorough analysis. They determined, these experts - Margaret Mead was one of them who helped study this thing - they determined that the implications of contact with extraterrestrial intelligence would be so disturbing to the body politic, the sociological balance of society on this planet, that they recommended that… we cannot release this to the public. The masses of people out there cannot handle this and cannot deal with it. So, [being the self-appointed experts] we are not going to tell anybody about this. That's when the lid came down. But you cannot close the lid on Pandora's Box. No, you can't close it because they (pointing skyward again) have been continually, gently and subtly trying to educate us as to their presence and to their reality. Not only that, they have been trying to sociologically, psychologically, gently help us grow into a level of maturity, which we are not at the moment, so we can accept their presence and our place in the Universe. That process is under way. They have been conducting it for centuries, but they have been

increasing and raising the level of exposure over the years."

As it turned out, the Disclosure event's live webcast was interrupted from the beginning. This was due to the size of the audience logging on. This was the second largest National Press Club event in history, second only to Monica's Blue Dress of the Clinton scandal. Media from every corner of the world was in attendance.

In a spirited discussion following the witness testimonials, one Washington D.C. reporter stood up and answered an audience question as to why the news doesn't report these events., The reporter said: "We don't report it because we're not allowed to!"

When these stories come in, the news agents are told to turn a blind eye, just as I had experienced all those years ago as a young woman anchoring the nightly news. Some things are simply not allowed to be told.

Sadly, the event received almost no coverage in the U.S. media. News directors squelched the story once they found out it wasn't a freak show, rather, a carefully laid out testament to the complicity of our government and shadow governments in obscuring and denying information that should rightfully be made available to every citizen. We live in a multi-verse with a vast number of other cultures beyond our solar system. When do we take our place as a conscious species among them? The answer to that question takes us down conspiracy lane, which was alluded to in Robert Dean's comments. It's a place I would later tread to expand my education into the deeper workings of the world's governments. Meanwhile, if you are interested in the anatomy of government cover-ups of extraterrestrial presence, read Nick Pope's The Rendalsham Forest Affair.

I was never informed as to why Steven Greer refused my participation as a journalist and attempted to discredit me as a person. He had told others I was an infiltrator from an agency. I am guessing this is because I could remote view and was a stranger to him. Paranoia is part of the conspiracy scene's deep psyche, sometimes for good reason.

I chose to walk away from it, deepened by the experience, which was invaluable. I also scrapped any plans to produce UFOs: Hard Evidence. If this was the mentality that prevailed in this underground world, then I could use my energy in more productive ways, which turned out to be a good decision. But I would often return to the story of extraterrestrial life and the phenomena of UFOs in the following years.

## Chapter Thirty-Two:
## *Adventures Between Dimensions*

Back in Sedona, Linda and I had begun setting our alarm clocks for 4:00 a.m. because it seemed there was something much more potent where meditation was concerned during these quiet hours before dawn. I can understand why monks in robes of all colors use this hour to contemplate before going into the chores of their days. The world is quiet, the veils are thin, and one can contact energies that are off the radar during the busy-ness of the daylight hours.

Both of us were familiar with strange energies and experiences, but we wanted to do something more controlled, with intention. Usually, events happened to us seemingly unexpectedly. We would be repeating a mantra or something equally mundane when a Being would come alongside us and perhaps stroke our shoulder, or ruffle our hair. We would often get goosebumps, then become filled with a sense of excitement or anticipation as each phenomena-based event revealed itself, like putting clues together in an Agatha Christie novel.

It seemed that the environment of the octagonal foyer with the pyramid, along with our past experiences, provided the perfect place to conduct experiments. In this sacred meditation space, we were able to contact supportive beings, spirit guides if you will, relatively effortlessly. This was particularly true of Linda who has phenomenal inner sight.

We were becoming more of a Sedona cliché by the moment. Did we really need all the new age tools to move between fields of consciousness? Perhaps not. But it cannot be argued that geometry, copper, crystals, and water all have great conductive and focusing properties. It can't hurt. That's how we viewed it. Besides, the pyramid was artistically exotic and hypnotic to look at.

As for our intention to open new doorways to the unknown, a year or so before moving to Sedona, we had been given a clue of particular importance by our new guide who called himself "Arasham, the connector to The Guardian." It allowed us to move through an energetic matrix into another dimension. We had only attempted this a few times as this was not an expedition one should take lightly. While I am generally up for an adventure, there are times in life when one should use a little restraint and humbly accept guidance.

Once the energy in the room was prepared as per instruction from our unseen allies, we felt there was support for the inter-dimensional expedition. This was followed by using the protocol that had been given to us by Arasham to pass through a portal to another field of density/dimension. On the count of three, we would take the leap together, metaphorically speaking.

There are no words to explain the physical sensation of shifting frequencies, and I only wish there had been a digital video camera present so we could see what the space around us looked like. Once we took "the leap," we were simultaneously sucked into a fast-moving tunnel of light.

The cells of our bodies felt as though they were flying apart into billions upon billions of particles of light. It was as though there was a powerful charge at the center of each particle, which translated to the physical body. It felt as though every cell in our body, even the hair on our heads, had undulating waves of chills running through them. Fortunately, this part of the journey doesn't last long. Soon we would recombine these "particles" of light into a new, unfamiliar, less dense body.

In one such adventure, we landed in a place that was undefined other than the perception of a couple of grandmotherly Native American women on the periphery. They seemed to be there essentially to babysit us. As this was occurring, Linda and I could speak to each other as we were traveling in tandem and delighted to experience these lighter bodies.

During one adventure, we noticed we had tiny little feet but could not stand on them, because we were floating, finding it hard to position the body in an upright angle. Everything felt so much lighter than in our world. We would explore, giggle, and allow ourselves to be amazed as we were being trained to commute to other sub-dimensional fields. We did not see any pale disembodied entities, giant cockroaches, reptilians or anything else unpleasant, perhaps because we were being looked after from the other side. It was simply quiet, dark, clean, and gave a feeling that there was nothing but space in which to learn and play. We could breathe and feel unencumbered by the weight of earthly bodies, minds, and emotions.

We would simultaneously know when it was time to return to the earth experience, because the feeling of lightness, or the visual scene around us, would begin to dissipate.

Though we felt what we had experienced was very real, there is always a question as to this kind of phenomena. We knew, however, that there was a precedent for this kind of tandem out-of-body experience as detailed in physicist and engineer Tom Campbell's book My Big TOE, in which he and his "traveling" partner, Dennis Menerich, would regularly meet in OBE experiments conducted under laboratory conditions by Robert Monroe.

> "His [Monroe's] instructions to Dennis and I were to go up above the lab, meet there in the out-of-body state, and then go on an adventure together. We were in these isolation chambers. So, we did that, and it probably took close to two hours for us in this out-of-body thing, and it was very eventful; saw a lot of things, had a lot of conversations, talked to each other. It wasn't a dull time and we had been doing this, now, for probably at this point two years. What we're talking about is three sessions a week with Bob. The sessions lasted from about 6:30 p.m. in the evening to about 2 o'clock in the morning, and then we'd go home. I'd go home at 2 o'clock in the morning and practice until it was time to get up to go to work, and then I'd go to work. It was like having two jobs.

He had Dennis and I go out; we had this adventure; we come back. You know we'd been there for two hours and it's been dark, you know, and we're—he's trained us to go and come back and report and talk. So, we stumble out into the light and it's always, you know, bright lights, and you get down to the end of the hall, and you have to know Bob Monroe, but he had a very sardonic and dry wit. So, we come there and he looked at us and he grinned and he says, 'Do you two really think you were out together?' And, we looked at each other, and I said, 'Well, yeah, it seemed that way.' And he said, 'Yeah, it seemed that way.' He (Bob) said, 'Well, listen to this,' and he reached out and he flipped the two tapes, which was Dennis's audio and my audio. Now, of course, we couldn't hear each other. He talked to us individually. So, he asked Dennis, 'What are you seeing?' And then he'd ask me on a separate line, you know, 'What are you seeing?'

> .... there was Dennis and I, out-of-body, having conversations, answering each other's questions, seeing the same things, having basically the same experience. Now, it was through Dennis's interpretation and my interpretation, you could see, just as if two people went on a vacation and they were both talking about it; it's different, but it's the same.

It was a validation I needed, and at that point—like I've told others—I probably walked around for two weeks in a bit of a daze. This is real! This is real! And, that was a big turning point. Now, after that I didn't need to ask the question whether it was real, anymore. I knew that it was real; it was objective; I was having those experiences. OK, now I had context for the fact that we were doing one-in-a-million data collection that was paranormal. I really had a sense of it being real. Now, I'm a physicist. What I do for my career is understanding how things work. That's what physics does. How does the world work? What's the Reality Model that describes this? So, that was my passion; that was my aim after that experience, to figure out what is going on here? What are the rules? How do you go out-of-body? You know, what does that mean? What are the limitations? So, I spent the next 35 years, 40 years exploring, doing research, doing experiments because you could eliminate some variables. What does this mean? How far does this go? How can I manipulate this?"

As physically disconcerting as these out of body experiences were, coming back into the body was equally as challenging, perhaps more so. The physical pressure of coming back into the density of this earth life is almost suffocating in comparison, like sinking into mud. We would return heavy-headed, finish the meditation, and then silently stumble to our respective rooms to go back to sleep and transition back to our earthly "reality."

We have never fully understood what we were being "trained" for because we had one last experience that frightened us so badly we didn't dare go back.

One morning, at the usual hour, we went to the pyramid. My little dog, a Bichon Frise named Genie, dragged her white, furry little body behind us to "meditate." She didn't like being left out and always managed, in spite of her advanced years, to rally with us at this dark and quiet hour. Not once through all the years of 4:00 a.m. meditation had she made a noise to interfere with our experience. That's because she slept through each meditation. The hint that she wasn't seeking enlightenment was her soft little snore.

This time, when we asked to meet with our guides, our connection was more nebulous than usual, but we could feel them - somewhat. The same when we went through the protocols of previous "journeys." Dim, but still there. That sounded good enough for me. I asked Linda how she felt about taking the plunge into the unknown once again. She said "Sure. Why not?"

We leaped as we had before. But this time there were no Native elders, there was no protection. If you've ever found yourself in a part of town in which you did not belong, this is what it felt like. It was grayish blue, dull. The only other beings we saw were a couple of men who seemed to be watching or following us. They were lurking around corners, in what looked like some kind of otherworldly industrial scene.

By the time we realized that something had gone wrong, it was too late. We alerted each other about the creepy feeling, trying to find a way out. I looked up, and it was as if there was a glass ceiling, one that could not be broken through. We realized we were trapped with no idea of how to escape this dark place.

As I looked back at the experience some time later, I realized that we were likely in a lower density astral plane, one in which the entities were not at peace. We hadn't had the clarity and frequency sufficient to go to a more refined field this time - we just barely made it off the ground, as it were, and this is the last place one would want to end up on a spiritual field trip!

As we began registering fear, my little doggie angel, Genie, suddenly woke. She jumped on Linda's leg, Linda screamed, and I came slamming back through time and space into my body with a horrible thud. We felt awful, but we were back, and wondering what the hell that was all about.

A few days later, I had a dream in which I looked at myself and saw that the entire right side of my body was black, virtually without energy. Then a voice came into the dream and told me that I had only eighteen months left to live if I didn't find a way to repair the hole in my aura. I awakened with a start, but just slowly enough to remember the dream.

The next day I met with Chris Spheeris, the musician I mentioned earlier. I relayed my dream to him. He suggested that I go to the Crystal Castle to have a photograph taken of my aura and see if there was indeed a problem on my right side. He went on to explain that the Kirlian type photography had advanced to the point where you could actually see components of the aura, rather than the diffused cloud of color one generally saw in older versions of the technology. I was doubtful, but I stopped there on my way home anyway. The store manager assured me that the fifteen dollars would be well worth the investment.

I stood in front of the camera and allowed my presumably damaged aura to be photographed. A few minutes later he handed me the photo, which left my mouth agape. There it was, a very large black field on the entire upper right side of my body - no color, no energy.

Now I was nervous. I went home and told Linda what I had discovered and asked her if we could go to Arasham, directly through a channeling. She was still a very reluctant channeler, so I had to be very respectful in my requests so she wouldn't feel pressured or used.

I guided her through the usual process, but this time, instead of Arasham notifying me that he was present and available for questions, Linda's hand went up and fixed itself to the right side of my face without a word. I was both surprised and curious because the right side of my face had been in terrible pain since our misadventure. It had developed what I can only guess to be neuralgia. The nerves were on fire, hurting when I chewed, spoke, or even blinked my eye. It had happened a couple of times in the past, so I knew it would take time to disappear, sometimes a week or two.

After allowing the hand to transmit energy for a few minutes, Arasham blurted out, "Don't ever do that again!" A little surprised at his tone, I asked what he was referring to, while at the same time noticing that the pain in my face had disappeared entirely. It only took a second more to deduce he was speaking about our early morning adventure of a few days before.

"Did you have permission to do this?" asked Arasham.

"Permission?" I thought. I had never heard this very patient guide overtly agitated with me before.

He went on to say that the portal had not been correctly set up for such a journey, and wanted to know why in the world we felt it was okay to proceed with such a delicate undertaking.

My answer was something like, "Well, we could see the sign, it was dim, but we could see it." He proceeded to inform me that this should never again be undertaken without the clear support of our guides. This was very dangerous without the proper protection, he continued.

I was not in a position to argue this one as I had a gaping black hole in my aura. So I began telling him about my auric troubles. He stopped me and said, "It has been taken care of."

No follow up questions were necessary as I had apparently been the beneficiary of some energy healing, thrilled that my face was pain-free. Whatever had been transmitted through Linda's hand had an impact on me. I don't remember anything else about that session as I was feeling somewhat humbled and embarrassed.

A few years later, I was reading Secrets of the Pyramid by Tony Bushby, the pseudonym for an author that some say is rumored to be a former Anglican priest. Whoever he is, I have a great deal of respect for his work.

I was intrigued by much of this book and had come to the

opinion that the rites of passage so assiduously practiced by the Freemasons and others were simply a ritualized method of going where Linda and I had found ourselves on those few occasions: of leaving this dimensional field and returning.

In this book, Bushby spoke of three priests known to have gone into these other dimensions. Of the three priests, one of the men died, another went crazy, and one remained to speak of the experience.

I was shaken to read this. Not to be overly dramatic, but it occurred to me that I might have been the one who died had it not been for the dream, the aura photo, and Arasham's hand-on-my-face-healing. In truth, I can't imagine that my guides and my own soul would have allowed me to die over a simple misadventure, but one never knows.

I did learn that this is not a phenomenon to be played with for the sake of curiosity. We were being groomed for something, heaven knows what. Until now, however, neither Linda nor I have been willing to give it another try. But, as they say, "Never say never."

Meanwhile, I had other lessons waiting - lessons of the heart.

## Chapter Thirty-Three:
# The Connection

Our improperly executed journey wasn't the only item up for discussion with our guides. They also had something to say about my love life. To assist you in understanding their perspective on such mundane matters, I would like to share an encounter with them regarding this subject that had taken place about a decade prior, somewhere in the early 1990s.

Exasperated, I asked about my pitiful, aching loneliness at not finding a partner to whom I could relate at a deep level. It had not yet occurred to me that I might be the common factor in my lack of deep, intimate relationships. Wagon Wheel, my father's nick name for me as a toddler, didn't like to be vulnerable. Though I was struggling with this part of my life, I recognized that profound lessons and gifts had accompanied each significant relationship.

Once again, I was dogged by a feeling of being unheard and un-met at a profoundly personal level. Knowing I was unlikely to find a sympathetic ear with our esteemed, invisible guiding companions, I was nonetheless desperate enough to take my love woes to them for advice. It went like this:

ME: "I feel as though I haven't had a truly happy

relationship in thousands of years."

THEM: "You know that you are not an easy match, don't you?"

ME: "What do you mean?"

THEM: "You have a different kind of vibratory pattern that is not compatible with much of the population of the planet. So, it is difficult for you to find such a match."

ME: "But it's been THOUSANDS of years!"

THEM: "That's not so long."

ME: (Crying now) "But it is for a human! That's a really long time!"

THEM: (no comment)

So much for guidance from beyond. I could have turned to a counselor, but I knew it would not change the reality of my experience with the men in my life. Something profound was missing. I heard the part about vibratory patterns but I hadn't fully come to understand the implications of this comment. I reasoned that I was living in Sedona now and if Sedona couldn't provide a match, or at least bring more in-depth understanding, then I was marooned without a phone to call home on this one.

As my lesson on surrender continued, I followed Lilli toward Chris at the outdoor concert. Sparks of light flew between our eyes in the literal sense. Linda was watching it and recounted it later.

Chris and I agreed to meet at another musical event later in the evening. I brought Linda with me as I generally do for safety and company. He met us as planned, but I was a bit self-consciousness about it all. I was the new woman in this small town and a private person, and he had a larger-than-life reputation on many fronts. I felt we were being watched, which we were.

After the performance, he suggested that we all go across the street to Lizardhead, another watering hole with live music, the third venue of the day. I agreed, and he left for a few minutes to freshen up before the rendezvous. As I drove out of the parking lot to drive to Lizardhead, I made a split-second decision to turn left, for home, instead of turning right toward the place of our planned rendezvous. Just as that decision was making its way to my awareness, I saw Chris running down the street toward our meeting place. It was all happening in slow motion. It appeared he was running to see me as we would both have been a bit late at this point. My heart lightened at the thought, but I still turned left - toward home, not our rendezvous. Why was I doing this? It's not like me to stand someone up.

Inch by inch, I felt my car move through the turn, my head turned over my shoulder watching him running in slow motion, then turning my attention back to the road ahead and driving away, away from the man that was to become a deep part of my internal landscape for years to come. I still don't know what part of me made that decision, but I believe it was the part that no longer wanted to put everyone else before me. I had been a pretzel for too long, and I could become lost in this man. I was tired and needed rest, another meeting with him would have taken a good amount of energy.

It didn't take more than a day or so to run into him again. This encounter brought an invitation to join him, another musician, and some of their friends for a weekend of music al fresco in a ghost town high atop some nearby mountains.

Lilli, Linda, and I packed overnight bags and started the dusty journey up Bloody Basin Road toward the long-forgotten town of Crown King. The only remaining signs of life and commerce were a tiny grocery store with a few items on the shelves, a motel, a tiny post office, and a surprisingly large motel/restaurant. Who in the world would venture here, 35 miles up a dirt road, for these amenities?

The weekend was magical. Chris and his friend, Anthony Mazzella, played all day and night at no charge to the concert-goers, taking breaks for meals and conversation here and there. I tilted my chair back and watched the tall, thin pine trees swaying high overhead in the breeze, a breeze that did not reach the ground of this protected little place. I was feeling mildly euphoric, boosted by the promise of a romantic encounter. I made a note to myself to snap out of it. It didn't take long for my mind to take its place behind the steering wheel once again. It began asking some very fundamental questions, such as whether or not this man was available to me for any deeper dialogue. I had no idea about the nature or condition of his own internal love-scape, but I had heard the rumor that he and his girlfriend of a few years had split up. Good enough. At least this was a starting place.

Until this point in my life, relationships had a start, a purpose, and an ending. Sometimes it was difficult to identify the purpose postmortem, but there was certainly a beginning and an end. I had no idea I was about to learn about the notion of relationship from a place beyond linear time and space, where beginnings and endings have no meaning.

## Chapter Thirty-Four:
# Love and Free Will

I was so deeply impacted by the connection with Chris that I asked to speak with Arasham to get a higher perspective as the worldly view held no wisdom for my experience.

He began by telling me that "This Being" [Chris] had been there for me in other lifetimes and had offered an open and helping hand whenever I was in need. In this lifetime, it was my turn to offer a hand as his Being was experiencing challenges. Also, he said, the possibility of our coming together in an intimate union existed. He continued, "You must hold him with a loving heart in the highest view with no attachment to outcome." I was also informed that this proposition was not certain as there was always the matter of free will, which often trumps soul agreements in earth life. It could go either way, and it would be his decision, not mine. I should simply envision a clear and high outcome then let it go.

Arasham continued, telling me that I was never to fantasize about this man. He said that to fantasize was to consume the creative energy before the intimate union occurred. When one does this, the game feels over before it begins, the connection has already been experienced and the person is left with the feeling of "Is that all there is?"

Arasham shared that this is particularly true of people who have strong mental and manifestation abilities. If this ability is not so strong, it doesn't hurt to fantasize as the energy put into the fantasy is not powerful enough to use up the creativity before the intimate encounter. For me, it was a no-no.

After eighteen months of holding the intention and sending unconditional love, Chris chose his old girlfriend and then a new one, never me. I had surrendered to the unknown, far beyond my experience on the tango floor. I was told from the beginning that it could go either way and it would not be my choice.

I had the privilege of learning about unconditional love - to surrender to an uncertain outcome without attachment. This is not to say that I did not have my moments of frustration and sadness, but on the whole, I had come through with my heart intact. I felt that I had upheld my part of the agreement to the best of my ability.

As time has passed, greater clarity has emerged. Chris and I transitioned into a timeless friendship, with a better mutual understanding of what "unconditional" feels like. Meanwhile, it was time to move on.

## Chapter Thirty-Five:
## Time to Heal

My life in Sedona continued to blossom surrounded by beautiful terrain and beautiful friends, both men and women. Looking back, it was like a dream in many ways.

There were deaths among our tribe; sons, mothers, babies, and friends. We gathered together with music, drumming, streams of water, and poetry to honor their lives. We gave one another many shoulders to cry on, many embraces and compassionate words. One only needed to be present to be the beneficiary of the loving acts of kindness, not to have somehow earned the privilege. It was the way the world should be, the way I envision our future as a species. Sedona was, for me, a new Avalon. Magic was everyday. What would generally be handled without grace in the outside world, was blessed by this place and its people.

As we went through our various hardships together, the temptation to enter into the mean-spirited taking of sides was tempered by a higher group understanding that it was in no soul's best interest to participate in pettiness. We genuinely tried to put events into a higher perspective of the soul's journey. From this place, no one can judge the journey of another, only offer a supportive hand and assuage any upset in whatever way feels meaningful.

I have come to believe that my Sedona family is part of a larger tribe that has come into this time to experiment with social structures and to be way-showers. There was a choice to live life from a higher consciousness, as is true in other conscious communities on the planet.

My journey was becoming more intriguing all the time as dreamtime wove more seamlessly with my waking time. Sometimes the dreams were instructive and empowering, reminding me of what was approaching. The following was a very powerful dreamtime experience regarding preparation for taking on the role of healer again:

I was among a sparse group of people standing facing the same direction and looking to the sky. We were silent, with our arms hanging flatly to our sides like a surreal Magritte painting. The location was the Bay Bridge, looking from the Oakland side to San Francisco. I was living in a small house on the Oakland side of the bridge, virtually underneath it.

The sight that had caught our attention was a solar eclipse that was being shadowed by a UFO. As the UFO passed over the sun during the eclipse, I had the clear, intuitive feeling that it was going to come over to me. I was dreading this because I did not want to draw attention to myself.

As the UFO came my way, it stopped and hovered above my head and downloaded energy into me for a few seconds, like electrical impulses coming into the crown of my head. After I was "filled up," I became aware of the people around me again and, embarrassed that they had seen what had happened, turned and went inside my home. I went to the stove to cook something, picking up a pot holder in the process. When I touched the pot holder, it caught fire.

It was then that I noticed blue flames coming out of my fingertips, melting the tips of my fingers. While there was no pain, I began trying to put the flames out and mold my fingers back to their regular appearance. Then a voice said that it was time for me to start my healing work once again. I was to use the blue flames in my fingertips to heal people.

This is not the kind of dream one forgets, nor was it long before I would understand why it had come into my awareness at that moment.

Within a day or two, I happened upon a car crash in which the young female driver had been thrown into the cacti. I ran to her and put my hand on her back gently, allowing the blue flames to merge with her. As I did this, her entire being calmed and she began breathing normally. Her pulse slowed, and we waited for the ambulance to arrive. She needed to be calm to be extricated from the cacti, making this rescue operation a thorny affair indeed. It was one of those scenes that makes any human cringe with empathy, but she was calm and under control now.

I was attending an outdoor wedding a few days later, not advisable in the desert during the summer months. The mother of the groom began to experience heat stroke, and her family was panicking. I asked if I could be allowed to help.

Again, I used my mind to direct the healing blue flames in my fingertips and within minutes her mind was clear again, and her body temperature had dropped. She asked what kind of 'voodoo' I had done as she did not believe in the supernatural. I assured her that this was not voodoo, just a little good juju!

The healings continued when later that week I went to the dry cleaners to drop off some clothing. Upon entering the shop, I witnessed a horrible sight. The owner of the cleaning establishment had become poisoned from the chemicals used in dry cleaning and had developed what is called Lobster Skin. Her entire body was encrusted in thick, swollen, red, dry skin - like a lobster. She was miserably uncomfortable and self-conscious. She had been to a variety of healers to no avail.

I asked if she would be willing to close the doors to the business for two to three minutes while I worked on her. I asked her to choose a place on her body for an experiment in healing. She chose her ankle. I focused on the energy coming from my fingertips while applying a soothing cream to the chosen part of her ankle for extra effect. When I left, I was overwhelmed with empathy for her plight but assumed that there was little I could do for her.

A week later I went to pick up my dry cleaning order, and I asked how that spot on her ankle was doing. She said, "Here! Look at it!"

The spot I had focused on healed over completely with new, pink baby skin. The entire surrounding area, meanwhile, was still covered with the thick, parched lobster skin. We were both thrilled.

Had I the courage, I would have done the same thing to her entire body to help relieve her pain, but I couldn't bear to touch the swollen, rough skin. It made me feel sick. So I did not, and I've felt guilty ever since. Fortunately, I was told she sold her business shortly after this and her body healed. Nonetheless, I had not done all I could and bore the burden of my cowardice.

And there were other such events. The dream was simply to alert me to put my blue healing gloves on because they would be needed and I might not otherwise recognize that I could be of service in the moment. That's how my guides work with me. They know I am a busy type and sometimes hard to get through to. So they go out of their way to catch my attention when they have a message for me, and they are very clever in their methods and the timing of such messages.

## Chapter Thirty-Six:
## Love Comes Again

Nicholas Richard Scott Meredith was living with his friend Ray in London after being ejected from his life in the United States on the heels of 9/11. Foreigners were deemed unsafe, and, in spite of his innocent and sparkling clean energies, he was a foreigner, a Brit, thus an apparent threat to our nation's security.

Upon being invited to stay in the upstairs room at Ray's home, Ray's wife informed Ray that she was leaving him. Ray's wife was also Ray's business partner.

Ray was in shock; he had not seen it coming. Feeling guilty, Ray's wife asked Scott if he would be willing to go on the couple's long-planned vacation to the United States in her place to keep Ray company.

Ray and Scott flew to San Francisco to begin a tour of the western states, ultimately finding their way to Las Vegas. Bored after a couple of days of glitz and noise, they remembered they had a long-lost friend and work associate in Sedona from some business dealings in London two decades before. They had seen him on a British television program featuring spirituality and art. The program was shot in Sedona. It was only a five-hour drive from Las Vegas, and Sedona would be beautiful even if they did not connect with Lawrence, my now constant social companion.

They stayed at the Matterhorn Motel uptown and began their search for Paul Lawrence. The clerk at the first store they stopped by said to go across the street to another shop where they might carry Paul Lawrence's artwork. As is the Sedona way, within ten minutes of beginning the search they had connected with their old friend.

Paul invited them to meet him, along with a few friends, at Osho's the following morning. The "friends" were me. He wanted to show me off to his buddies from England.

Upon seeing Scott for the first time, I noticed his impish handsomeness and his light-filled energy. He was a giver of energy, not a taker and appeared to be cheerful and adventurous. I took a liking to him immediately.

Shortly after our introduction I had to go to the restroom, perhaps a similar reaction to house hunting? As I was in the "loo," Scott said to Ray that if he were ever going to marry someone, it would be me, or someone like me.

Paul Lawrence, meanwhile, had hopes for a future with me himself and his face drained of color as he saw the connection taking place between Scott and me.

After breakfast, Lawrence invited everyone around to his place to look at the paintings in his Women of Honor series, which featured me and a handful of other Sedona women.

As we gazed over Lawrence's paintings, Scott and I spoke a little further about our various business ventures in life and discovered that we had some common ground in television production. We were increasingly becoming intrigued with one another but had no time to explore further potentials. I had to finish up some work before visiting family for the holidays.

Both Scott and I were seeing other people at this time. He was flying out in the morning to spend the Christmas holiday with his Canadian girlfriend at actor Colin Firth's apartment, and I was flying to Sacramento with a man I was seeing to visit my family, including Stuart, for Christmas. Stuart at this point was attending Arizona State University in Tempe, Arizona, studying philosophy, and was going to Sacramento to see both sides of his family for Christmas.

As I drove away, I thought it was a shame that we had not advanced enough as a species that someone could have a deep affection for a member of the opposite sex if they were in a relationship with someone else without that someone else having their nose bent out of shape. Human possessiveness is not one of our more admirable traits.

Scott and I each flew west with our companions and, lost in holiday festivities, forgot about one another – ships passing in the night, as they say.

Five months later I was in Sacramento once again, to visit my family.

On the twelve-hour drive from Sedona to Sacramento I contemplated my life. I was at a standstill on the various projects I was trying to manifest and couldn't see a way forward. For the first time in my life I was seriously considering throwing in the towel to enjoy life as an ex-pat someplace where I could live comfortably and inexpensively.

As I drove along the mind-numbingly boring stretch

between Needles and Barstow, I said to my guides and the universe, "We need to make something happen now, or I am going to move to India or Mexico, live on the cheap, bake cakes, and do psychic readings for fun." I calculated that if I could live for under $1000 a month I could survive for a few years. The easy life was beginning to hold some allure for me.

My sister Denise was also looking for a little easier life. Having taken a short break from her stressful career as a cardiac nurse, she was working for me handling the administration for Regina's Vegetarian Table. One of her duties was to answer the email that came in from viewers around the world.

One afternoon, Denise and I were discussing whether I should go to England to be with my British friend Anna who had flown home after learning her mother was gravely ill with bladder cancer.

My finances were a consideration in whether I would be able to join Anna because they were becoming as frayed as Anna's nerves. I ultimately decided to book a cheap ticket and keep Anna company during what was shaping up to be a difficult transition for her mother.

About an hour later Denise, still going through the email, said, "I would normally put this kind of email in the trash, but there's a picture on the bottom of the email, and he's really cute!"

"Let me see," I said. When I looked at the thumbnail picture at the bottom of the email, my heart leaped. "That's a man I met a few months ago in Sedona, but he had a girlfriend. Let me read the email!"

In the email, Scott said that he'd had a dream about me the previous night in which I had beckoned him with my index finger, like in the movies, but the energy was very sweet and calming. Touched by the dream, he said he just wanted to say hi and see if I remembered him.

I wrote back and told him that I had literally just made the decision to fly to London in two weeks' time. Perhaps we could get together.

He replied with an invitation for me to stay at Ray's home after the ten-hour flight so I could sleep and freshen up for my trip west to Yeovil, where Anna was caretaking her mother. There was plenty of space for me at Anna's mother's home as her mother was now in a hospice facility.

I took a London taxi to Ray and Scott's home where Ray was awaiting my arrival. Scott was out, installing wireless technology in someone's office. Ray and I walked to the Parson's Green neighborhood Starbucks around the corner from his home. I needed a little caffeine fix to stay awake until a reasonable hour to synchronize with the local time zone.

As Ray and I caught up on love and life, Scott rode up on his BMW motorcycle. After taking off his helmet and revealing his helmet hair, he proceeded to tell me how he was conflicted about going to Canada to see his old girlfriend and how he had reconnected with his old high school love. This barrage of news had come before he even sat down at the table! The bubble of excitement at seeing one another again burst quite abruptly, and I refocused my energy on my departure to Yeovil the following morning. Had I missed some encoded message between the lines of his emails? They had seemed warm and friendly enough.

After two weeks with Anna, watching Coronation Street with her quiet and dignified mother Olive, painting Olive's toenails pink and adorning her foot with a toe ring while she was in a morphine sleep, Olive was feeling more alive, Anna was more relaxed, and I was ready to return home.

I tagged two more days onto my trip so I could attend the Egyptian Exhibit at the British Museum, a favorite of mine, and visit with Ray and Scott.

On the final day, as I left for my museum outing, Scott asked if he could walk me to the underground stop. We made a short detour to Starbucks along the way. As we sipped our lattes, he nervously told me that his intentions toward me weren't strictly professional. I said, "Nor are mine" and we exchanged a tiny kiss.

Love is amazing. It doesn't matter how often it comes nor how many decades we have walked the earth, it's always like teenagers connecting for the first time. In this way, Scott and I walked to the underground.

Halfway to the underground station, we stopped at an intersection to say goodbye until later in the day. It had started drizzling and we were sharing an umbrella. At that moment, a tiny man stepped outside onto a small landing of a church and announced: "You are the most beautiful couple I have ever seen!"

I was embarrassed, and Scott was flabbergasted. When he turned around to look at the man again, he had disappeared, just like that. He looked like a leprechaun in an overcoat, and Scott said people in England just don't say things like that to strangers. He believes to this day that it was a little man angel who gave us a message so we could speed up the process of our union because I was leaving for the United

States in the morning.

Later that night we sat on a park bench in Parson's Green and pondered what would come next. He had to follow through on obligations with his old high school sweetheart and then decide what to do about the trip to Canada. I left him, clear once again that the decision was his. I had already made up my mind that I would be happy to pursue the relationship if he were free.

I waited while Scott cleared up his obligations and decided to explore the possibilities with me. The United States had not been kind to him in the past and he was in no mood to revisit that. But he was in the mood to revisit me, so he arrived in Sedona six weeks after our previous meeting to see what this strange American woman's life was about. This might be a situation in which ignorance indeed is bliss. "Enigma" was becoming an often-repeated description of me and my life.

I picked Scott up at the Phoenix airport. Since we had such a short exposure to one another in London, we were nervously hoping that we were each as the other remembered.

The affection was instant, and two days into his visit we decided to go to Los Angeles to his storage locker to bring some things back to my house. Oddly, this seemed a completely natural thing to do in spite of our days-old romance. This was to be the precursor to a lightning round of getting to know one another and settling in together.

We picked up the rest of his things by December and founded Conscious Media Network the same month under its original name of The Broadband Learning Channel. Everything was evolving as though the barn was on fire and there was not a minute to waste. There was just one major inconvenience.

Scott had to exit the country every 90 days due to visa restrictions, which became both an emotional and financial burden. So we decided to marry, in spite of my growing belief that I was not the marrying kind.

We had been told of one nightmare after another regarding post 9/11 immigration. One attorney told us the process would take up to four years and would cost thousands of dollars in attorney fees to submit all of the proper paperwork. Scott decided to try it himself being the self-starter that he is.

We drove to Phoenix to appear for our first immigration meeting and apply for his residency as a spouse. Recounting some of the considerations depicted in the film Green Card, we went over our favorite colors, foods, and other stories while waiting in the Immigration office to be seen. We did not want to be caught with inconsistent stories as we were still getting to know one another.

We had technically jumped the gun and had already married in a beautiful ceremony in the octagonal meditation space in my home. It was a modest, yet absolutely beautiful love-fest with all of our friends and family in attendance - a truly magical day.

The two immigration officers asked us how we met. We told them our story, complete with the first dream and the little leprechaun man.

They said: "Your visa should be ready in about six months. You'll need to have proof of a physical exam and vaccination record." We were dumb- founded. That's it? No more interviews? They told us we would need to come in one more time to get signed off. That was it.

We laughed, holding hands, as we left the building. On the one hand, we felt as though we had been given a great deal of help from our clever little "Leprechaun." Practically speaking, however, we had also ascertained that we were an easy call compared to many of the other couples in the immigration office. Among them were unconventional pairings such as sixty- or seventy-year-old white men with twenty-five-year-old Thai girls. We happened to look like a "normal" couple, and that was good enough for the post 9/11 United States Department of Immigration.

## Chapter Thirty-Seven:
# CMN Travels

Conscious Media Network was never birthed as a proper business, though the proper papers were filled out and filed with the appropriate agencies. It was an expression of our hearts, to offer something useful at a time when confusion and anger were reaching a new peak in the western world. There was no time to focus on business plans and partnering potentials. We felt the changes in the winds of human evolution, and we needed to gather all of the information we could and offer it to the world free of charge. Surely good karma would prevail, and people would voluntarily support our efforts.

*Travels with CMN, L. to R. - Scott Meredith, me, David Icke, Stuart Campbell*

We were not short of opinions from friends and family. The first question was always: "But how do you make money from this?" Actually, that has been the first question from many of our interviewees and colleagues as well. We seemed reckless and irresponsible for staking so much on an unsustainable business model. But we couldn't stop. We were the only such video site on the internet at the beginning of 2005. There were others driven by a host/star, as well as internet radio programs, but no video archives devoted to consciousness on a broad array of topics such as our fledgling online video network.

For the first time in my professional life, I felt as though I was complete. No topic was prohibited, and I could use my intuition to create our programming without fear of ridicule. I wanted to explore all of it, including that which had frightened me in prior times.

One of our investigative journeys led us to Israel, which would become a turning point in both our lives.

I had been in relationships with two Jewish men during my dating life. I was also deeply programmed by the American media to fear Arabs. This was the extent of my Middle Eastern education other than having enjoyed personal friendships with the Persian elite who had fled to America when the Shah was removed from power. I found the women in particular fascinating and wrote a little ode to them in my cookbook Regina's International Vegetarian Favorites.

Meanwhile, I held a completely different belief of what the Palestinians, for example, were. Photographs of Yassir Arafat cloaked in white robes and his black and white checkered keffiyeh, the headgear that is a symbol of Palestinian heritage, sent a shiver of fear through me. The media had done its job well as I had come to believe Palestinians to be murderers and socially undeveloped. My fear of Arabs began to change on September 11, 2001.

Linda was in Kansas City, looking after her elderly mother on the morning of 9-11. She called me at 6:30 in the morning with an urgent tone in her voice and told me to turn on the television quickly. It flicked on just as the second plane was about to hit the second tower. I watched the surreal, historic-making event with one part of my brain while the other part was telling me to turn the television off and meditate - now!

I did as I was guided to do. Within a few seconds an image came into my mind of covert American forces, CIA, meeting with Arab factions somewhere just above the Eastern US-Canadian border in Canada (which, within days surfaced in the news as a known Arab activist stronghold).

In the vision, there were roughly eight to ten agents from both sides in the room, symbolic of collusion. An inside job? I had never contemplated anything quite so sinister to this point in my life as I was not involved in conspiracy communities.

Within hours disturbing evidence began pouring out via alternative media sources. Much of the information has since been validated - stock option transactions on United and American Airlines the day before 9/11, NORAD's lack of response, Andrew's Air Force Base not scrambling jets, no airplane debris at the Pentagon, and on and on - though still relegated to the category of "conspiracy theory." Oddly, while researching a topic in this genre, I came across a quote that impacted me deeply: "Conspiracy theory is just another phrase for 'unspeakable truths.'" If the words of one of my interviewees are right, then the truth would be unspeakable indeed.

Dr. Judy Wood is a former professor of engineering mechanics, structural mechanics, materials engineering, and deformation analysis at Virginia Tech. She also has authored over 60 peer-reviewed papers. In short, she is a heavyweight in terms of materials and structural analysis.

In my interview with Dr. Wood, she shared dozens of images and pictures demonstrating her analysis that the destruction of the towers was done with exotic energy technologies. She believed it to be directed particle beam weaponry, i.e., a Tesla energy weapon. Once you read her book, Where Did The Towers Go? you will not look at 9/11 the same way.

On a more personal level, Dr. Wood is a sweet nerd. She is not a conspiracy theorist and has no real political interest in who used the weapons, but rather a respect for the power of the technology if it could be used for positive purposes.

On the day of our Gaia interview, Dr. Wood had received a note from her father stating that he was proud of the work she had done. Until then, he, along with others, could not wrap his mind around her theory. He was now convinced.

At the end of our interview— one of the most profound I have ever done— Judy began crying, saying that she had finally been accepted by her father. It had been an impossibly long and challenging journey with trolls of every kind trying to discredit her work. And while her theory was unique, more than a thousand other engineers joined in with the analysis that airplanes could not have taken down the World Trade Center towers that fateful day.

Meanwhile, with so much attention drawn to the Arab regions of the world, I had begun questioning who the Israelis and Arabs really were in terms of modern history.

This led to investigations into Zionism and Palestinian terrorism.

Four years later, the invitation to go to Israel came as a surprise following our interview with Dr. Vernon Wolf, the creator of Holodynamics.

Holodynamics is a modality of balancing unresolved issues and energies within the mind and body by coming into connection with what Vernon terms our hyper-spatial counterpart, the part I call our True Self. His work is influenced by the work of the famed physicist Neils Bohr and other well-known researchers in the field of quantum mechanics. I found it to be an elegant and approachable method of unifying with our higher self to release past trauma and tap into hidden potential.

During my interview with Vernon, he spoke of an experience he had in Jerusalem ten years prior. He was touring Israel as part of an international peace mission accompanied by other spiritual luminaries including social visionary and author Barbara Marx Hubbard.

One day, while separated from the group, Vernon wandered into a Palestinian owned antique shop in the Old City. He struck up a conversation with two young men, one of whom owned the shop along with his father. He asked about the intifada (Palestinian revolt against the occupying Israelis) and how the young Palestinians had experienced life in Ramallah, which is the capital of the Palestinian Territories. They angrily told of their fear and hatred of the Israelis and of their personal family histories.

The boys had spent most of their young lives in prison. Throwing stones at passing armor-plated bulldozers, which served as wrecking balls for their ancient family homes in the Palestinian territories, is a jail-able offense. From age five, onward, the boys spent their prison time teaching each other history, English and French as their mother was multi-lingual and well educated.

Meanwhile, Vernon conducted a Holodynamics session on the two young shopkeepers. They began crying at the release of the fear and hatred by the end of what shaped up to be a life-changing session and asked if Vernon would meet with one of their friends.

Over a lifetime of on and off again imprisonment, hardness had set into their hearts and some of their group had become affiliated with terrorist factions.

One boy, Mohammed, had turned to revenge when Israeli soldiers, on a shooting spree in Ramallah, shot his father in the head through the window of their family kitchen, killing him instantly. There was no reason given and no apology. The bullet hole in the kitchen wall sparked a wave of anger deeper than most of us will ever know, and Mohammed vowed revenge. He began training with other young militants.

Mohammed was eventually caught and kept in a small wooden crate for five days, too small to stand up in, but too tight to sit down. His feet and face were smashed with gun butts. The two young men in the antique shop asked if Vernon would meet with Mohammed to help him resolve the hatred and violence in his heart before he ended up dead. Vernon agreed.

Vernon was picked up in a van after darkness fell over Jerusalem, and after curfew. The young Palestinians, well accustomed to living on the edge of incarceration and physical danger, transported Vernon into Ramallah. This was before the wall was constructed, but dangerous business nonetheless.

Vernon and Mohammed met. A transformation of unimaginable proportions occurred when Vernon facilitated a Holodynamics session with the angry young man.

Mohammed vowed to love all men as he would love his own family as he now saw all mothers, Palestinian and Israeli alike, as his mother. His life was permanently changed, his soul retrieved from the darkness of hatred.

Vernon wanted to make a return visit to Jerusalem and the people he had met a decade before. He wanted the entirety of it documented. He asked if Scott and I would be interested in accompanying him as the documentary filmmakers. We, meanwhile, wanted to film Mohammed and the two shopkeepers to see how their Holodynamic experience had served them over time.

*Frustration and anger among Palestinians in Jerusalem*

Vernon explained that it could be a bit dangerous as we would need to go back into Ramallah, now shuttered from view behind the Wall. Nervously, we agreed. We had two weeks to prepare for our departure.

Our party consisted of Vernon and some Holodynamic practitioners – Paulette (Vernon's companion), Ryah and Timothy plus Scott and me. We knew nothing more of what laid ahead other than that our accommodations had been arranged.

Our first stop was Geneva, where we changed planes to an El Al flight bound for Tel Aviv. It was early in the morning and the Hasidic businessmen in their customary black clothing and fedora felt hats, turned en masse to the rising sun and began saying morning prayers. Most of them carried large black briefcases, filled with gold and jewelry from their business dealings in Switzerland. A guard with a machine gun watched. It hadn't escaped my notice that this was the only gate at the airport that hosted an armed guard. I was beginning to have a glimpse of the world we were about to enter.

We were told to keep quiet and let Vernon do the talking as we entered the Tel Aviv airport, which was festooned with soldiers and more machine guns. He explained we were on a peace mission. Visas were granted, our passports stamped, and we quickly made it to the rental car agency, at which Ryah had reserved a van. Within a short time, we were on our way to Jerusalem.

From the moment my feet touched the paving stones of the Old City, I felt that they had walked here before. I was in a near hypnotic state with my skirts flowing in slow motion as I loped down the long stone staircases. While my heart was as alive as it had ever been, the severity of the land and culture kept shocking me back to reality.

In the old city, the religions of the world intersect in a few-square-block area of old Jerusalem. The Via De La Rosa is said to be the street through which Jesus carried the cross to his crucifixion. Located in the Arab quarter of the Old City, today it's lined with curios and antique shops, falafel stands, spice stalls, rug shops, and clothing vendors. Every so often you stand aside while a solemn group of Christians re-enacts the carrying of the cross. The cross can be rented from a shop nearby.

Arab shopkeepers, leaned against their storefronts, casually smoking and chatting among themselves. They quietly watch the Christian procession. The hawking of rugs and other wares continues in the wake of the re-enactment.

The Jewish quarter is much more orderly with modern business establishments. It feels quiet and deserted in comparison to the color and busy-ness of the Arab section.

The Christian quarter, meanwhile, has at its core, the Church of the Holy Sepulchre, which is believed to be the site of the tomb of Jesus. The Church has been an important Christian pilgrimage site since the fourth century. It's a stunning though dank and restrictive remnant of the Holy Land's historical roots. Nearby shops sell crosses, crucifixes, and statues of the Mother Mary.

At the center of these historic quarters are the Wailing Wall and the Temple Mount. At one end of the Wall, the women cry and plead to God to relieve their suffering. At the other end of the Wall, the men pray and do business. Our traveling companion, Tim, in blissful inappropriateness, wandered into a cave to the side of the men's Wall where he was greeted by a suspicious and unfriendly group of men. He was not welcome but managed to stay long enough to be privy to business dealings being conducted in English. As a non-Jew, he was

*Temple Mount, the most disputed building in the world*

told to leave.

As we wandered Jerusalem, what was perhaps the most unsettling aspect of this adventure were the numbers of guns. You could not enter a coffee shop, grocery store, mall, theater or virtually any other business without being searched or at least passing the watchful presence of a machine gun-toting soldier at the entrance.

We settled into our local lodging, which I call Boris's Bunker. A young strawberry-haired Russian Jew and devotee of Holodynamics, Boris, had agreed to give up his apartment to accommodate Tim, Scott and me. The three of us would become intimately familiar with each other's bodily functions and habits as the Bunker had minimal insulation, separating doors, windows, or heat for that matter. It did, however, have an abundance of mold and mildew.

Sneezing, snoring, breaking wind, bowel movements and belching - I felt as though I had been transported to some teenage frat movie.

Scott, being British and, thus, conscious of boundaries, was not happy with the arrangement. Within days, however, Tim's vivacious lust for living won us over. We began traveling Israel as friends. Scott dubbed Tim "Delightfully inappropriate at all times."

The time had come to join Vernon in his reunion with the two Palestinian shopkeepers.

Some things cannot be fully articulated with words. Passing through the Wall into Ramallah, the capital of the Palestinian territories, is one of them.

As our elderly Mercedes taxi honked and pushed through the procession of other decrepit taxis toward the Wall, the energy became more desperate with each passing meter. The increase in emotional intensity was visceral. My anxiety levels began to rise, though I had no idea what awaited us on the other side. Vernon had not been here for a decade, and much had changed since his last encounter with the young Palestinian men he had arranged to reconnect with.

When we stepped out of the taxi, Paulette and I were highly visible as the only ones in sight with uncovered, no less blonde, hair. As we walked out of Israeli territory and onto Palestinian land, my entire body started weeping. Everything in me was shocked by the horror of this existence, and I could not stop the tears.

Palestinian men approached us, their eyes hollow and hungry. They attempted to sell us anything they felt free to part with. An orange, a pair of used children's socks, a hammer. Their desperate need to feed their families amidst perhaps the highest unemployment rate on the planet, filled the air around us making it hard to suck in the next breath.

After the first shock, my senses became aware of the lack of green living things. There was not a tree, flower or shrub to be found. What passed for pavement was rubble from the many homes destroyed by Israeli bull dozers. We were told the trees had been uprooted and taken to Israeli territories.

We were welcomed into Hammed's home, one of the two young men Vernon had met in the antiques shop ten years earlier. His mother offered us apricot juice and tea in gilded juice glasses on a lovely service tray. They were wealthy as Palestinians go, having been in the antiques industry in Jerusalem for several decades.

A few minutes later we were introduced to the former terrorist, Mohammed. Modest, diminutive in size, and wearing a mechanic's coveralls, it was difficult to imagine him as a terrorist.

Scott began rolling videotape while Vernon, Paula and I listened to his story.

His life had changed irrevocably since his first meeting with Vernon, he told us. The scars on his hands, now covered in mechanic's grease, and the wounds in his eyes still spoke of his past, though his words spoke of his future.

Mohammed told us that from the moment he discovered peace with Vernon he would never support violence as a means to an end. He had taught his brothers and friends, along with his children and the children of others, that hatred and revenge will never bring them peace. I asked him how he felt about the Wall, which was still under construction.

With armed Israeli guards in watchtowers in direct eyesight of the living room in which we gathered, he said he felt the Wall was perhaps a good thing. It was true that it allowed for little movement, hope, or freedom for his people, but he said that maybe it was best to keep the two sides apart. He felt that over time the tension would cool and Israelis and Palestinians would be safe around one another again, but not now. He then quietly went outside to pray while we surveyed this bleak and hopeless land.

We thanked him for speaking with us, quietly thanked Hammed's mother for her hospitality, and stepped outside and into a waiting taxi. On the way out, I noticed that Hammed's family home did have a few little plants and trees in its yard, which was as beautiful as any oasis in the desert amid the surrounding rubble and guard towers.

When we arrived back at the Wall, we had to go through Israeli security, a frightening affair.

Hammed and Scott were told to go into one line. The women and old men (Vernon) could go into the other. Paulette, Vernon and I walked through the gate with little interaction with the guards.

Once on the other side we waited for Scott and Hammed. And we waited. I was carrying the videotape so Scott would not be questioned. I could feel my heart beating in my ears as the time passed. I would quiet myself and meditate, repeatedly receiving the message that they would come through safely. I was also nervous because we were going to be late for a meeting at the Knesset where we were to meet with the head of a Parliamentary committee that afternoon.

After an hour or more, Scott and Hammed emerged through the Wall. Scott, red-faced, whispered under his breath to me, "Those f------! Let's get out of here." As we climbed into the taxi back to Jerusalem, we had no words. Each of us was dead silent. The profundity of what we had seen was too shameful to speak of.

Scott later told Tim and me of his experience going through Israeli security. The border police would turn on green lights and red lights and have the Palestinians move from one line to the other randomly. Jostling would begin as the long lines were comprised of men trying to get to and from family and work. Trying to pass through the Wall by car would mean a five-hour delay. Tensions would inevitably rise through the frustration. Men who lost their patience and began to jostle for position would be pulled aside and questioned, often denied passage. Scott said it was an unending and unnecessary "mind-f---" designed to create frustration. They had also given Hammed a difficult time.

Hammed, however, had learned patience after having once been shot in one of his testicles with a rubber bullet. It had taken a good while to recover. He would toe the line now, but his eyes bled with humiliation, resignation, and anger. He did not want to jeopardize his upcoming business trip to his shop in Los Angeles. Plus, his family lived in Ramallah, and he would do nothing to bring harm to them as had happened with so many of his friends who had rebelled.

After sleeping off the intensely draining experience in Ramallah, we took the next day off to enjoy the holiday spirit. Hanukkah, Christmas, and Hajj all occurred during our time in Israel. There was very little sign of any festivity unless one went into Bethlehem. There were the usual holiday sales at the western style Jerusalem Mall, with sweets being distributed on the morning of Hanukkah, but this was about the extent of any public holiday revelry. This was when I learned that the majority of the Israeli population is secular and do not practice Judaism.

At the outset of our stay in Jerusalem, we had been assigned to the loving care of an Israeli Holodynamic devotee named Marsha. Marsha was a divorced mother of two boys who came to Israel from South Africa upon her divorce. She would help us find our way around, learn the customs, and interpret signage.

We asked Marsha for a ride to Bethlehem on Christmas Day to experience a touch of the holiday spirit in the Holy Land. She was visibly shaken at the request. Bethlehem is Palestinian territory. She told us she could not do that, she would be killed. We said that was crazy thinking, no one was going to kill her. She told us stories of the murderous things that Palestinians do, the things she had seen on the news.

This began a series of discussions in which we told her of our experiences with the Arabs. We told her of their kindness and generosity to us. She said, "To you perhaps, but not to a Jew!" It was then that we began to see the collective psyche at work. She genuinely believed that Arabs were primitive, hateful beings who live to taste Jewish blood, just as I had believed watching American media.

Her son's bedroom, meanwhile, was decorated with a single metal road sign that depicted an Israeli soldier, gunning down tourists with a machine gun. This disturbed her too, she said. The thirst for blood goes both ways, it appears, and this bothered Marsha.

When we told her of our brief experience in Palestine, she began to cry. She had no idea that the people were living in such devastation, like fish in a barrel.

Christmas Eve arrived. Hammed invited our little group of Americans to dinner at a cafe in the Arab section of the walled Old City. We were to be his guests.

We invited Marsha to join us. She quickly refused. With some persuasion that this could be an excellent opportunity for spiritual growth and expanded awareness, she very reluctantly agreed to join us.

In Arab style, the dishes were sumptuous and beautiful. Wine was served with each course for the Americans, finished by a delicious array of desserts. The group of twelve spoke of everything under the sun, sipped espresso, and took tokes on a hookah filled with sweet-smelling dried apple-laced tobacco.

Marsha was beaming from the inside, softening her features and showing a lovely side we had not seen. Not only had she made it through the meal with her life, she told us that this was the most beautiful night she had had in many years. Our hearts were bursting to have been part of this one small healing of ancient misunderstandings and grudges.

Part of Vernon's agenda was to introduce a new type of energy technology to the Israelis and Palestinians so that each could become energy self-sufficient. His web of contacts in Israel positioned us for a visit to the Israeli Parliament where we would meet with a man named Shlomo Shoham.

Small, bald, and shining from the inside out, Shlomo had been a judge in the Israeli judicial system. At the same time, he was a practicing mystic, with a deep understanding of the nature of humankind. At the time of our meeting, he was the Minister for Future Generations in the Israeli Parliament. It was his young legal team's task to evaluate all legislation as to its impact on the population for up to seven generations into the future. One of his committee's triumphs had been to keep Coca-Cola out of the school system, which had proved a sizable challenge politically.

During his tenure on the bench, a defendant named Mayer, an Israeli Arab, had come before him. Mayer had committed some very bad crimes as a member of the Syndicate, an Israeli mafia group. He had come up before the court many times before, served time and been released, only to come before the court again. This time he stood before Shlomo.

Shlomo listened to the latest story from Mayer. Something told him to take Mayer's word describing his newly reformed attitude to be truthful. He said, "I will let you go on probation this time. But if you break the conditions of parole, you will serve the full seventeen-year sentence. There will be no negotiation, no parole. Do you understand?"

"Yes," said Mayer.

A few months later Mayer and his friends had taken a trip to the Dead Sea to do some drugs and have a good time.

As he entered a particular area, he spied a group of people in white clothing meditating. To his astonishment, the judge who had given him his freedom was at the center of the group. Shlomo invited him over and asked Mayer if he would like to join the circle. Mayer hesitated, but, as an adventurous type, agreed to sit in the middle of the group.

Shlomo directed the group of skilled meditators to focus loving intention on Mayer for a few grace-filled moments. Mayer began to cry, looking into Shlomo's eyes, wondering who this beautiful man was; the man who had freed him when he was guilty. From that moment on Mayer became devoted to Shlomo in every way.

He returned to his party of friends and told them to go on without him, he would find his own way home.

Many years had passed by the time we entered their lives, and it was Mayer, having also studied Holodynamics, who had made the introduction of Vernon, Paulette, Scott and I to Shlomo and obtained access to Parliament. Mayer was still a mover and shaker and had inside connections of many kinds, which he now used for bettering mankind rather than criminal activity. We had grown fond of this intense and powerful former mobster. His heart was soft as petals at the core, which was revealed to me toward the end of the journey.

On our second to last day in Israel, he had asked to speak with me privately.

Softly, as if embarrassed, he told me of a dream the night

before. In it, he saw me across a field of beautiful flowers. I beckoned to him with my index finger, as I had to Scott at the inception of our union. Mayer said he walked toward me in the dream and took my outstretched hand at which point I told him he could sleep peacefully now. He fell into a deep, deep sleep.

When he awoke the next morning, he realized that he had slept peacefully through the night, which he had not done in many years and couldn't wait to tell me his story. Deeply touched, I smiled and said to Scott, "I wonder who else I am beckoning with my index finger during dreamtime!"

During our time in Israel, other events unfolded on the international political scene. Ariel Sharon had been found guilty of taking millions in bribes and payoffs. It had made the front page of the Jerusalem Post.

The next day Sharon slipped quietly into a coma. Had he been declared dead, an election would be required to take place within a few weeks. It was explained to us this was not desirable to certain factions.

Meanwhile, an acquaintance whose brother worked as a doctor in the emergency ward where Sharon had been admitted told us a different story than what we had read in the newspaper. We met him two days after the onset of Sharon's coma and he said to us that his medical colleague had told him that Sharon was, in fact, dead. Nothing in this strange land would have surprised us by now, though we left room for the possibility that the unflattering headline news may have precipitated the aneurysm.

Meanwhile, the media descended on the small hilly town of Ein Karem, where Sharon "remained in critical condition," awaiting news of his recovery or death. The press eventually went home. His condition, interestingly, remained "unchanged" for eight years until his actual death was announced.

Ein Karem is known as the birthplace of John the Baptist. There are two churches in this tiny village honoring the rebel religious figure. One is the Church of St. John the Baptist. The Catholic-Franciscan order now oversees the chapel, baptismal well and prayer cave. I had never heard of the cave above the baptismal well and was intrigued. I love the energy in caves, so pristine and protected from outside frequencies and interference. I had regularly hiked to them for quality meditation time in Sedona.

On a free day, I headed, like a moth to a flame, to the tiny decorated shrine in the meditation cave that sits above the baptismal well. Scott and Tim followed me and stayed for a moment or two. I remained and took a seat on one of the miniature meditation/prayer stools. It was apparent within moments I was about to have an experience.

No sooner had my eyes closed than the visions began. Caught off guard by the grandeur of what was unfolding, I sat stunned but observant. Bizarrely, with all of the media nearby and the Christmas holiday drawing crowds of tourists, I was the only person in the cave and remained undisturbed for the entire length of what was to be a pivotal mystical event for me.

As my eyes closed, I became aware of an enormous golden yellow sphere descending from the ceiling of the cave. A female Being, semi-transparent and dressed in white, floated diagonally down toward the ground. I just observed without interaction.

I felt other, more familiar, Beings around me, including my

"journeying" partner Linda. Sensations at the top of my head, neck, and shoulders commenced as energetic adjustments were transmitted. My hands floated up into specific positions without my direction or effort. I was then shown the meaning of all the hand positions and alignments portrayed in the Egyptian hieroglyphics.

I understood everything in that moment. This ancient artwork wasn't merely a stylized depiction of the lives of the Pharaohs, queens, priests and other prominent figures. Each hand position was as meaningful as the other hieroglyphic images themselves. The information flew past me at lightning speed as I, on some level, downloaded this knowledge.

At the end of this phase of my cave journey, I asked the female who had floated toward me to give me her name. Clearly, this experience was not random, and I wanted to know who had orchestrated it. She said what I thought to be the name "Maa-nat." I asked her what this event was about.

She told me it was an initiation. From this point forward "I" would be in much closer connection with my body - my soul and my body would act more in concert, and greater understanding would be available to my conscious mind. Okay. Thank you, I thought. Suddenly the entire scene dissipated and I was left alone on my little prayer stool stunned.

I exited the cave and excitedly dug my cell phone out from the bottom of my purse and called Linda to tell her what had occurred. Though it was still early in her time zone, I felt it appropriate because her energy was among the Beings in the cave.

She didn't answer so I left a message telling her to call me back ASAP. I heard from her about an hour later.

When I answered the call, she said, "I'm sorry I didn't answer before. I was sleeping, and in my dream, I was with you somewhere." I started laughing and said, "You have no idea!"

When we arrived back at Boris's bunker early that evening, I chose to stay in by myself while the others went to an event in Tel Aviv. I needed some time to process what had happened.

I had interpreted the words of "Maa-nat" to mean that I was to be more "in my body," which is not where I generally reside. I relaxed and became very still. I then used all of my will to pull my true self down into my physical body.

A horrid kind of pressure began to accumulate in the top of my skull and brain. It was as if I was trying to stuff a down comforter into a sock. The physical sensations were increasingly painful as I continued trying to pull myself through the eye of a needle, now down to my eyeballs. Enough! I had to stop.

I sat on the edge of Boris's saggy bed feeling as though I had failed. I didn't know if I could bear to live if my life were so severely restricted as to live within the confines of the physical body, even though sages throughout the ages tell us it is desirable to be in our bodies. It was just too limited, too painful. With a heaviness and great sadness, I ultimately drifted off to sleep.

A month had passed. Our trip to Israeli, home to past lives and previously unfathomable modern agendas, had changed us. A part of us had become more serious, more informed, and more dedicated to unearthing hidden truths. This had been the journey of a lifetime on more levels than we could fully understand.

## Chapter Thirty-Eight:
# Ma'at Joins the Team

Back in Sedona, still profoundly impacted by my experience in the John the Baptist cave, I asked Linda if we could go directly to Arasham. She agreed. I needed to speak frankly, without any chance of misunderstanding about what happened in the cave.

I told of my experience at Ein Karem, to which Arasham said: "Sometimes it takes a bit of a show to get your attention."

I asked about the woman who called herself Maa-nat. He said, "The name was close, but not exactly that. The proper pronunciation is Ma'at."

"Ma'at? As in Egyptian mythology and history?" I asked. "Yes," he said. "She has been with you for a very long while, but you have had no awareness of her. She felt it was time to establish that relationship on a more conscious level."

I was comfortable with this as ancient lore believed her to be aligned with Truth, Balance, Order, Morality and Justice. She has also been noted to be the personification of the fundamental natural order of the universe.

"What did she mean when she told me I needed to be more in connection with my body? I tried to pull myself in and I couldn't do it," I asked.

"This was not what was meant. That would be a waste. It's not for you to live inside your body, this is not how you are designed."

He continued, "The strength of the connection between the two parts, the body, and soul, is critical and was further established. This is not to be confused with energetically living inside the body as this is too restrictive and could be damaging to you."

I was relieved and no longer felt like a failure in my attempt to "integrate" body, and soul. I thought about how it must be for others. Do each of us feel differently about our relationship with our bodies? I realized that I have no idea how another person feels in their own skin, nor they about me in mine.

The nature of my education on the importance of Egyptian hand positions as depicted in Egyptian artwork was a natural bridge to the information I was being given. Arasham had once told Linda and me that if we wished to know the future of mankind, we should take the time to uncover the true meaning of the knowledge embedded within the hieroglyphics. "The Egyptians did not create art for beauty and the sake of art, but for the preservation of knowledge." He also stated that the current understandings of the hieroglyphics are, for the most part, incorrect and incomplete. There is profound information from distant civilizations preserved in hieroglyphics awaiting humanity for the time of the awakening, he said.

Back in Sedona, the trip to Israel beginning to fade,

Conscious Media Network consumed most of our time and just about all of our money. The inevitable day had arrived, which was unceremoniously announced to me by my higher guidance upon waking. No sooner had I surfaced to consciousness from my sleep state when I heard the words that it was time to leave Sedona. I was to sell the house and move. There was no time to waste!

I was momentarily shocked, as I generally am when I get these strong "suggestions" from the voice that only I can hear. My mind struggled to integrate the implications of this directive. But I love Sedona! My friends are here, I love our home. I don't want to leave this life I love.

In truth, there was little choice. I had not fully allowed the reality of our financial situation to sink in, nor had Scott. Being an optimist, I had believed that something miraculous would happen, that the people who enjoyed CMN would voluntarily choose to support this work. Alas, this is not human nature. Most people don't choose to support what is already free, especially on the internet.

We had made the strategic choice to make our network's offerings free so nothing would stand in the way of the flow of this esoteric knowledge. I kept thinking of college students with no spare change, people from other areas of the planet who had no access to debit or credit cards. We offered it free for the first five years, but after year two we were broke and out of credit.

I waited until Scott was awake and told him about the message. He was accustomed to such things by now and had proved to be incredibly flexible in his response. If "The Voice" said it was time to move, then it was time to move. It hadn't misled us yet.

The message to sell the house and leave Sedona had come toward the end of May 2006. The real estate bubble was still inflating, and my house was growing in value while our savings were dissipating. By the time we were able to complete minor house repairs and give the house a little makeover, four months had passed. It was time to engage a realtor, quickly, because we had only enough money left to make a few more house payments, no less pay for the rest of our needs in life.

December 24th, with only enough funds for one more house payment and no remaining credit available, we received an offer on the house. The market had just begun what historically became a long and painful downward spiral. We were touched by good fortune to sell our home for a profit at the near peak of the market. The equity in the house would be enough to carry us for a couple more years with CMN.

Scott and I thought this might be the opportunity to relocate to Vancouver, British Columbia as we had both enjoyed a love affair with this beautiful city in years past. Scott had lived there for a period of six to seven years in the 90's and had always wanted to return, while I had visited Vancouver in the summer to see friends on numerous occasions. In the interim, we had to vacate our home and take care of some business in Sacramento.

A week before escrow closed, Scott left for California with a van full of furniture to get a head start on some business there.

I called my Sedona friends together for one last gathering at my home, which had become a favored place for people to join together to eat, meditate, celebrate, dance, and enjoy life.

Toward the end of the goodbye party, I asked everyone to

join me in the meditation space around the pyramid. I told them all how much they meant to me and how Sedona had provided me with a glimpse of life that I had never imagined. Crying now, I looked at each of them and told them I would never forget them. And I haven't. This was my soul family. The party dissipated with one long embrace after another.

Our friend Jim, Stuart, Linda and I, along with a small hired crew, loaded the moving truck during the heaviest snowstorm I have ever witnessed in Sedona. Dazed and confused, I ineffectively wandered about trying to direct which items came with us and which stayed. I couldn't think clearly; I was still traumatized at the reality of leaving my beloved Sedona.

We pulled out of the driveway in the mid-afternoon. Jim and Stuart drove the truck, Linda and I left in the car. As I looked over my shoulder at the rock formations behind the Chapel in the Red Rocks, I began to sob and continued to cry until the last red rocks were behind us. Even amidst the emotional trauma, however, I never seriously doubted that CMN was worth the sacrifice.

## Chapter Thirty-Nine:
# India, The Sedona Afterlife

We temporarily landed in a spare bedroom at my father's home in Sacramento.

Because I had never experienced any kind of prolonged mental depression, I didn't know what the signs were. I did notice that I was not feeling joy. There were no friends to have tea with in the morning, no beautiful rocks with their protective arms around me. The green, blue, and red of nature had dissolved into suburbs and the endless gray of freeways. I no longer experienced an array of hugs and inspiring conversation at the grocery store. I had, in fact, become an invisible entity walking amongst strangers, like disincarnate beings wandering in the astral world not yet aware of their circumstance.

Vancouver was not shaping up for us. Canada requires that an immigrant bring lots of money before they can become part of the system and we did not have that kind of money available. So, we settled into life in California until further notice from "The Voice."

A year after the move, Scott and I attended a luncheon in Sausalito for the opening of a spiritually-based recovery center. The featured speaker was Dan Millman, of Peaceful

Warrior fame, whom I had previously interviewed. As happens so often with the people that I interview, there was an instant recognition between us, and we wanted to stay in touch.

During the event, a blonde woman and former Australian news anchor named Miranda asked if she could take a seat at my table. We began the natural kinds of inquiry.

She explained that she was a spiritual counselor and would be part of the staff at the recovery center. Her passion, however, was taking groups of spiritual seekers on tours to India, a city to which people, Indian and outsiders alike, make regular pilgrimages. She expanded her explanation telling me about tiny saintly women with hair down to the floor who live in silence, and with whom you can meditate. Their energy was sublime, she said.

Something in me said, "Go!"

Scott had returned from a motorcycle vacation with his brothers a few months earlier and suggested I might want to take a vacation - to have an adventure of my own.

I agreed it was time for a shift in energy. The conversation with Miranda had nudged me over the edge in my decision to go to India. Perhaps there, in a cave far removed from my world, I could integrate my new reality and come to peace with it.

Because of my adrenal insufficiency (the original birth defect detected at Stanford University as a child), I cannot travel alone. The side effect of this birth defect is that my body doesn't create cortisol in reaction to stress. Heat, food poisoning, sleeplessness, travel, etc., can all incite what is called Addison's Crisis in me. This requires an immediate trip to the emergency room to be given intravenous cortisone and electrolytes. Unfortunately, I have been to emergency rooms all over the world because death is the end result if not treated.

Needless to say, I was thrilled that Stuart had some free time and enough money to purchase an air ticket to join me (I would pay for the rest). He had been to India the previous year during his post-graduation gap year. The two of us had always traveled well together and looked forward to the adventure.

We decided to join Miranda's group but also to connect with two friends who were living in Pondicherry, which is the home of the ashrams dedicated to the Oxford scholar and visionary Indian sage, Sri Aurobindo, and his counterpart, The Mother. Our friends Gaia and Mitra were on a six-month pilgrimage of meditation and reflection, living in what was formerly The Mother's house in separate rooms due to residential chastity requirements.

Pondicherry, renamed Puducherry in 2006, is a lovely French Colonial city that was under French rule from 1742 until 1954, when the town was taken back by the Indian government. Pondicherry was one of the principal cities in the freedom movement, and British educated Sri Aurobindo was the predecessor to Gandhi in seeking sovereignty from the British.

Today, the city blocks are studded with saffron-colored walls and bright coral and blue courtyards, the streets lined with tuk-tuks (small motorized rickshaws), street vendors, and bazaars. There is also the occasional elephant staked to the ground, performing tricks for its master before "blessing" the tourists and taking their money with its dexterous trunk.

There was no sign of Western attire among the women, who moved slowly in the heat with brightly colored saris floating around their bodies. Gold bangles graced the wrists of even the poor - their dowry and sole possessions - and bare or sandaled feet were weighted with heavy pewter or silver ankle bracelets.

The poorest of women, the widows, wore saris without the customary short sleeved blouse underneath, their shriveled breasts exposed beneath the part of the sari that crosses the chest diagonally and continues over the shoulder. Some of these women were selling platefuls of cow dung, a necessary fuel for the modest Indian home.

I was initially taken back by the intensity of the Indian gaze into our eyes. Without self-consciousness, they were trying to see who was within. As they looked at us, they would often smile, a gleaming white expression of intrigue and curiosity. As a rule, we do not look into one another's eyes in the United States unless we are well acquainted. Maybe for a brief moment or a quick business transaction, but we fear to be in such intimate connection or being seen as inappropriate. This was quite a shift in human interaction, disconcerting at first, but I found I liked the intimacy.

Stuart and I had settled into an ashram guest house. We were furnished with a bucket for our bath water and a towel each. Mosquito nets were draped above our bunk beds, and we were provided with a top sheet. At the center of the guest house were a verdant little garden and a dining room with chai and pastries, which were available for 50 cents. The cost was $1.75 per night.

What we could not figure out was the bathing arrangement. There was no warm water available in our room, and it was not until our final day that we understood the use for the bucket. There was a communal tap in the hallway that provided the guests with hot water. You were to carry it into your toilet room, which had a drain hole in the ground, and doubled as the "shower." Once you get the hang of it, bucket showers can be very sensual with the deluge running over the head.

We connected with our friends Gaia and Mitra on the second day. They showed us the safe restaurants, the Aurobindo Ashram, and the ocean walk. Plans were made to go to Auroville, which was the focal point of stopping in Pondicherry before joining Miranda's group in Tiruvannamalai.

A tuk-tuk drove us over bumpy and dusty roads to the outskirts of Pondicherry, toward the Auroville community, which was an experiment in self-governance, self-sufficiency and global unity.

Aurobindo devotees from around the world had gathered to build their energy- efficient, off-the-grid homes, which were arranged in clusters. This small cluster of houses would serve as their primary community with communal restaurants and shops at the hub of the larger body of Auroville. Gardens connected the space between the homes.

Policy, however, developed as slowly as that of the European Union. Coming to consensus with so many cultures represented was difficult. This stalled the growth of this high concept city of visionaries.

At the hub of Auroville was the Matrimandir. A gleaming, golden, other-worldly sphere covered in golden concave medallions, the Matrimandir (Heart of the Mother) was the vision of The Mother. It was built by the community of global artists, architects, and craftsmen to help facilitate the upward progression of human consciousness into a new age of enlightenment.

I recognized this spherical meditation space as something different than I had ever experienced - this was Atlantean energy. Through hypnosis, I had visited distant past lifetimes in Atlantean culture and, as mentioned in an earlier chapter, I was familiar with the circular temple rooms. A relic of Atlantean memory was re-emerging in this magnificent, intention-infused temple. If I felt invisible in Sacramento, I felt fully alive here among the energetic imprints of every enlightened being that had ever been inside the Matrimandir.

The sacred sphere is set at the center of a park, near a sacred tree with which it works in harmony. The tree was the only living thing when Auroville was conceived in the 1960's. It had been a dry patch of land spoiled by erosion, a veritable wasteland. Incredible amounts of creativity, faith, and hard work were required to turn this into the vision of the Mother and Sri Aurobindo. The experiment was roughly forty years into its progression when we arrived.

Gaia and Mitra had managed to arrange our entry into the Matrimandir for a meditation session, which is generally only available to Auroville community members. They had spent a good amount of time in Auroville and had developed friendships within the community.

As we entered the sphere, we were asked to take our shoes off, as is customary everywhere in India. We began ascending a large, seemingly self-supporting spiral staircase. The interior walls were like the inside of a clamshell, a softly illuminated pinkish white color accented by the geometrical framework of the globe, which is invisible from the outside.

Halfway up we entered a chamber, the meditation room. The circular room was pure white - white columns, white walls, white carpet, and white meditation cushions. Above was an opening in the ceiling that allowed the sun, assisted by a computer-directed set of mirrors, to direct its rays down through a three-to-four- foot-in-diameter crystal ball, which was placed in the center of the meditation chamber. The light shone through the ball and was reflected down to the space below.

We took our places. Stuart and I positioned ourselves in front of one of the columns across the room from one another. Quietly, without guidance or fanfare, everyone in the group silently went into our own private meditations.

Mirroring my experience in the cave in Israel, I felt myself stretch up high above my body. I understood that I was sitting in the temple of myself. My guiding forces spoke with me and images flooded my mind. I had never felt such a sublime, refined, life-enhancing energy in my life. Bubble girl was home. This was my dream structure, as I had always told Linda and anyone else who would listen, that my dream home would be a glass dome amidst the redwoods. Over time, I had come to realize that my life-long fondness for dome dwellings was no more than a remembrance of abodes I had enjoyed in my ancient past.

The next sensation was that of invisible hands pushing me forward so I was completely bent over my crossed legs. The "hands" then began working on my back energetically. I had experienced this before when I was having pain in my hip and lower back. At the end of one particular meditation, the pain completely disappeared after being worked on by invisible hands. On this occasion, the same internal voice said: "All has been healed" as the "hands" pushed me back into a seated position. I felt wonderful!

My initiation into what would transpire during the following days in India had begun. My heart felt full and free with the restrictive feelings of my new life in Sacramento left far behind. I reluctantly, silently, descended the spiral staircase to exit the Matrimandir. Indeed, I felt as if I had experienced the Heart of the Mother, and the Mother was me.

After sharing some beautiful meals and suiting up in Indian attire, we said goodbye to Gaia and Mitra and took a taxi to Tiruvannamalai, which is in the state of Tamil Nadu. I felt an overwhelming pull to do a quick meditation before the taxi arrived to pick us up for the three-hour ride.

In the brief meditation, I was told that I would not like what I was going to see when we arrived at our destination but to "be patient, it will grow on you." Uh oh. What have we gotten ourselves into? I thought.

Our taxi driver was a thin, dark man named Debashish who took his job seriously. He arrived on time, ushered Stuart and I and our belongings into his white Morris taxi, turned on the air conditioning (for which we had paid extra) and set off. Stuart mentioned that I might not want to look out the window when traffic was approaching. He tends to be disarmingly understated in both his humor and his advisories.

My heart nearly stopped on numerous occasions during the three-hour taxi ride to Tiru. I had not heeded Stuart's warning. I wanted to see it all, and I did.

Until then, I would not have believed it spatially possible for a taxi, passing an overladen bus, passing an oxcart, passing a bicyclist, passing a person on foot against a similar pattern of oncoming traffic, to occur without a loss of life.

As we arrived deep into the "tourist" part of the city, a feeling of heaviness and restriction came over me. Dislocated-looking people from around the world were wandering glassy-eyed amidst a sea of garbage in the streets. Cows, tethered to stakes in the ground, were eating any refuse left behind. This nutrition would be transformed into milk, then yogurt by morning.

Again, Stuart advised me not to look as we passed some commotion on the street. An elderly sadhu (holy man), draped in orange robes, lay dead at the side of the road, apparently hit by a taxi. I didn't look this time.

Old women begged aggressively and the city stank of open sewage. My levels of anxiety rose. I was to live here for two weeks? Before exiting the taxi, I wanted to turn around and return to Pondicherry. Stuart reminded me of the message I had received earlier that morning - "Be patient, it will grow on you."

The cityscape is dominated by one of the great Shiva temples, Annamalaiyar Temple, and is in the shadow of Mt. Arunachala. The homes of the Indian people are very simple and sparse, most without running water and electricity. The houses of the local working-class people who provide the goods and services to the city are peppered among more sophisticated abodes replete with verandas, patio gardens, and servants. The endless flow of garbage does not discriminate as to where it lands. Simply put, there are no waste removal services of any kind. The most aesthetic and hygiene-conscious residents burn their piles of garbage, but most just let it fall where it has been consumed or opened.

We arrived at our four-star hotel outside the heart of the city. The complex had a large swimming pool and beautiful grounds with traditional Indian buffets available twice daily and a restaurant to cater to our needs in between. Hot water, however, remained elusive.

We connected with our group of Americans and Brits and were informed as to the rhythm our lives take beginning the following morning. For a laid-back spiritual pilgrimage to India, there were to be few spare moments.

First on the agenda the next morning was a hike up Mt. Arunachala, which would lead us to the caves in which Ramana Maharshi had lived for several years. The trek began at the ashram dedicated to Ramana, followed by an uphill climb, which is not strenuous in and of itself. But when combined with 90 degrees-plus heat and humidity, it was challenging for we pale folks.

The meditative retreat that awaited us midway up the mountain, however, was worth the discomfort. The cave I preferred was small and crowded but was imbued with decades, indeed centuries, of intention. Once settled on our little patch of stone flooring, I felt myself rising up and sitting in the temple of myself once again. Communication with other realms was easy and clear.

We took a breakfast break after the morning hike and meditation. Afterward, we were guided to our second meditative experience of the morning - fifteen minutes with ShivaShaktiAma. She was one of the diminutive women with floor-length hair that Miranda had told me about at our first meeting back in Sausalito.

ShivaShaktiAma quietly entered the room full of aspirants, the suffering and meditators alike, and took her chair. In typical hierarchal style, it was surrounded with blossoms donated by the attendees. She had not spoken in 30 years in spite of bearing many of children and remaining in a marriage for much of that time. The energy she was able to maintain by not wasting it on superfluous words poured from her eyes and body. By not attempting to communicate with the outside world, she was able to remain consciously connected with her true self, her soul, directly all of her waking hours. She had a perpetual upturn to the corners of her mouth from a life spent in prayer and contemplation and few outside distractions.

*My sketch of Shiva Shakti Ama, the silent saint*

Once the room calmed into closed-eyed meditation, everyone sitting on cushions or blankets on the cool marble floor, she would scan the auras of the people and select a few of them. She would then begin transmitting loving and healing energy to them.

Stuart and I both kept our eyes open during a few of the meditations to watch the dynamic at work. She chose during those times to connect with us. The energy she sent felt like a physical sphere of warmth and love, but with a cognitive power behind it. It was up to each person to make of it what they wished. The environment carried the vibration of peace and goodwill and was our twice-daily retreat from the garbage and stench, to which I had quickly become accustomed as my guidance had told me. Our lives had taken on a slow, grace-filled rhythm.

One day after the morning climb and cave meditation, I stopped at the Ramana ashram. I was alone in a room in which there was a portrait of Ramana reclining on a sofa along with another picture of his face. As I passed the portrait, he winked at me and smiled. I blinked a couple of times and looked again thinking I might still be dazed from my earlier meditation. He did it again!

A broad smile crept across my face, I couldn't wait to tell Stuart what had happened.

To put this into perspective, as Ramana was in his decline, a disciple of his cried out, "What will we do without you?" Ramana responded by saying something to the effect of "Where else would I go?" He said he would remain with the people in this place. Devotees say he chooses certain people to communicate with in his wonderfully tricky ways. I felt honored.

I loved Ramana's face. There was a type of open honesty and intelligence in his eyes, and he lived an uncompromising life dedicated to his connection with the divine, and the lifelong inquiry into "Who Am I?" He, like ShivaShaktiAma, lived in silence, and he believed that one could look nowhere else than inside if they were to find happiness.

To validate my experience, toward the end of our trip one of our newly acquired friends, Michael, told Stuart in private that Ramana's portrait had smiled at him. He was concerned that he was going mad as some of his other meditation experiences had challenged his sanity. Michael was relieved to find that he wasn't crazy, just the honored recipient of contact by Ramana.

I was finding the path of silence intriguing and powerful and found myself speaking less than I ever had. There was peace in the silence, which I had become comfortable with through meditation, but did not practice outside of meditation in my daily life at home. In fact, I can be quite the chatterbox with questions on everything under the sun, often attempting to answer the same questions simultaneously as I ask them. It can be a bit taxing on those around me as my mind goes into warp speed at times.

While this silence was feeling good, my body was screaming from the heat and I had apparently come down with an infection of some kind. I was feeling tremendous surges of energy and heat coming out of my hands and feet. Stuart placed his hands about six inches from mine and said, "Wow mama! You have energy spiking out of your hands!"

We went to a local cafe to have some cooling foods and beverages so I could calm the energy. Stuart suggested I discharge my energy into a spoon via spoon bending. He said I should visualize my energy flowing into the spoon as the molecules of metal became "liquid." He had learned this while attending a Buddhist university the summer before our trip.

I had never tried spoon bending before, but thought this would be a good opportunity to learn. I did as Stuart had instructed.

Voila! The head of the spoon bent forward and twisted a full turn around with ease. In Stuart's not so delicate observation: "Mama! You bent the shit out of it!" Proud as I was, my new skill did not assuage my burning discomfort.

I slowed down my participation in the activities of the day to give my body a rest but still insisted on a day trip to Pondicherry. We called our favorite taxi driver, and Stuart and I packed for an overnighter. I remembered to pack everything - except the cortisone injections I carry in case of a physical emergency.

I woke at 4:30 the next morning in Pondicherry with a gnawing and rumbling feeling in my stomach. The identifying symptoms began - slipping into incoherent thinking, tingling in my fingertips, shivering in my spine and the sensation that my energetic matrix had dissipated. All of this precipitates many rushed trips to the toilet. I was becoming very weak but didn't want to wake Stuart, so I waited until 6:00 a.m. By this time, I was not feeling well at all and knew I was in danger, with no ability to pull myself out of the downward spiral of the Addison's Crisis as I had no cortisol with me. I was becoming frightened.

Stuart called Gaia and Mitra, who, in turn, called a local doctor they knew, who, in turn, called the local ashram hospital. He sent us directly to the endocrinologist on duty. Both of the Indian doctors earned their medical degrees in America.

When I am in this state, I am vulnerable to everything around me. It hurts and drains me even to look at things. With eyes necessarily open so that I could walk with assistance, we entered the hospital. It was a beautiful colonial building across from the shoreline of the ocean, and was as peaceful as an ashram.

Women in beautiful saris silently swept the shiny tiled floors with the locally gathered brush made into brooms. My brain found this slow, graceful repetitious activity comforting.

We were soon called in. The doctor asked a few questions and immediately knew what was going on, so gave me a strong injection and allowed me to stay until I recovered. I did not need an intravenous drip this time. On the way out, we passed a wooden box labeled "Donations."

I've been in emergency rooms around the world as I mentioned, but I have never had such a kind and comfortable experience as in Pondicherry. No waiting, no paperwork, no antiseptic smells, just care, a doctor who listened and cared for me, immediately.

As our time in Tiru drew to a close, it was hard to imagine going home to the lists of chores, busyness, and work load. My Being had become more integrated - the physical and spiritual - and had quieted. Flavors were more vibrant, colors more alive, meditations more profound, and I had learned to understand the nature of garbage - I was smiling again. We were scheduled to fly to London the next morning to rendezvous with Scott and do an interview before returning to America.

When we arrived at Heathrow, my nerves were assaulted with the dourness of the people bustling about, gray and humorless with everyone pressed to be somewhere several minutes ago. My energy began constricting for its own protection, and I felt overwhelmed with the harsh monochromatic quality of the sights and sounds.

As happens with most people who have been impacted with the flavorful and slow pace of India, I was sporting fusion clothing - black street pants, black turtleneck covered with a knee-length Indian dress, Indian scarf, and wool coat. There was little guesswork as to the country from which we had just arrived.

Scott was to meet us at the airport, but his flight followed ours by five hours. I was exhausted and fell asleep on a restaurant bench, as did Stuart. Scott, Stuart and I stayed at Scott's parents' home in Winchester while we conducted some CMN business. Our primary objectives were to videotape a lengthy interview with Manjir Samanta Laughton on her book Punk Science, and to spend the day with our friend David Icke on the Isle of Wight. The English countryside provided enough greenery and spaciousness to serve as a segue back into Western life, which was waiting for us in California.

## Chapter Forty:
## *Reality Sinks In*

California is beautiful. I often slip when speaking of it and call it a country, and, as it is the eighth largest economy in the world, it essentially is.

From vast dry deserts to dripping wet fern and redwood forests, oceans, and pine studded mountain lakes, to say nothing of my birthplace, San Francisco, there is little of natural beauty you can't find in California. Still, I was feeling blue.

The information Scott and I had been receiving via some of our more prominent interviewees, as well as our own research, pointed to some severe hardship for California and the United States. Those who were "in the know" seemed to have already considered the possibilities and made arrangements.

We did not want to be caught off-guard for the impending financial meltdown, which was to begin in 2008 according to Devi Kidd, George Green and others we were in contact with. The need to remain stable and protect CMN became a deciding force in how Scott and I chose our path.

While on business in Vancouver BC, we took a trip to the breadbasket of British Columbia, the Okanagan Valley. As we passed fruit orchards and vegetable gardens and well-disguised cannabis farms, admiring the abundance of life in this rural garden spot of Canada, I turned to Scott and said: "This is what we need. A place to grow food that has its own water supply. If all hell breaks loose, we can sustain ourselves and any friends who end up turfed out of their homes when the economy goes down." It was now the summer of 2007, meaning the autumn of 2008 we had been warned of was just around the corner.

Within a second or two we looked at each other with the same thought: We already have that!

Not to waste the heat of an inspired moment, I excitedly called my father and asked how long the current tenants had on their lease of my mother and father's home in a tiny farming community in the Sierra Foothills. Though they had not built it until I was in my early 20's, it had become our family home, complete with five acres of land, private water supply, and a mandarin orange orchard. Dad had long ago moved into the city so his new wife, May, could be nearer her family.

As it turned out, the tenants were set to move out in six weeks. The hand of fate herself must have been guiding this, I thought! How convenient! Scott and I agreed to rent the property from my father, but within a week we thought why not just buy a part of dad's estate with a portion of the equity left over from my Sedona home after paying off some of the loans we had incurred to keep CMN going?

Being a number seven in the Enneagram, which is a personality profiling science, my excitement at new adventures can blur the bigger picture at times, and my seven was dominating this conversation. That said, unbeknownst to me, Scott had always been drawn to the verdant peacefulness of the family farm, so it took no arm twisting to convince him that maybe we had the perfect solution right in front of us.

Our plan to move from Sedona to Vancouver was fading. Vancouver was to have been the reward for having to sell our beloved home in Sedona, a happy new life in Canada.

But that plan was far from my mind now. Nothing was manifesting as we had expected. I was thinking more along the line of whether or not the interior of the family farmhouse should remain buttery yellow or be changed to something more surprising, like a cherry red or turquoise. The Plan had dissolved, unbeknownst to me, along with my internal moorings.

We chose the buttery yellow, and planted marigolds, petunias, a few more fruit trees, and a vegetable garden. My heart was happy as we woke to the sounds of birds, farm animals, and the occasional locomotive passing by. The buttery yellow color cheered my mind as we created a veritable poster home for Pottery Barn. Everyone who came to visit slept well and loved the energy of the farm, many not wanting to leave, which was fine with me as I missed the company of my Sedona friends.

In the past, I would have invited them to live with us as I had so often before, but I had to consider my partner now. Scott enjoys his sovereignty and privacy. I had never personally embraced these attributes. If I liked someone, I was happy to share my home with them, especially now that I was feeling isolated.

My mother had handled the isolation of country life

differently. She became over-committed to one charity and religious or political group after another, anything to keep her close to people. She was not cut out to be a rural wife. Nor was my dad's new wife, May. And, as I was learning, nor was I. I found my heart and mind regularly being pulled back to the Red Rocks, my friends - my soul family.

As my research and time spent with our interviewees is a constant source of soul connection and enrichment for me, CMN was becoming my primary raison d'etre. It was at this time that "The Voice" told me to write a book about my life experiences, about my soul's journey. I didn't understand the purpose of this and was concerned my life was not sufficiently interesting for anyone to want to read about. But change was in the wind, so I listened and began writing the book - this book.

As had been predicted, the economy crashed in the fall of 2008. The value of my Sedona home had begun dropping like a stone. We had made it out just in time to save some of our equity.

About this time, I had a brief meditative vision in which I was walking onto a TV set with Oprah. She was interviewing me about my new book that had just been released. It was one of those quick snapshots - a metaphor for my book being well received - in which I could see everything, but ask no questions nor analyze. Okay, I thought. I will finish the book.

A few weeks after that brief vision, I received an email from two producers in Los Angeles who asked to speak with us at our earliest convenience. Scott and I decided we would meet with them while returning from what was becoming one of our quarterly road trips to Sedona.

Sitting in their Beverly Hills office, overlooking the gritty, gray city of Los Angeles, I felt something shift inside me. Was I ready to go back to the world from which I had escaped? At what price? Could I release my current role with CMN if it became necessary? I had some priorities to sort through.

What I came to understand was that I had not journeyed this far into my dharma to abandon it. Yes, I could go back into the world of television, or any other media world, once again, if I could feature the kind of information we were producing for CMN.

As it transpired, one of our two new business partners, Suzanne DePasse, was a friend of Oprah's. Suzanne and her business partner, Madison's, idea was to place a program in which I would be the host covering subjects based on psychic phenomena and consciousness on Oprah's new television network (OWN) that was in the works.

Meetings took place, Oprah's people were contacted, but I came up short in the first round. The producer for OWN said they were going to take more of a popular approach featuring shows on basic personal improvement. What I had to say about quantum leaping, aliens, remote viewing, and healing with intention was just a bit beyond the average viewer's personal spiritual makeover plan.

In the summer of 2010, Oprah put out a casting call to America. Anyone with a $100 flip cam was invited to do an audition to garner support for their own show on OWN. Several CMN viewers urged me to enter the contest, but I felt that if our business partner was a personal friend of Oprah and that didn't work, there was little point in joining the fray with hundreds of thousands of other aspirants. On an ego level, I also found it a bit demeaning after a 30-year career in television, truth be known.

At the eleventh hour, I decided "Why not?" I pulled up the entry form, which had a long page of legal requirements. Because my brain freezes at the sight of legalese, I emailed the document to my niece, Kelly, an attorney.

"Kelly, I want to know if they will own everything I send to them if I enter this contest. I'll make you any kind of cookies you want for looking at this contract." I had intended to make it easy on myself by sending OWN the opening video on the index page of CMN as my video. It pretty much tells my story in one minute and fifteen seconds. No point boring people.

The next day Kelly sent an email with comments and excerpts of the document enclosed. "Yep, she would own everything - your URL, video, logo for your site, everything. I'll take peanut butter cookies with chocolate chips. I need some cheering up. My law partner's being a bitch."

I must say they were some of the better peanut butter cookies I've made, particularly buttery and crisp. We were both cheered up. My vision regarding Oprah, however, remained a mystery. Meanwhile, Kelly and I decided on a name for her new business - Will Counsel for Cookies.

## Chapter Forty-One:
## *Conspiracy*

I have spent much of my life in a man's world. Small talk of babies, curtains, neighbors and daycare holds little attraction for me except for food, books, friendship, films, and lipstick. In spite of my resonance with the things men talk about, except for sports and the stock market, I do embrace the feminine.

It was not until my life in Sedona that I understood that women with deep and open minds and hearts are the most interesting people of all for me. We can scale universes in our conversations without having to couch our opinions behind the quotes of an expert or university study, which men often require in conversation. That said, some men can also go to this free-wheeling mental place.

Conscious Media Network was a working nirvana in this regard because it insisted that I honor the mantra of the greeting card that is on my bathroom mirror: "I would rather have a mind open by wonder than one closed by belief." This has taken me to places I would never have believed existed, no less would have chosen to explore. This includes the "dark side."

While conspiracy theory held little fascination for me until about twenty years ago, I have since stepped somewhere near the center of that stage upon occasion, interviewing high profile people.

I was first drawn in by a video of David Icke in the mid-1990s in which he informed the audience as to the exploitive economic practices that emanate from the City of London. I was fascinated as I knew nothing of the world of the financial institutions and elites that create money for their own purposes. Much has been exposed on this topic since then through well-researched books and documentaries such as The Money Masters and Inside Job.

The next exposure I had to a cloaked world of knowledge was Gregg Braden's slim volume titled Zero Point in which he explained the dynamics of the magnetic field surrounding earth and its dissipation. He said this phenomenon would lead to profound geological changes around the turn of the millennia and throughout the next couple of decades. I wanted to know more.

Then came the subject of extraterrestrials. This came into my line of sight when I attended my first Prophet's Conference in Palm Springs, California, as mentioned earlier.

Shortly after that, covert military black ops projects came to my attention along with new information regarding underground bases. This became personalized when two friends of mine, who are extreme hikers, had witnessed large cables poking out from red rock formations in a remote area outside of Sedona. Military personnel were also encountered, waving my friends off with machine guns. This was later captured in James Redfield's work of "fiction" titled The Twelfth Insight. Redfield's Sedona home was just around the corner from mine.

What are they hiding in the middle of the Arizona high desert? I later learned from a man who was a former military intelligence that there were a number of underground bases within close proximity to my above-ground rainbow-filled life in the city of Sedona. This became symbolic for me.

What shone under the deep blue desert skies from the rivers and rocks and people's eyes was one world. What was buried beneath was rumored to radiate something very different.

In truth, conspiracy theories, be they individually real or not, have consumed many people in my field. This subject is fraught with frauds, disinformation, outraged activism and brave hearts with swords bared. In the end, there is little satisfaction to be had as official channels of power remain tight-lipped.

We can debate until our last breath who, or what, may be controlling the human race's perception of reality and will likely stumble on aspects of truth from many quarters.  In the end, it's up to us to find our own way home.

## Chapter Forty-Two:

# Letting Go

For seven years Conscious Media Network had offered hope and viable options for new thinking to tens, if not hundreds, of thousands of people over its existence. But Scott was becoming tired. He had worn too many hats for too long and the day to day responsibility had taken its toll on his spirit.

People regularly wrote to us thank our organization for the beauty we were bringing to the world. They asked whoever received the email to please thank Scott and Regina for our good work. That email generally landed in Scott's inbox first as there was no one else but the two of us. It shocked many of our viewers to learn that this network was the work of just two people. But everything has its price.

Upon awakening one morning in January of 2012, my sleepy thoughts roamed to seeing myself on a small TV set surrounded by a production crew. I was laughing with them before the camera began taping. I had no idea where this "TV set" was located, only that it was intimate in its size and feeling. The name of the show was Open Minds.

Once I got up out of bed with a cup of tea to get the day rolling, I began producing a pilot show. It was a roundtable discussion - like The View - with a guest and a panel of three women in dialogue. Within a few days I had contacted some of my CMN interviewees who lived within a 100-mile radius and invited them to the videotaping of the pilot show. I also brought in two women I had interviewed to be part of the panel. To complete the feel of the show, I had white coffee mugs with the words "Open Minds" printed on them in front of each of us, positioned toward the camera.

We shot the pilot shows in one day at a studio in Auburn, California. Scott began the editing process only to realize that one of the three cameras had been shooting on an incompatible format. The shoot was a bust - no one would see the film. I put the "Open Minds" coffee mugs up on the top shelf in the dinnerware cupboard. Each time I opened the cupboard, I noticed them and wondered what that endeavor had been about. It only took a few months to learn that that act of faith and action on my part had planted a seed within the cosmic consciousness.

In May of 2012, five months later, I received a call from Jay Weidner. He wanted to know if I would be interested in meeting with him and the founder of Gaia to talk about doing a show for them. After hanging up from the conversation I meditated and knew that the phone call was about much more than a show. I "saw" that Gaia was going to offer to buy Conscious Media Network. I agreed to fly to Boulder, where I was offered a buyout just as I had been shown in meditation. I was also offered a show. When asked what I would like the show to be called, I smiled and said "Open Minds."

Scott was tired and thus, relieved at the offer. He couldn't carry the technical aspects of operating CMN any longer. We had gone into this grand endeavor with a financial model one could call economic suicide: we would just put it out there and hope that CMN had enough value that people would support it. We were barely paying the bills in spite of having peaks of more than 500,000 unique viewers a month. So, we sold our baby to Gaia, Inc.

There was an automatic role for me to transition to at Gaia as host of Open Minds. I began commuting to Boulder, Colorado every week, living at the St. Julian hotel three nights a week. For Scott, the future was less certain. He needed a break. After adjusting to the brutal travel schedule, I received a call from my cousin, Lilli. She told me that a girlfriend of hers had been walking by my former Sedona home that morning and a "For Sale" sign had been put up in front of the house. My beloved home was for sale, and I had some money in the bank!

The market was at a low after several years of recession. I was lucky enough to have sold at the high, and now I was going to make an attempt to buy back at a low. The price had fallen to half of what I had sold it to the current owners for. The profit I made from the original sale had allowed CMN to continue for five additional years. I still view this as divine grace. Just as grace stepped in on Christmas Eve of 2006 with an offer to buy my home, grace now intervened to bring my home back to me.

Scott and I moved back into the Sedona home in March of 2013. I nearly cried as the mural with my personal symbolism embedded within it that Paul Lawrence had painted thirteen years earlier fit perfectly back into its place. The words, drowned in my tears six years earlier – "I'll be back" - had come true. I now understood why my Guides had told me to have the mural painted on something that could be removed, much to my protest at the time. I had sworn that I would never leave my Sedona home. They knew thirteen years before that my journey would take me away from my home and temple and, just as surely, return me to it one day! How vast is their vision?!

For the most part, the furniture I had sold with the house was in the same position as when I had left it. Some of the artwork and rugs were there as well. I had it repainted from the original peachy color to "chai latte," a soft buttery golden color. The pyramid went back in the foyer along with the palm plants and amethyst crystals. The temple was restored.

In the frenzy of my weekly trips to and from Boulder, Scott and I were becoming quietly estranged. He did not feel purpose any longer. The exhaustion and dissolution of CMN had taken its emotional toll on both of us. On Halloween 2013, the day before Scott's birthday, we quietly agreed to split up. There was no argument from either of us. We posited that the birth of CMN may have been the underlying, unconscious reason for the relationship, though we were unaware of it at the beginning. Perhaps. The glue that bound us together had disintegrated, and we were handling the change in a dignified manner.

On New Year's Eve 2013/14, I drove Scott to the airport where he would join friends in Chang Mai, Thailand for a few months of R&R. I hugged him longer than normal as I said goodbye. As I left the airport, stuck in traffic for an hour, I began to sob uncontrollably. We had put all of ourselves into CMN, and now Gaia for me. There was nothing left for our relationship, and it had ended. I did not know what the future would bring as I stepped off the ledge of certainty into what felt like a free fall, once again.

## Chapter Forty-Three:
# Entanglement

The void that occurs at separating from a long-term relationship is highly nuanced. At first, there is a sense of freedom. I could listen to French folk-pop for breakfast, dance around the kitchen, enjoy a pot of my exotic tea as often as I wished. I could even turn the light on in the middle of the night to write down a dream without disturbing anyone. But then there is this odd sense of energetic loss. We have no genuine understanding of what it means to live so closely with other living beings, be they human or even house pets.

Our auras are intermingled, always adjusting to, giving and taking, from one another. This very real phenomenon took a while for me to distinguish. There was an emptiness, which I filled with work. Having to provide eight interviews a month for Gaia was enough to keep me afloat with research and travel. A deeper sadness settled in as I realized that my life had become a repetition of function. This was a startling new take on my life, which, to this point, had thrived on being pulled forward into the unknown. There is a secret fear and a thrill of not knowing what the soul is going to move us into, pull us toward - provided we're open to its voice. For perhaps the first time it seemed as though my soul was not speaking to me.

A couple of years passed and I began a very patterned thought process of thinking that went like this: My son, Stuart, would ultimately marry, have children and I would become his stalker, following his little family from place to place to have a sense of belonging. I realized that there was something very wrong with this strange way of thinking. It even occurred to me that I might be depressed. Having no experience with depression, I wasn't aware of the diagnosable constituents, but I was certainly feeling blue.

As happens in my life, another life-changing dream came in February 2016, two years after Scott and I had split up:

I was in a kitchen space when "The Voice" came into my awareness. It told me that I was going to be attending a dance and that my partner had already been chosen for me. I perked up and began clueing into my surroundings.

A man was sitting at a wooden table across from me. He had wide-set blue eyes, a salt and pepper stubble on his face, and he was silent. I realized that this man would be my dance partner. I wanted to reach out and touch his face when "The Voice" admonished me, "NO! Not yet, the dance has not yet begun." Not to be denied, I reached out to his skin with my etheric hand and touched his cheek – his skin felt so familiar.

Soon after, I noticed that the man was stepping into the shower in preparation for the dance. As he opened the shower door and stepped in, I noticed his beautiful, well-proportioned body. Like a girl, I experienced a little tingle of energy over the knowledge that my dance partner was so beautiful.

The scene then changed back to us sitting across from one

another at the wooden table. I asked him to please tell me his name to which he replied, "Rama." I thought that this could not be his name, as it was the name of the Hindu God. But I thought this could have a meaning embedded within it, perhaps symbolic.

When I awoke, I was bathed in a sense of knowing. I had a partner on his way; one who had been carefully selected by my Soul and would be brought to me by my guiding forces. I felt warm and hopeful for the next week or two as though I was living a parallel reality.

Within a couple of weeks, I was researching a book titled Transforming Economy for a Gaia interview. The author was Zeus Yiamouyiannis. As I read through the pages of his book, I had a feeling that this man and I would have a natural collaboration in our work as we envisioned a similar future for a newly emerging kind of humanity.

After finishing the book, I went online to find more blogs to flesh out my research. I came across a low-quality photo, one taken from his computer camera in a Skype conversation. His right eye (on the left from my perspective) drilled into me. The thought and feeling flooded my brain that if we were in the same room, I would fall in love with him. That thought was quickly followed by another: that this would be terribly inconvenient as 1) I needed my wits about me in an interview and, 2) I was under the impression that he was married with a young child.

On March 16th, 2016, Zeus and I met for a pre-interview dinner, which is a common practice in my work. As we walked toward The Kitchen restaurant on Boulder's Pearl Street, an energetic aspect (etheric double) of my hand was wandering over to him, looking for his hand. I was shocked at the forward nature of my body's reaction to him.

We were seated at a small wooden table, very similar to the one in my dream – his eyes were wide-set and blue, his stubble was salt and pepper.

We chatted for three hours. As fate would have it, he was divorced. We said goodnight, and my research complete - on more levels than one - I drifted off to sleep. That night I had another dream that shocked, titillated, and frightened me:

In the dream, I saw a close-up version of myself with a man standing behind me. He reached over my shoulder and handed me a gift - something wrapped in white gossamer fabric and tied with a bow. I opened it and found a gold wedding band. I thought, I don't even know you, but the answer is 'Yes.' I accepted the ring. As I awoke "The Voice" announced: "Zeus is your husband, and you are Zeus' wife. This has already occurred in another realm."

I woke up startled at the directness of this dream. If I had lived a normal life up to this point, I would have disregarded this as a typically feminine romantic vision. But, I knew better. Dreams such as these, in which "The Voice" speaks directly, are always instructive and informative in nature. To ignore them is at my own peril.

I arrived at the Gaia studio, nervous. I struggled to keep my focus after being given what one could safely call TMI, or Too Much Information.

Zeus took his place across the table from me in the Gaia studio. A lovely energy flowed between us, and the interview proceeded without a hitch. When it was finished, he was to be quickly whisked away by the driver, back to his hotel. I felt a small sense of panic and followed him to the back door. During a heartfelt hug, I whispered, "I hope we see one another again" to which he replied, "Oh, we will."

My heart expanded beyond my chest, my breath became shallow, and I drifted into faraway places. This was audacious as he was a virtual stranger, yet the future had been laid out in two dreams and one meeting. I would wait to hear from him. I thought of his name, Zeus/Rama, the name of Gods. The dream.

During this same stint at Gaia, I was to meet Belinda Womack, a woman I now call my Earth Angel. She was to be a guest on the subject of Angel guidance, an interview in which I had bucked participating. I had become jaded on the subject as I know far too many people who purvey messages from the angels, many of whom have either misinformed angels or whose angels are playing tricks on them. The information is often either wrong or too lofty to validate. I had had a belly full of this. However...

While speaking with Belinda's publishing agent, I told her of my misgivings when discussing whether or not she would be appropriate for my show. Jane Lehr said, "She's different. She's the real deal." Reluctantly, I scheduled her for Open Minds.

At the end of our interview, we took off our mics and wandered back to the green room, happy with the direction the show had taken. We hugged, and Belinda told me to call her anytime I would like her to check in on something or do a reading for me.

I get a lot of these offers, as you might imagine, and I don't always take my guests up on them. This time would prove different as that night was to be my first meeting with Zeus, my world destined to tip upside down.

Three days after my interview with Belinda, I emailed her and said that I could use a little peek at something. We scheduled a meeting for Monday, two days later. By then I was becoming edgy, waiting to hear from Zeus, again.

Belinda did a quick reading for me in the morning during which she said of Zeus and me: "This is going to happen faster than the speed of light and there is nothing either of you can do about it." There it was. It was living in some other dimension than my own imagination.

Within hours, I received an email from Zeus that was peppered with such words as "delightful." We were off to the races. Within five months he had relocated to Sedona, and we were living together. I was the more impulsive and flowing one between us, but he is open to going with the flow when life makes an invitation that is too good to turn down.

As for the nature of this kind of relationship, we are both still attempting to find words to describe our connection. It is time folded in on itself, from the ancient past to the more ancient past, and threading itself through now and into the future. So familiar that I can't tell my skin from his, yet so different from the independent imprints of lifetimes apart.

Each iteration of "us" bears its own signature of memories and emotional imprints. In this lifetime, we made a pact that we must be truthful and transparent at all times.

*Wedding vows in the redwood forest*

I don't need to say that this presents

challenges for the very private person I am. But this agreement to remain open and truthful has become the backbone of our relationship. If it can be seen and known, we can work with it. What remains in the dark, under the surface, is what corrupts relationships and I had let too much lie in the dark in times past, i.e., unaddressed desires and needs I wouldn't stand up for.

Our pact to be one hundred percent truthful with one another would also be our saving grace with extraordinarily challenging times waiting just around the corner.

## Chapter Forty-Four:

## More Letting Go

One year later, just as it seemed our worlds were about to expand into the blessed state of the extended family with our sons, our fates changed.

During the summer of 2017, Zeus and I were simultaneously faced with estrangement from our respective sons.

Stuart had begun an uncharacteristically secret liaison with a young woman. Prior to this, our lives had been an open book to one another as we took joy in sharing life's journey. Looking back, our lifelong friendship as mother and son had been so harmonious that it might have supplanted needs for any number of other relationships on a certain level. We were confidants to the extent it was appropriate and, at the very least, we always supported one another's choices in partners and friends. We both cherished and cherish the notion of extended family and community. My girlfriends were his 'Aunties,' and I was often called 'mom' by his friends and girlfriends. Neither of us knew it any other way.

With the arrival of his new partner, as Stuart explained it, he kept the liaison a secret until it had time to strengthen. By the time Zeus and I learned of it, a couple of months had passed and Stuart was ready to share a home with his new love. Upon being told of this new secret affair, Zeus and I independently felt a sinking feeling in our stomachs, in part due to the secrecy. Why wouldn't you want to shout to the rooftops your new romantic love with others you love? Something just felt wrong.

Within a few short weeks, what seemed to me to be a minor disagreement effectively ended my relationship with my son. After a year and a half of attempts to reach out and establish a meaningful connection once again, I have resigned myself to the current reality that I no longer have a relationship with Stuart. This is an event that I had never believed possible and it feels as though I have had a limb amputated. The phantom pain of the heart is constant, like a low grade emotional fever.

Over the course of the last year and a half I have had to learn about 'letting go' on a level that is unfathomable to me. Who are we when we are not the things we cherish any longer? Above all else, I cherished being Stuart's mother and friend. While I hold out hope for a change of circumstance in the future, I am left at this time with the fact that I enjoyed thirty-five beautiful years of camaraderie with my son. This is more than most people ever have. Still, the awareness that he is here on the planet and has brought his own son into the world regularly catches me by surprise and brings sorrow at the knowledge that I am not part of it.

Simply put, I never saw it coming. No one did. But perhaps I should have.

Stuart never rebelled. He was a thoughtful, reflective and agreeable child and man in every way. He was born this way. He, like me, didn't voice needs and frustrations well. He would never rat-out someone else, even when he should have. He held any pain close to his chest and put on a helpful and kind face, which endeared him to everyone who knows him. Those he still interacts with also enjoy his grace and kindness. His recent rebellion against his family and friends is born out of something he could not clearly articulate, which is why none of us saw it coming. But never, not for a moment, do I forget how beautiful a Being he is.

And, the story isn't fully written as long as we have breath left in our lungs.

During this same time, Zeus' former wife went into a custody dispute with Zeus, which kept him from his ten-year old son, Phoenix, for nearly a year and a half. Zeus was heart sick not to be part of his son's life other than a couple of Skype calls each week while his son remained with his mother in the Philippines.

When his son was three-years old, Zeus, and his then wife had gone to the third world on what was to be a one year 'adventure' that stretched to several. Zeus left the relationship and country at the three year mark of the 'adventure' as it had turned out to be anything but an adventure.

In addition, the ex-pat lifestyle lacked the spirituality Zeus craved and the blithe self-absorption did not fit with his nature. Add to this foul air quality, massive traffic congestion and a day-to-day consumerist mentality. Zeus was like a fish out of water. He pled with his former wife to come back to the United States so their son could have a healthier upbringing, but she refused. Help is cheap and the money through her banking job is good. With a deadening sense of hope for his and his son's future, Zeus departed for the United States to rebuild his life until the day came when he could care for his son again in a stable environment.

Mediation is underway at this moment to find some semblance of balance between mother and father, which we hope will bring peace to all concerned. But the attorneys and courts across four jurisdictions has done little to brighten our outlook on institutions. The Philippines has no Hague Treaty agreements with the United States. A resident there can make decisions with virtual immunity from the law, making it very difficult to achieve a fair agreement.

This has taught Zeus and I a great deal about how the mind, individually and collectively works. Institutions are not there to serve anything other than themselves. The best laid strategies mean nothing when the people involved are not ready to embrace them. As Zeus says, "We cannot expect to have a higher consciousness solution through lower consciousness institutions and thinking." Ultimately, each of us is a sovereign soul and will learn what is needed in our own time. The passing of time under challenging circumstances can feel excruciating, but time is only time, and it waits for us to fill it with meaning.

This is a theme that is also playing out in the world around us, and it is now up to each of us to choose when, and how, to engage. We are engaging by getting on with our lives.

## Chapter Forty-Five:
## Beginning Again and Again

"Life goes on" as they say, and Zeus and I have one another. Though I didn't know it several decades ago, the learned skill of compartmentalization has helped me through this challenge more than any other single factor, besides Zeus. I can continue on with my life, relationships, and creativity by merely giving my focus to these things rather than the pain of loss.

My life strategy is simple: if you do not have the power to change something then develop the grace to accept it. If it causes personal pain and robs you of peace, then distance yourself from it if possible. This does not preclude working on the inner planes toward a resolution. I send my love to Stuart and his son every day, visioning Stuart as healthy, happy, and at peace with his own life and, ultimately, with me.

Meanwhile, the professional itch has begun again. Toward that end, I launched www.reginameredith.com in the fall of 2017. It is a free video streaming site where I have free will to interview whomever I like. It feels good.

While it may seem like a move backward to my Conscious

Media Network days, it is not. Yes, creating a video site based on donations was financially challenging in the past. Yes, I am doing it again. But this time I have grown new parts that allow me to engage this altruistic aspect of myself. I am dedicated to people accessing thought-provoking information without having to whip out a credit card. The intimate retreats I hold a few times a year, and my presentations at conferences and such like now supplement the donations. In addition, I have expanded my financial model to include affiliate fees with products and services that I believe in and personally use. This is the new way - helping one another forge a cleaner, more responsible new world.

I feel my spirit rising as I once again hand pick my guests and cover the subjects that fascinate me and inform. My days feel happier, if a bit more sober. Zeus and I know that, at the end of the day, no matter what court document has come via email, or what sighting of Stuart by a friend or acquaintance may have occurred, we can curl around one another at night. We can wake up at 3:00 a.m. and know that we can talk about our dreams and frustrations or whatever is on our mind in those dark and quiet hours.

Zeus is teaching me to have the deepest faith in myself. I am teaching him to trust in his soul - and his son's - that it will never fail him, even when the outside world does. Together, we have made it through our darkest times and are grateful every day that we found our way to one another. Our relationship continues to grow and embrace new ways forward.

Our wish is that our union of spirit, thoughts, and ideas will extend to others in building a new community. Zeus's most recent contribution is his book The Spiritually Confident

Man, which helps men re-envision their place in the world to offer the best of their masculinity to family, loved ones, and society. My book, Accidentally on Purpose, simply illustrates how one person's life is fashioned by listening to the whisperings of her soul and guiding forces as her sole roadmap.

And, so, it came as no surprise that, while meditating one morning, I was "shown" that I would be leaving Sedona - again. Shortly after this message, we were at our family farmhouse in California. During our stay, my father experienced an unfortunate event that indicated he can no longer shoulder the burdens of managing his orchard.

Dad and I have had an arrangement for several years that I would manage the house and immediate yard, and he would manage the acreage, which features his beloved Satsuma mandarin orange orchard. He can't do that any longer as his body is beginning to fail him in essential ways. In addition, it's difficult for him to get on and off the tractor and hold his weight up.

On one Autumn day, when the unfortunate event occurred, my father sat shaken and hunched over atop his old tractor. After hearing what had just occurred, I said, "Dad, Zeus and I are planning on spending more time here. We have even talked about a potential move here one day." My father nearly cried, saying "Dearie, nothing in the world would make me happier than to have the two of you move back here." At that moment I knew we would leave Sedona and my magical home - never to return.

Sedona had served its purpose, as it is said to do for all who come to her. She has deepened my sense of purpose, connection, service, and love. She has done the same for Zeus. We carry this with us now no matter where we place ourselves. The only question left is whether we take the mural with us this time.

I sold my home to a dear friend, Greg, who has always loved the time he has spent there. He asked if I would leave the furnishings again – along with the mural. "Yes," was my answer with the caveat that if I ever asked for the mural, he would hand it over, to which he said, "Of course." But, the cosmos may have it otherwise!

'The Best is Yet to Come!' Selfie of me and Zeus at the San Francisco Opera

Just this morning I was driving through town and a clear thought and image came into my mind that the mural may want to follow me to my home in California once again. I didn't think much of it. An hour later I spoke with Greg about some Facebook business. Before we began the conversation he said, "Regina, the strangest thing happened last night! The mural literally fell over on me as I walked by!" I laughed and told him about my thought this morning. That mural is wedged in its place pretty tightly and has never loosened from the wall until now. It looks like I need to call a shipping company.

Meanwhile, the move felt more peaceful this time. My home would remain in "the family," the filaments of her energy flowing to me whenever I conjure her in my mind.

Zeus and I have a future to create, which will ultimately take us to many places. My father and my sister, Denise, and her children are in California. Our son's futures are yet to be determined, but we feel will resolve well one day. Our California country life feels right… at least for right now.

## Chapter Forty-Six:
## Many Hats

I have worn many hats - the barrel racer hat as a fake cowgirl, the hair helmet of the news anchor, the metaphoric toque of a home chef, and the tinfoil hat of those on the fringe of conspiracy. It's time for the hats to come off and stand as myself, to throw off the images imposed by others and reveal what has simply been there all the along.

My life so far has resulted in a blossoming of intuitive abilities, knowledge, communications skills, wonderful friendships, and intimate relationships. This is all that I need to be of service in the way that I can to a world that is fraught with confusion and fakery. If we can find our clarity, we can be of service to one another, holding up a true mirror (rather than a distorting one) in which to examine ourselves. I believe in our innate intelligence and creativity to begin again, and again, and again. And so, with my merry band of comrades, we travel to parts still unknown - the boundary-less expanse of the spirit and the place where it informs us. The only requirement throughout this journey is to maintain an open heart and mind. Toward that end, I will continue my commitment to be there for others who, like me, are choosing to grow.

The motto of my website runs like the motif of my life: "Sovereign mind. Open heart. Engage with possibility." It is my strong desire that people begin to see behind the manipulation of their reality and make decisions in a more powerful way. Once we can see our own truth clearly, it will require that each of us look at the way we have been living our lives. Is our life sustainable? Is it vital? Does it contribute to refinement, balance, and elevation? This living truth can involve our economic lives, emotional lives, vocations, relationships, family affairs, and spiritual lives. It's my goal to help people liberate themselves from conditions and mindsets that no longer serve us and, at the same time, gather sustainable and beautiful options for living, even if it means we have to rearrange our lives.

Life is meant to be lived by the great virtues of truth, love, and beauty. If we are exhausted from living a lie, being lied to and treated disrespectfully, then it's time to unplug from a matrix that demands obedience but provides nothing of value.

Why not encourage each other to unplug from mindless or unhealthy activities? To me, this means rejecting non-organic foods, digging our fingers into the soil to grow a garden, being open to a different story of who we are, where we came from, and where we are going, learning to heal our emotions through playing music. To me, this means lifting our consciousness by using nature's bounty of beauty, color, and scent, or taking time to dive deep within.

According to sidereal astrology, I chose to be born with Pluto - the ruler of death, rebirth, and transformation - impacting every other planet in my chart. This has given me great strength, resilience, and commitment to my purpose. I will not allow life to keep me down for long because I know the winds of change will come blowing again. My chart also indicates that I am a rebel, a revolutionary, an anarchist, and a mystic with a soft spot. I am also stubborn and willful, which may be why I have been such a handful to the men in my life. But these traits suit me perfectly for the path I have chosen.

Beyond this, I am told that "the best is yet to come!"

I believe it. I really do.

# The Author

Regina Meredith is a pioneer in the world of Conscious Media and is one of the most respected TV hosts and bloggers in the world of esoteric studies, health discoveries, politics and secret agendas. As the co-founder of Conscious Media Network, host of OpenMinds on Gaia TV, and the founder of her own free streaming video network, Regina has reached millions with messages of hope and enlightenment. Join her community at www.reginameredith.com

Made in the USA
San Bernardino, CA
09 February 2020